John Philip Newman

The Thrones and Palaces of Babylon and Nineveh from Sea to Sea

A thousand Miles on Horseback

John Philip Newman

The Thrones and Palaces of Babylon and Nineveh from Sea to Sea
A thousand Miles on Horseback

ISBN/EAN: 9783337236946

Printed in Europe, USA, Canada, Australia, Japan

Cover: Foto ©Andreas Hilbeck / pixelio.de

More available books at **www.hansebooks.com**

THE GARDEN OF EDEN.

THE
THRONES AND PALACES
OF
BABYLON AND NINEVEH

FROM SEA TO SEA

A THOUSAND MILES ON HORSEBACK

"Look ye! master traveller, unless ye note something worth the seeing, and come home wiser than ye went, I would not give a stag's horn for all your travels."
Old Play.

By JOHN P. NEWMAN D.D.
MEMBER OF THE LONDON SOCIETY OF BIBLICAL ARCHÆOLOGY

NEW YORK
HARPER & BROTHERS, PUBLISHERS
FRANKLIN SQUARE
1876

Entered according to Act of Congress, in the year 1875, by
HARPER & BROTHERS,
In the Office of the Librarian of Congress, at Washington.

Inscription.

TO HER WHO WAS THE CHOICE OF MY YOUTH, WHO IS THE JOY OF MY
MANHOOD, WHO ACCOMPANIED ME IN MY TOUR AROUND THE
WORLD, WHOSE LOVE OF THE BEAUTIFUL, APPRECIATION
OF THE ANTIQUE, AND ENTHUSIASM IN EXPLO-
RATION WERE TO ME A PERPETUAL
INSPIRATION, THIS VOLUME
IS AFFECTIONATELY
INSCRIBED.

JOHN P. NEWMAN.

WASHINGTON, D. C., October 5, 1875.

CONTENTS.

CHAPTER I.

Up the Persian Gulf.—Brilliant Anticipations.—Memorable Historic Lands.—Preparations for the Journey.—Our Party.—Steamer *Burmah*.—English Travelers.—Pilgrims to the Shrine of Dwaka.—Kurrachee.—Its History and Commerce.—Civilizations Compared.—Worshiping Alligators.—Oriental Gamblers.—Looking for a Harbor.—Guadur.—Appearance and History of Muscat.—Its King and his Kingdom.—Delicious Dates.—Ornamented Women.—Reign and Forts of the Portuguese.—Terrible Massacre.—Sunset at Sea.—Arabian and Persian Mountains.—Persian Gulf Described.—Bunder Abbas.—Portuguese and Ormuz.—Fire-worshipers.—Islands in the Persian Gulf.—Kishm and Larrack.—Lingah.—Pearl-divers of Bahrein.—Pearl-fisheries.—Costly Pearls.—A Sea of Blood.—Bushire.—Tragic Scenes.—England's Lion Share.—Ancient and Modern Persia.—Brilliant Phosphorescent Display.—Slowness of the Orientals.—Dreadful Storm.—Farewell to the Persian Gulf.—Great Shaat-el-Arab.—Beautiful River Scenery.—Sheikh of Mahomerah.—First Stage of our Journey Ended.—Commerce of Busrah.—Enchanting Rivulet.—Busrah.—Home of Sindbad the Sailor.—Ancient Ruins.—Garden of Eden..Page 17

CHAPTER II.

Historic Lands.—Anticipations and Emotions.—Steamer *City of London*.—The Three Great Rivers.—Confluence of the Tigris and of the Euphrates.—Steaming up the Shaat-el-Arab.—The Floods Prevail.—Shepherds and their Flocks.—The Garden of Eden.—Its Appearance.—Inhabitants and History.—Sail up the Tigris.—Wild Boars of the Forest.—Daring and Successful Lion-hunt.—Tomb of the Prophet Ezra.—Scenes on the Banks of the Tigris.—Grand Mountains.—Arab Villages.—Ruins of Ancient Seleucia and Ctesiphon.—First View of Bagdad.—Guests of Captain Holland.—Wonders of Bagdad.—The People, Bazaars, Mosques, Churches, Tombs, Baths, Jews, and Christians of the City of "The Thousand and One Nights."—Turkish Railroads.—Commerce with the United States.—American Petroleum the Light of the World.. 63

CHAPTER III.

Five Days among the Ruins of Ancient Babylon.—Preparations for the Journey.—Early Start.—Bridge of Boats.—Crowd of People.—Celebrated Tombs.—Raising Water.—Luncheon by the Way-side.—First View of the Ancient Ruins.—The Pilgrim's Khan.—First Night among the Ruins.—Again in the Saddle.—Ancient Walls.—Arab Villages.—Telegraph Poles.—The Old Canals.—Remains of Belshazzar's Palace.—The Famous Hanging Gardens.—Daniel's Lion's Den.—Harps on the Willows.—Rivers of Babylon.—The Euphrates.—Immense Palm-groves.—Bridge of Boats.—Modern Hillah.—Our Khan.—American Petroleum.—Telegraph Station.—Call upon the Pasha.—Playing with a Lion.—Sail on the Euphrates.—A Night in Hillah.—Start for the Tower of Babel.—Dangers in the Way.—Wonderful Ruins.—Ascend the Tower of Babel.—The Fiery Furnace.—The Glory of Babylon.—Progress of its Decline.—Prophecy Fulfilled.—The Warriors of the Desert.—Return to Bagdad........................Page 122

CHAPTER IV.

Sail on the Tigris.—Perilous Situation.—Shrines of Kathimain.—Modes of Traveling.—Making a Bargain.—Departure from Bagdad.—First Night's Experience.—Half-way House.—Delli Abbass.—Adam's Fleas.—Den of Robbers.—Hills of Hamreen.—Beautiful Flowers.—Karateppeh.—Storks, and their Habits.—Jebarah Portrayed.—War of Words.—Walking Qualities of the Arab.—Town of Kifri.—Turkish Soldiers.—Day of Rest.—Storm on the Desert.—Crossing the Dreaded Dooz.—Dooz Khurmuttee.—Changeless East.—Conscripts.—Dandy Officer.—Village of Tavok.—Singing Dervish.—Robbers.—American Songs.—City of Kerkook.—Traveling with the Pasha's Wives.—Excitement in the Hills.—Altoon Kupri.—Remarkable Bridge.—Ancient Arbela.—Battle between Darius and Alexander the Great.—Greater Zab.—A Night with the Shepherds.—Habits and Customs of the Bedouins.—Eleventh Day Out.—Domes of Mosul, and Gates of Nineveh.—Crossing the River.—Mine Host.—Mr. Rassam.—Splendid Residence.—City of Mosul.—Mosques, Churches, and Bazaars.—Easter-Sunday.—Elegant Ladies.. 185

CHAPTER V.

Among the Ruins of Ancient Nineveh.—Historical and Scriptural Allusions.—Nimrod, the Mighty Hunter.—Asshur and his Colony.—Extent and Duration of the Assyrian Empire.—Extent and Glory of Nineveh.—Its Walls, Gates, and Palaces.—Identity of its Ruins.—Jonah's Visit to Nineveh.—His Mission and his Tomb.—Sail down the Euphrates.—Beautiful Scenery.—Selamiyah.—Donkey-ride.—Birthplace of Saladin.—Great Image of Nebuchadnezzar.—Exploring the Ruins.—Tower of Nimroud.—Ancient

Temples.—Wonderful Sculptures.—Palace of Asshurizir-pal.—Splendid Remains.—Palaces of Shalmaneser II., and of Tiglath-pileser II.—The Marble Obelisk.—Palace of Esar-haddon.—God Nebo.—Horrid Night with the Arabs.—Return to Mosul.—Grand Palace of Sennacherib, and its Magnificent Sculpture.—Annals and Will of Sennacherib.—Palace of Sardanapalus, and its Splendid Bass-reliefs.—Assyrian Wars.—Fall of Nineveh.—The Last Battle.—Prophecy Fulfilled.....................Page 253

CHAPTER VI.

Discovery of the Royal Library of Asshur-bani-pal.—Rawlinson on the Nature and Style of Assyrian Writing.—Eminent Cuneiform Scholars.—Layard's History of the Process of Deciphering the Cuneiform Characters.—Triumphant Success.—Specimens of the Translated Tablets.—Promissory Note.—Bill for the Sale of Slaves.—Deed of Conveyance.—Religious Views of the Assyrians.—Forms of Prayer.—Death of a Righteous Man.—Harmony between the Bible and the Assyrian Records.—Daniel in the Lion's Den, and his Companions in the Fiery Furnace.—Modes of Punishment.—Chaldean Account of the Creation and of the Deluge by Berosus.—Original Account of the Flood by the Assyrians, Discovered by Mr. Smith, and his more recent Translation of the Same.—Copy of the Record.—Its Agreement and Disagreement with the Bible.—Probable Future Discoveries, and their Bearing on Biblical Interpretation.—What the United States should do in the Work of Exploration................. 321

CHAPTER VII.

Christianity in the East.—Origin of the Nestorians.—Their Great Learning.—Their Vast Missions.—Letter from Mr. Hormuzd Rassam on the Eastern Churches.—Syrian Jacobites.—Syrian Catholics.—Chaldean Nestorians.—Their Chaldean Origin.—Opinions of Ancient and Modern Authors.—Language of the Chaldeans.—History and Creed of the Nestorians.—Their Present and Their Future.. 362

CHAPTER VIII.

Departure from Mosul.—Horseback Ride of Six Hundred Miles.—Last View of Nineveh.—First Day's Ride.—A Night with the Devil-worshipers.—Hills of Kurdistan.—The Kurds.—Stuck in the Mud.—Xenophon's Retreat.—Sabbath of Feshapoor.—Crossing the Tigris.—Traveling in Mesopotamia.—Girls of Uznaoor.—Beautiful Scenery.—Nisibeen and the Nestorians.—Roman Ruins at Dara.—The True Ararat.—Heights of Mardeen.—American Mission.—Jacobite Christians.—Missionary Meeting.—Dance of the Devil-worshipers.—Attacked by Robbers.—Great Caravan.—No Water.—Beautiful Orfah.—Abraham's Fishes and Birthplace.—Ur of the Chaldees.—Armenian Christians and their Creed.—A Letter to Christ.—American Church.—Roman Roads and Reservoirs.—Milking Sheep.—Picturesque Town of Birijik.—Crossing the Euphrates.—Traveling in Syria.—American Petroleum.—Three Hundred Camels, and their Habits.—Aleppo and its People.—A Funeral.—Commerce.—American Mission.—A Beautiful Lady.—Charming Scenery.—The Flood.—Roman Roads.—Wild Pass of Beylan.—First View of the Sea.—End of the Journey..Page 392

ILLUSTRATIONS.

	Page
THE GARDEN OF EDEN ... *Frontispiece.*	
MAP OF ROUTE FROM BOMBAY TO THE MEDITERRANEAN SEA ... *To face*	17
IDOL TEMPLE AT DWAKA	22
FEEDING THE SACRED CROCODILES	28
CITY OF MUSCAT	33
THE PEARL-FISHER	46
WILD BOAR OF THE TIGRIS	73
A LION HUNT	76
TOMB OF EZRA	79
ANCIENT CTESIPHON	90
CAPTAIN HOLLAND'S HOUSE	97
MARKET-PLACE OF BAGDAD	105
NATIVE CHRISTIAN WOMEN	115
THE KHAN	126
ANCIENT BABYLONIAN CANALS	132
BELSHAZZAR'S PALACE	135
HANGING GARDENS	139
DANIEL'S LIONS' DEN	142
THE CHARM-BOWL	143
TOMB OF EZEKIEL	150
TOWER OF BABEL	153
BRICK FROM THE TOWER OF BABEL	154
PLAN OF ANCIENT BABYLON	163
FIGHTING PILGRIMS	181
BRIDGE OF BOATS AT BAGDAD	187
TOMBS OF KATHIMAIN	190
TOMB OF ZOBEIDA	191
A KHAJAWAH	196
INTERIOR OF A KHAN	201
TOWN OF KIFRI	210
RAFT ON THE TIGRIS	233
SHEPHERD'S TENT	235
ARAB MAN AND WOMAN	239

ILLUSTRATIONS.

	PAGE
CITY OF MOSUL	241
LANDING AT MOSUL	244
INTERIOR OF A HOUSE AT MOSUL	245
JOSEPH ADO	250
ENTRANCE TO A TEMPLE	266
TUNNEL IN THE TOWER OF NIMROUD	267
ENTRANCE TO A TEMPLE	269
STATUE OF A KING	271
ENTRANCE TO THE GREAT HALL OF THE NORTH-WEST PALACE	273
EXCAVATIONS	275
TIGLATH-PILESER IN HIS CHARIOT	279
THE GOD NEBO	283
THE MOUNDS OF KUYUNJIK	287
A WINGED BULL	290
TOMB OF THE PROPHET JONAH, AND THE RIVER KHAUSSER	292
PALACE OF SENNACHERIB RESTORED	294
BASS-RELIEFS	296
SCULPTURES IN RELIEF	298
REMOVAL OF A COLOSSAL LION	301
SENNACHERIB ON HIS THRONE	304
PLACING A HUMAN-HEADED BULL IN POSITION	305
INSCRIBED TABLETS	308
INSCRIPTIONS ON THE WINGED BULLS	309
JEWISH CAPTIVES	313
TORTURING THE CAPTIVES	316
SPECIMEN OF A CUNEIFORM INSCRIPTION	329
THE DELUGE TABLETS	349
CHAMBER WHERE THE TABLETS WERE FOUND	351
HORMUZD RASSAM	366
A TUKHTERAVAN	393
VALLEY OF SHEIKH ADI	398
CHIEF OF THE DEVIL-WORSHIPERS	400
DANCE OF THE DEVIL-WORSHIPERS	401
HIGH-PRIEST OF THE DEVIL-WORSHIPERS	403
YEZIDI WOMEN	404
KURDISH WOMEN	405
CHRISTIAN GIRLS OF UZNACOR	414
GREEK AND ROMAN REMAINS AT NISIBEEN	417
CITY OF MARDEEN	421
CITY OF ORFAH	429
ABRAHAM'S MOSQUE AND POOL	433
TOWN OF BIRIJIK	439
THE DROMEDARY	446
ARAB CAMELS	447
HALT OF A CARAVAN	449

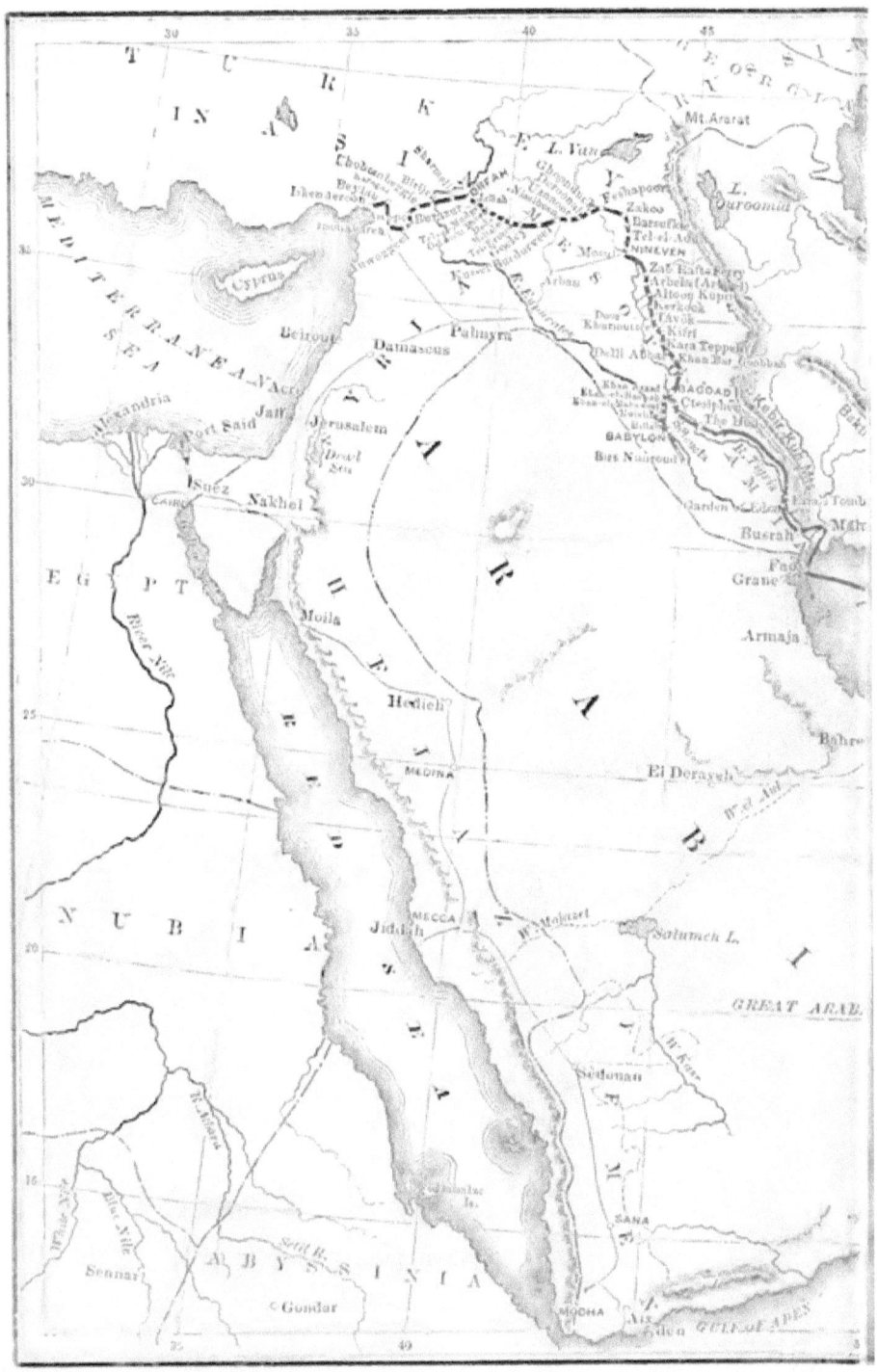

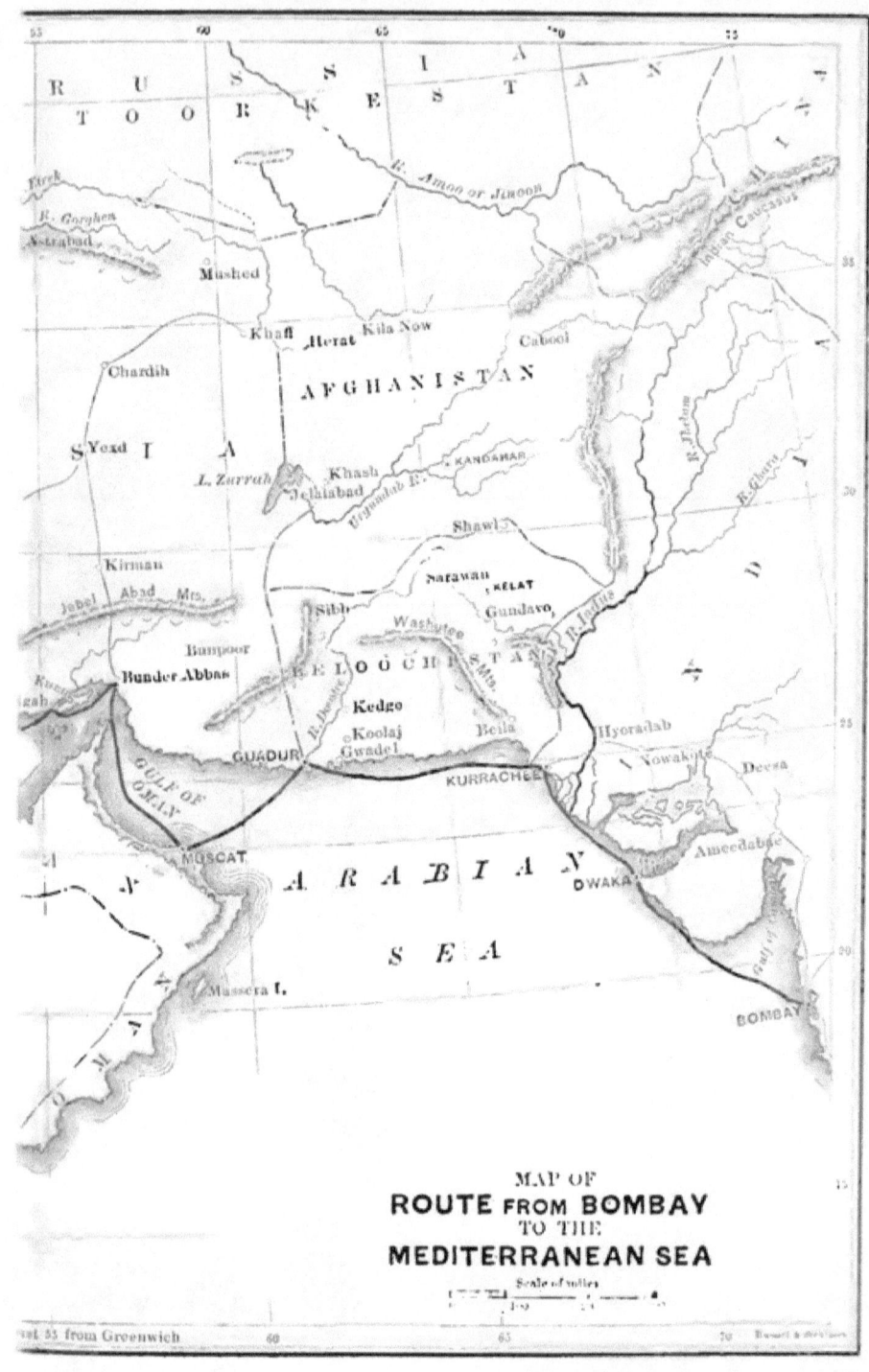

MAP OF
ROUTE FROM BOMBAY
TO THE
MEDITERRANEAN SEA

THRONES AND PALACES
OF
BABYLON AND NINEVEH.

CHAPTER I.

Up the Persian Gulf.—Brilliant Anticipations.—Memorable Historic Lands.—Preparations for the Journey.—Our Party.—Steamer *Burmah*.—English Travelers.—Pilgrims to the Shrine of Dwaka.—Kurrachee.—Its History and Commerce.—Civilizations Compared.—Worshiping Alligators.—Oriental Gamblers.—Looking for a Harbor.—Guadur.—Appearance and History of Muscat.—Its King and his Kingdom.—Delicious Dates.—Ornamented Women.—Reign and Forts of the Portuguese.—Terrible Massacre.—Sunset at Sea.—Arabian and Persian Mountains.—Persian Gulf described.—Bunder Abbas.—Portuguese and Ormuz.—Fire-worshipers.—Islands in the Persian Gulf.—Kishm and Larrack.—Lingah.—Pearl-divers of Bahrein.—Pearl-fisheries.—Costly Pearls.—A Sea of Blood.—Bushire.—Tragic Scenes.—England's Lion Share.—Ancient and Modern Persia.—Brilliant Phosphorescent Display.—Slowness of the Orientals.—Dreadful Storm.—Farewell to the Persian Gulf.—Great Shaat-el-Arab.—Beautiful River Scenery.—Sheikh of Mahomerah.—First Stage of our Journey Ended.—Commerce of Busrah.—Enchanting Rivulet.—Busrah.—Home of Sindbad the Sailor.—Ancient Ruins.—Garden of Eden.

THE lights along the lengthened bund* burned dimly as we steamed out of the spacious harbor of Bombay. The evening star shone over the Caves of Elephanta. The elegant villas and woodland slopes of Malabar Hill were on our right when we made our exit to the sea. We were *en route* to the most ancient and renowned

---

* Wharf in India.

lands known to history, whose monumental ruins bespeak a civilization earlier than that of Greece and Rome, and whose exhumed annals contain the record of events coeval with our race. The dreams of other years were soon to be realized, and long-maturing plans were at the point of consummation. Guided by the studies of former days, the imagination dwelt with delight upon the pleasures that awaited us. We were to enjoy the delicious excitement of

"Moonlight over Oman's sea;"

scent afar the spicy breezes of "Araby the blest;" linger in the date-groves of Muscat; gather pearls from the shores of Bahrein; behold "Kishm's fair isle;" roam through the Garden of Eden; sail up the Tigris and the Euphrates; stand on the Tower of Babel, and explore the ruins of ancient Babylon; stroll through the bazaars of Bagdad, the city of "The Thousand and One Nights;" examine the remains of Nineveh, and wander through the palace of Sennacherib; traverse the whole length of Mesopotamia, where Job lived, where Abraham was born, where Jacob wooed his beautiful Rachel; pass over the battlefields of Cyrus, of Alexander, and Trajan; follow the "Retreat of Xenophon and the Ten Thousand;" visit Nisibis of the Nestorians, Mount Masius of the Romans, and Antioch, where "the disciples were first called Christians."

Such was the fascinating vision that floated before our imagination, and allured us by its entrancing hopes. It was not easy, however, to obtain accurate and reliable information necessary to make the tour. The route is not frequented by ordinary travelers, and only a few have made the journey for research and exploration. Nine-tenths of the persons of whom we made inquiries discouraged the attempt. We were told that terrific storms frequent the Persian Gulf; that robbers infest those countries; that competent guides could not be obtained; that there were no places of entertainment for the accommodation of the traveler; that numberless streams, swollen by the melted snows from the Hamreen and Taurus Mountains, would prove impassable; and that a journey of a thousand miles on horseback must be performed. Stories were related of personal hardship, of robberies and murders, and confirmed by Buckingham, by Ainsworth, by Layard. But occasionally we had met some brave, hopeful, intelligent person, whose encouraging words were an inspiration. And, fortunately, we were favored with letters of commendation from the high officials of British India to the English consul at Bushire, at Busrah, and at Bagdad.

Happily our party was small. If great hardships were to be endured, there were but few to suffer. If lives were to be sacrificed, there were only three to die. One of our companions was a lady whom we had known for eighteen beautiful years, and could rely upon her courage in danger, her endurance in fatigue, her enthusiasm in exploration. The other *compagnon de voyage* was a gentleman who had seen the beauty of sixty summers, who was quiet, intelligent, and brave.*

Our steamer was the *Burmah*, of the British India Steamship Navigation Company, and was bound for Busrah, on the Shaat-el-Arab, the end of the first stage of our journey. Of a thousand tons, the *Burmah* proved an admirable steamer. Her saloon was large, tastefully ornamented, and furnished with mirrors, sofas, and a library. The state-rooms were not inferior in size and convenience to those on the Atlantic and Pacific steamers.

---

* Mr. C. B. Collins, of New York.

The bill of fare was good, the attendance excellent, and the officers were competent and gentlemanly. Our captain was a thorough seaman, and a thorough Englishman. He was a sailor among his crew, a gentleman among his passengers. His vigilance knew no cessation; and although the first officer was one of the most efficient seamen I have ever met, yet the captain remained on deck from sunset to sunrise. In conversation he was genial and entertaining. He was familiar with the ancient and modern history of the Persian Gulf, and seemed happiest when reciting some legend of the sea. Although small of stature, he was every whit a man. Gifted with a merry laugh, he drove dull care away. Born to command, his stentorian voice rose above the storm. He had the habit of omitting the *h* where he should have put it, and of putting it where it did not belong. One day when sailing along the Persian coast, I inquired: "Captain, what peaks are those?" "Those hare the Hass's Hears, sir," was his aspirated response.

On board the *Burmah* was an English party bound for Bagdad, and consisted of the Hon. E. H. Ellis, his mother, Lady Howard de Walden, and his sister, the Hon. Miss Ellis. He was a young gentleman of fortune, and traveled for pleasure. His previous voyage over the same route had made him familiar with every island, peak, and river, and his genial manners rendered him a delightful companion. He was an amateur photographer, and his proficiency in the art is best evinced by some of the pictures that illustrate this volume. His mother and sister kept a pictorial journal of their tour, and sketched in colors each town and temple and ruined tower, each quiet bay and beetling crag, each emerald isle and palm-date grove, with a rapidity and accuracy that excited our admiration. Stately in her bearing as

IDOL TEMPLE AT DWAKA.

a queen, the mother was a lady of much culture, and of extensive reading. The daughter displayed less reserve of manner, and gave expressions to her wit, which was as brilliant as it was caustic.

The first night at sea had passed, and the morning found us on the Indian Ocean, whose waters lave the distant shores of Arabia, and form the western boundary of British India, a prize coveted oft by earth's greatest conquerors. The wind blew hard, and the waves ran high; but as the day declined and we neared the land, the sea became calm:

> "All hush'd, there's not a breeze in motion,
> The shore is silent as the ocean.
> If zephyrs come, so light they come,
> Nor leaf is stirr'd, nor wave is driven."

At nine o'clock on Sunday morning we dropped anchor in the harbor of Dwaka, three hundred miles from Bombay. The small village of Dwaka is on a white sandy beach, and is the site of one of the richest idol-temples in India. We had stopped to land two hundred and fifty Hindoo pilgrims, who had come to offer their devotions at this most sacred shrine. The occasion was a méla, which occurs once in twenty-five years, and thither these devotees had journeyed to worship and to *pay*. On leaving port, they had expressed their superstition by throwing cocoa-nuts into the sea to insure a pleasant voyage; but the gods of the deep had been indifferent to their offerings, and the sea continued rough. The women were extravagantly ornamented with ivory anklets, with gold ear-rings, and with silver rings in their noses; but they were thinly clad, and suffered much in the keen winds of February. According to report, these Hindoos save the earnings of a quarter of a century, to present them at this famous shrine; and such is the accumulated wealth of the temple, that the eyes of the gods are diamonds, and the priests live in princely magnificence. Dwaka is a walled city, and within the walls is a spacious arcaded court, adorned with miniature temples. In the centre of the court stands the great temple, a cluster of buildings, crowned with a dome of white marble, above which is a pinnacle of the same material, magnificently gilded. In the sea-front of the tower are a series of ornamental balconies, and from its peak floated a banner bearing a curious device. To witness their devotions, we joined the vast procession of pilgrims, who pressed, with boisterous excitement, toward the idol-shrine. All the streets, all parts of the court, the temple itself, and the tower thereof, were filled with worshipers, whose offerings to the idol amounted to millions of rupees. From the temple the idolaters, old and young, male and female, priest and layman, hastened to the sacred tank, and to the streams that issued therefrom, and plunged tumultuously therein, believing that the waters were efficacious to wash away their sins. The enthusiasm of the devotees rose to madness; and, to prevent injurious results to life and limb, the soldiers on guard interfered, but with more violence than discretion.

In the gray of the next morning we sighted the red bluffs of Kurrachee, and soon thereafter saw the long, low, sandy beach, with irregularly formed hills beyond, and vast, gloomy mountains extending far away to the northeast. At noon we approached Manora Point, whereon is a light-house one hundred and nineteen feet above the level of the sea, and seen on a clear night a distance of seventeen miles. From the highest bluff floated the English flag, and within the bay were steamers, men-of-war, and native boats, quietly at anchor. As the bar across the mouth of the harbor is ever shifting, dredging-machines were employed to keep the channel open. From Manora Point there has been constructed a stone breakwater a thousand feet long, and on its extreme point is an iron lantern, wherein a fire is placed at night. The view from the deck of our steamer was exceedingly picturesque. On our left were the Government buildings, and near them was a pretty Gothic church; on our right was beautiful Clifton; to the north-east was Kiamari; and near us were rocks carved by the waves into fantastic forms. The most conspicuous object was Trinity Church, whose square tower is one hundred and fifty feet high, erected by a seaman to guide the inward-bound mariner.

Situated near the mouth of the ancient Indus, Kurrachee has a historical and commercial interest of more than ordinary significance. It was here that Alexander the Great, returning from his expedition into India, embarked to join his fleet on the Persian Gulf, under the command of Nearchus; and for a thousand years thereafter Kurrachee was the seat of an extensive trade. Prior to the eighth and ninth centuries of our era, the Red Sea was the chief channel of trade between India and Europe; but after the Mohammedans had seized Egypt, the merchants of the East sought a new channel of commerce through the Persian Gulf and the valley of the Euphrates. Since the decay of the Mohammedan power, trade has returned to the Red Sea, but not to the disadvantage of Kurrachee. Under British rule, it is the sea-port of the rich province of Sinde, and of the whole valley of the Indus, from Cashmere to the Indian Ocean. It is the most north-westerly port of British India, and the coming rival of Bombay for the trade of the great North-west. A railroad is now in process of construction along the banks of the Indus, extending from Kurrachee to Moultan, to Lahore and Peshawar, and, when completed, will not only connect Kurrachee with all parts of Northern and Central India, but will bring to its harbor the products of the Sinde, of the Punjab, of Afghanistan, and of Cashmere. At present, large quantities of cotton, wool, wheat, indigo, hides, and horns are brought here for shipment. In 1873, the imports were valued at nearly $5,000,000, and the exports exceeded that amount. During our late war, Kurrachee was the principal port for the shipment of Indian cotton, which was raised in the valley of the Indus, and which gave considerable importance to the place; but since the return of peace and the re-appearance of American cotton in European markets, the city has declined, and real estate is now sold for a song. The present embarrassment, however, is only temporary, and results from wild financial speculations rather than from permanent causes. Under the new impulse from railroads, trade will rapidly revive. Sooner or later, the Euphrates valley railroad will be an accomplished fact; and when that great work is done, Kurrachee will be the second commercial emporium in British India, and trade will be restored to one of the most ancient channels of commerce known to history.

Here, as in other parts of India, the effete civilization of the East is gradually succumbing to the better civilization of the West. By the liberality of the European residents, a library of six thousand well-selected volumes has been opened to the public. Adjoining the library is a museum, wherein are specimens of native minerals and petrified wood; a variety of cereals, of fishes, of red and white corals; a large number of stuffed birds, of deer and wild goats, and a quantity of Sinde pottery, rich and rare. Near the entrance to the museum are two pillars, each one resting on the back of an elephant, and each composed of a series of carved men and women in the grotesque costumes of India. Those pillars are the spoils of war. When the English captured the city of Beyt, they blew up a famous idol temple therein, and from the débris thereof carried away the pillars as the trophies of victory.

Here, as elsewhere in India, the light of a purer faith is sensibly dissipating the darkness of pagan superstition and ignorance. Houses of mercy, schools of learning, temples of piety, open their portals to the 30,000 idolaters of insular Kiamari, and the results are as beneficent as they are gratifying. But the darkness that remains is palpable. In the small adjacent village of Muggapoor are performed idolatrous rites debasing to all that is noble in man. Thither the people go to worship alligators, regarded as sacred animals, and daily fed by the idol priests. Near a temple, and within a large tank, are twenty of those hideous creatures, which are treated with more than human kindness. Pilgrims come from afar to offer sheep and goats to these horrid monsters. On the neighboring plains, the priestly shepherds keep large flocks to supply the pious market at a cost of two rupees per head. As an act of devotion, the pilgrim throws the purchased sheep to the alligators, which fight over the offering in a most ungodlike manner. But feeding them with sheep is a great improvement compared with the horrid custom of the past, when mothers threw their infants to the monsters that sported in the Indus and the Ganges.

At eight o'clock in the morning, the *Burmah* started for Gaudur, two hundred and eighty miles from Kurrachee, and nearly eight hundred miles from Bombay. The air was hazy, filled with a fine sand blown from the distant shore of Beloochistan. On our right was Ras Malan, where recently a whale had become entangled

FEEDING THE SACRED CROCODILES.

with the submarine cable, and, failing to extricate himself, had been completely devoured by the sharks. The number of our passengers had been increased by an addition of many Turks, Arabs, Persians, Jews, Parsees, and

Armenians. Whatever their wealth and their style of living at home, these Orientals never travel as first-class passengers. Their respect for caste, their religious superstition, their mode of cooking and eating, their pastime amusements, and their national self-conceit, render them exclusive. They prefer to sleep on the deck rather than in a well-furnished state-room, and to eat on their mat rather than sit with Christians in an elegant saloon. As they constitute the majority of travelers on all the steamers in the Far East, their wishes are respected, and the whole deck is accorded to them. They prefer midships, and the hatchway is their favorite resort. Once in possession of this, they will fight for it to the death. Rows frequently occurred, and blood was shed in the struggle for this preferable spot. Our hatchway amidships was held by five Arabs—four men and a boy. They were of the better class of their race, and their costume was of the gayest colors. Each one was a walking armory, and was armed with a Damascus blade, a nicely curved cimeter, a brace of silver-mounted pistols, and a rifle ornamented with mother-of-pearl. A Persian rug covered the spot they occupied, on which they ate and slept, prayed and gambled. At sunrise, at noon, at sunset, they made long prayers, offered with many genuflections. At sunset—fit emblem of man's dying hour—they seemed most devout. The coming twilight, the silence of all nature sinking to rest, added to the solemnity of the scene. Nothing diverted their attention. They appeared unconscious of the eyes that gazed upon them. How reverential was each act! how measured each sentence of prayer! how exact each prostration before the Lord and his prophet, Mohammed! Yet their religion allowed them to shed blood in defense of trivial and fancied rights. They retained possession of the hatchway even to blows, and threatened death to all intruders. Theirs is the religion of the sword. "Blood for blood" is a maxim of every-day life. The hours intervening between their acts of solemn worship were spent in gambling. They gambled for gold, for the swords they carried, for the jewels they wore. Occasionally, the game was suspended long enough for prayer, and then resumed with renewed zest. Their love for a game of chance was not peculiar to them, for it is a ruling passion in the East. Gambling is universal in Japan and China, in Persia and India, in the islands on the equator, in Egypt and Palestine, in the cities of Asia Minor, in the palaces of Constantinople, in the Turkish empire from the Persian Gulf to the banks of the Danube. Those who cast lots on Mount Calvary for the seamless garment have more followers than the prophet Mohammed.

We should have been at Guadur at 5 P.M. on the second day from Kurrachee; but the fog was dense, the harbor difficult to enter, the officers indifferent to the lapse of time, and fearful to make a bold venture. As night came on we *slowed*, and moved at the rate of a mile an hour till morning. The fog and the darkness passed simultaneously away. The sun rose clear and bright, but no one knew where we were. For twenty hours we steamed up and down the coast, looking for the harbor. Each man had his opinion, charts were consulted, landmarks were scanned, and each mountain and inlet was carefully viewed through the glass. It was apparent to every one *that we were all at sea*. For three hours we ran along the bold white bluffs of Ras Noo. All agreed that we were near the place. At length we sighted the low white sandy beach extending from Ras Noo to Castle Hill, a bluff five hundred feet high, composed of white rock, whose summit the elements had wrought into the semblance of a castle, which had given name to the place. Fancy could discern columns and galleries and pinnacles, and, when viewed in the moonlight, seemed weird, like the haunted ruin of some forsaken palace.

It was high noon when we anchored in the harbor, which, though difficult to find, is one of the best on the coast. As Kurrachee is the most north-westerly port of British India, so Guadur is the extreme north-western limit of Beloochistan. It is an insignificant place, but has long been the disputed ground between Beloochistan and Persia, and the battle-field of many a struggle for possession. It has a population of four Europeans and three hundred natives, whose rags their poverty proclaimed. Near it is a larger town, wherein is a telegraph station, the only sign of a better civilization.

Once more afloat, we were now bound for Muscat, Arabia, one thousand and twenty-five miles from Bombay, and located on the Gulf of Oman, which is intermediate between the Persian Gulf and the Indian Ocean. The bold bluffs of Castle Hill and Ras Noo

"O'er the deep their shadows flung,"

as in the evening twilight we turned our prow toward the Arabian shore. All that night, all the next day, all the ensuing night, we steamed over a placid sea, not faster than seven knots per hour. It was a run of two hundred and forty-five miles, and occupied more than thirty hours to accomplish. While yet the stars were bright, we anchored in the outer harbor, and waited for the dawn. And when the sun rose, the cove, the forts, the city of Muscat, lay before us. On our right and on our left were rock islands, the dreary home of fishermen and pirates. From out the sea appeared rocks, six hundred feet high, and beyond them, and far inland, could be seen the mountains of Northern Arabia. The increasing light revealed the deep caves along the shore, that echoed the roar of the waves; and far up the rugged rocks appeared Arabs in white, climbing the narrow, winding paths. On the boldest peaks were the old forts of the Portuguese, now the watch-towers of the Arabians. Conspicuous among the buildings of the town, were the king's palace, the English residency, and the custom-house. The scene in the harbor was no less pleasing to contemplate. The beautiful cove is a semicircle, and therein fifty vessels can safely anchor at the same time. A mile long and three-fourths of a mile wide, it is safe and well sheltered. When we arrived, an English gun-boat, a Turkish man-of-war, and many coasting boats, were at anchor in the quiet waters of the bay.

Commercially and politically, Muscat has had an eventful history. Three centuries ago, Alphonso d'Albuquerque, of Portugal, conquered all the islands of the Persian Gulf, and the Portuguese held them till 1707, when the Muscat Arabs gained the ascendency. On all the higher rocks commanding the entrance to the harbor the Portuguese constructed strong forts, that for two centuries bade defiance to Turk, to Arab, and Persian. During all those years of possession and prosperity the merchants of Portugal controlled the commerce of the gulf, and amassed immense fortunes. Under their prosperous reign Muscat became a city of wealth and luxury, and the genius and beauty of Europe adorned society; and under those Catholic conquerors, churches and monasteries were built, and priest and monk held undisputed sway. In the rocks by the sea are the cells of the anchorites, while here and there may be seen the prostrate column of some grand cathedral. But all now is changed.

The Portuguese were expelled by the Arabs. The cathedral became a mosque, the monastery became a harem, and from the summit of the rocks the monk and the nun were cast into the sea. Ten thousand Christians were massacred. The recluse was burned to death in his cell; the priest was sabred at the holy altar; and the Sister of Mercy, with her helpless orphans, were hurled from the precipice, and dashed against the rocks below.

CITY OF MUSCAT.

Originally, the kingdom of Oman embraced the southeastern section of Arabia, from Ras-ool-Hud, on the south, to Zobara, on the north-eastern coast. It consisted of two principalities; the capital of one was Rastag, and the capital of the other was Julfar. The male portion of the population was then estimated at eight hundred thousand, and furnished an army of brave warriors. But since the expulsion of the Portuguese, frequent quarrels have occurred between the Arabs and the Persians, resulting now in Persian conquest and anon in Arab ascendency. At present, Muscat is the capital of all that portion of the former kingdom bounded by the Gulf of Oman, and contains a population that fluctuates from ten to thirty thousand. Still retaining somewhat of its former commercial importance, the Banians are the brokers, the Arabs are the merchants, and the king is the chief trader. The present imaum, as he is sacredly called, is an independent sultan, whose will is absolute, and whose authority is maintained by the force of arms.

On going ashore, we called upon his majesty, who is now in his forty-fifth year, but in feeble health. On the left of the royal entrance is a lion's den, wherein was a young lion, the plaything of the king's domestics. Adjoining the palace is the sultan's harem, filled with young and beautiful Arabian women. Opposite the residence are the royal stables, well supplied with the best native horses, that were cleaner and fatter than the men who had them in charge. Near the palace is the custom-house, which presented a busy scene. Extending along the bund for hundreds of yards were stacks of wheat, wool, and dates in sacks, ready for shipment to foreign parts. The chief article of export is the Muscat date, considered the finest in the world. From four to six American vessels arrive here annually, and load with dates for the United States. Those sent to America are packed in bamboo sacks when fully ripe, by which process the rich juice is preserved, and hence they are called "wet dates;" but they are much inferior in flavor to the "dried date," sold here in the bazaars, and which constitute the principal article of food of the natives when on a journey. Were these dried dates shipped to America, they would be esteemed a luxury, and would find a ready market. In 1833, a commercial treaty was concluded between the United States and the Sultan of

Muscat that secured to us the advantages of an enlarged trade; but, owing to our limited merchant marine, England controls the trade of this port. But England has no other relations with the sultan than such as are stipulated by treaty, which, however, secures to her the superior advantage of the right to keep at all times one gun-boat in the harbor, and by which she has a commercial advantage over all other nations.

From the custom-house we wandered through the town, whose streets are crooked lanes, whose buildings are hovels, whose bazaars are gloomy and filthy. The bazaars were well supplied with English goods, with wet and dried dates, and with native wares. Each merchant had his gun by his side and a sabre in his girdle, not only in accordance with universal custom, but to protect his life and property, as neither is secure under the weak and miserable rule of the Mohammedan sultan. The Arabs, who had come from their farm and their fold to trade, were armed for battle and ready for the fray. The Arab sleeps, eats, drinks, trades, works, travels, marries, prays, and dies with his sabre, matchlock, and pistols on, ready for use at a moment's warning. In the bazaars, women were winnowing grain, and men selling their merchandise. Beauty is not an attribute of the women of Muscat. They had rings in their ears, rings on their toes, and rings in their noses, but beauty nowhere. A single robe of blue cotton cloth covered their person, and the tattered condition of that indicated the poverty to which they are reduced by a false religion and a despotic government.

From the market-place we ascended the rocks on the right of the town, and entered the old Portuguese fort. Over the entrance is the date "1588." Within the walls are rusty English, Dutch, and Portuguese guns of large calibre; and on one is the date "1625." From the parapet of the fort, six hundred feet high, the view of sea and land was extensive and enchanting. Inland could be seen the town, with its white buildings and the green valleys beyond; seaward, the prospect was grand and boundless. Around us lay the ruins of former greatness; and directly opposite was Fort Jilla Forsah, from whose frowning parapet, and down whose rugged sides, monks and nuns were hurled by their Mohammedan conquerors.

Amidst the golden splendor of an Arabian sunset, we left Muscat for Bunder Abbas, two hundred and fifty miles to the north-east, on the Persian shore. The peaks of Oman were the last to cherish the fading light of departing day. A brief twilight, and the greater and lesser stars came forth one by one to attend the crescent moon. There was a calm in the sky; there was a calm on the sea. On the *Burmah*, quiet had succeeded the excitement of the day. The thunder-tones of the little captain had given place to notes of softness. Pilgrim, traveler, and sailor felt the repose of the evening hour.

> "'Twas the voice of nature calling
>   Earth's weary children to repose;
> While, round the couch of nature falling,
>   Gently the night's soft curtains close.
> Soon o'er a world in sleep reclining,
>   Numberless stars throughout yond dark
> Shall look, like eyes of cherubs shining
>   From out the veil that hides the Ark."

That was the last night of the week. The Christian Sabbath dawned upon a land where its sanctity is unobserved, and where its benedictions are unknown. Our Mohammedan passengers prayed and gambled; the Persians ate and slept; the Jews counted their money; the Parsees examined their accounts; the Armenians read and sung; and six Protestants assembled in the saloon for Divine worship.

Late in the afternoon we sighted land—Arabia on the west, Persia on the east. On either shore the mountains were lofty and imposing. On the Persian coast was Ras Jashk, 1720 feet high; beyond was Mount Danghir, whose summit is 3133 feet above the level of the sea; and rising above them all in glory was Mount Biss, the height of whose highest peak is 4600 feet. On the Arabian shore, the mountains were higher and bolder. Mount Kewa rises 5800 feet above the level of the Gulf; further on was Fire Peak, whose altitude is 4470 feet; and higher and grander than all his fellows, was Sham Peak, whose lofty brow is 6700 feet above the surrounding plain. The summits of all the higher mountains were covered with snow, reflecting the rosy tints of the setting sun. When the day had ended, the last zephyr ceased to breathe. The sea became as a plate of glass, and the wake of our steamer through the phosphorescent light shone like a path of silver. As each wave rolled on with unbroken crest, it resembled a silver scroll thricely polished.

During the night, we had passed the imaginary boundary of the Sea of Oman; and when the morning came, we were on the Persian Gulf, which is six hundred miles long, from forty to two hundred miles wide, and has an area of eighty thousand square miles. In outline it describes a curve, and properly it is an arm of the Indian Ocean. Its entrance is through the Arabian Sea, the Gulf of Oman, and the Straits of Ormuz. The latter are less than thirty miles wide. It receives the waters of the Euphrates, of the Tigris, and of other less celebrated rivers. It is frequented by terrific storms, destructive alike to shipping and the towns along the coast. It is a classic sea, and rich in historic associations. In one of its harbors Alexander the Great rejoined his fleet, commanded by Nearchus; and over its waters the great Macedonian general returned to Babylon, to revel in luxury and to die in shame. During eventful wars, Greek and Roman, Persian and Parthian, Portuguese and Briton, have fought thereon for power and glory. On the bottom of this little inland sea are strewed the wrecks of the mighty navies of Europe and Asia, and amidst its corals are the bones of the gallant dead. For two centuries its shores were the seat of European commerce and luxury. One of its cities was the scene of some of the legends in "The Thousand and One Nights." On one of its islands lived the Fire-worshipers, described in Moore's famous "Lalla Rookh." For many years it has been the resort of pirates, whose bloody deeds are the bloodiest in piratical annals. The Joassamee pirates have long bidden defiance to Persia, to Turkey, and to England, and plundered the merchantman thereon, cargoed with the "wealth of Ormuz and of Ind." Nor is their occupation gone. Not a month before our arrival, they boarded a companion steamer of the *Burmah*, wounded the officers, and stole the immense treasure on board. And we were in like danger; but, happily, we were fully prepared to meet the pirates.

At two o'clock in the afternoon, we dropped anchor in the harbor of Bunder Abbas. We were now in Persia, whose warrior-kings fill so large a space in ancient and modern history. Situated on a sandy plain of crescent shape, Bunder Abbas is at the base of a lofty range of mountains. So shallow is the water along the rocky coast, that even small boats can not land. When within a hundred feet of the shore, we were carried to dry land on the backs of the boatmen. Hundreds of Persians and Arabs crowded to see us, and followed us in our wanderings through the town. Homely and untidy as were the women, they ran at the approach of the strangers. They were veiled, but not to hide their beauty, for with this they were not embarrassed. The dwellings are of mud, without form or comeliness. The custom-house has some pretensions to shape, and near it is a round tower, but a poor defense. The village contains a post-office and an English residency. In the bazaars were luscious oranges, a hundred for a dollar; and Persian rugs, the best, twenty dollars each. South of the town are extensive gardens, where the palm grows in its beauty. In summer the air is as the blast of a furnace, and mortal vapors are exhaled from the earth: the fields are then dry and black as if scorched with fire, and the people fly to the mountains to escape the consuming sirocco. Those mountains are high and grand. To the south was Shemil, whose altitude is 8500 feet; to the east was Ginnoch, 7690 feet above the sea; and far away could be seen Mount Bukan, 11,000 feet above the adjacent plain.

We were now at the centre of the commercial wealth and luxury of the Portuguese in the sixteenth and in the seventeenth century. On our right was "Kishm's fair isle;" before us was Larrack; on our left was Ormuz. Less than twelve miles to the south-west of Bunder Abbas the celebrated island of Ormuz is thirty miles in circumference. Its barren rocks are seven hundred feet high, and the peaks thereof are covered with a transparent ice-like incrustation of salt. Some of the soil is yellow with sulphur, some gray with copper, some red with the oxide of iron. Toward the south, the rocks rise from the shore like a vast cyclopean wall. Ormuz is an island of salt. In former days, the article was placed between the planks of ships to preserve them from the dry-rot; and, in later times, large quantities thereof were exported to Arabia, and to ports on the Persian coast. It is the driest island on the globe. It contains no water, save what is gathered from the clouds into immense reservoirs, some of which are centuries old. Its present inhabitants number four hundred, who fish by day and steal by night, and are among the strictest followers of Mohammed.

But how changed the face of this once fair island! Here lived in wealth and splendor forty thousand people. The merchants of Portugal made it the emporium of trade between Europe and India. Here were sold the jewels of Bokhara, the blades of Damascus, the carpets of Persia, the shawls of Cashmere, the spices of Ceylon, and the fabrics of Europe. It was the most splendid city in the East, the centre of fashion, and the seat of learning. From all parts of the globe, merchants were allured hither by the gains of trade, the splendor of the entertainments, and the polish of its citizens. The streets were covered with carpets; linen awnings were suspended from the tops of the houses, to afford shade and coolness; the dwellings were adorned with gilded vases filled with flowering shrubs and aromatic plants; wines from Persia, perfumes, and richest delicacies, tempted the appetite and intoxicated the senses; the citizens ate from plates of gold; they were banqueted with the music of the East, then in its highest perfection; and beauty and genius combined their charms to complete the circle of delights. Camels laden with water were stationed in the public squares for the use of the citizens and the accommodation of the traveler. In a word, extensive commerce, universal opulence, refined luxury, politeness in women, and gallantry in men, united to make the city the seat of pleasure.

Near the sea stood the palace of the captain-general, whose extraordinary splendor was the burden of many a song. From out the waters rose the castle, defended by the bravest troops, and contiguous thereto was the lofty column whose light, seen from afar, guided mariner and merchant to this metropolis of wealth and luxury. It was of this renowned city, in its palmy days, Milton sings:

> "High on a throne of royal state, which far
> Outshone the wealth of Ormuz and of Ind,
> Or where the gorgeous East with richest hand
> Showers on her kings barbaric pearl and gold,
> Satan exalted sat."

The last line is more than poetry—it is descriptive of a historic fact, confirmed by the dissipations of the people, and the terrible wars which occurred.

Unable to conquer the Portuguese without the assistance of a foreign ally, the Persians formed an alliance with the English, and the island was taken by storm in 1622. Nothing now remains of the former magnificence of Ormuz but a fragment of the old fort rising out of the sea, a portion of the conspicuous light-house that stood between the fort and the higher rocks, and a few of the large reservoirs designed for the accommodation of the public. It was not destined, however, to pass into oblivion, but rather to have other and better claims on the attention of mankind. It has been the asylum of the oppressed, and a city of refuge for the persecuted. When the disciples of Zoroaster, resident in Persia, were persecuted beyond measure by their Mohammedan masters, they fled to the caves of Ormuz for refuge, and, watching their opportunity, they migrated to Bombay, where their descendants are now known as the Parsees, who are distinguished no less for their wealth than for their intelligence.

At noon the next day we started for Lingah, one hundred and five miles up the Persian coast. We came in between Ormuz and Larrack, and went out between Larrack and Kishm. Larrack is the *Icarus* of Arrian, once famous for its pearl-fisheries. Its rocks are five hundred feet high, and are picturesque when viewed from the sea. Its ruined churches and warehouses proclaim its former prosperity; for it was here, in 1748, that the Dutch established themselves, and founded a flourishing commercial city, but from which they were driven, in 1765, by the Arabs, led on by the brutal corsair Miramhana.

To the north-east was Kishm, the largest island in the Persian Gulf. Fifty-four miles long and twenty miles wide, its form has some resemblance to that of a fish. Between it and the main, the channel is from three to thirteen miles wide, and is studded with pretty islets. On the plains are table-hills from two feet to four hundred feet high. Circular in form, they are broader at the top than at the base. Having been exposed to the action of the elements through countless ages, their sides have crumbled away, leaving many grotesque figures, which, when seen by moonlight, appeared to pleasing effect, and recalled a canto in "The Lady of the Lake:"

> "Their rocky summits, split and rent,
> Form'd turret, dome, and battlement,
> Or seem'd fantastically set
> With cupola and minaret;
> Wild crests as ever pagod deck'd,
> Or mosque of Eastern architect."

In the centre of the island is a barren rock, three hundred feet high, and steep on every side. Its summit is reached from within, through an aperture like a chimney, and is crowned with unknown ruins.

In the happier days of commercial prosperity, the island was inhabited by twenty thousand people, and on it were seventy towns. Most of the inhabitants were weavers, who produced a tapestry that equaled that of Persia. The chief cities were Kishm, Luft, and Bassadore. The latter has a good harbor, a small bazaar, and a limited population. It is now a coaling station for the English navy; and one of her majesty's gun-boats was in port for coal when we passed the place. The prosperity of this beautiful island continued under the Portuguese down to the incursions of the Joassamees pirates, who laid waste the fields, destroyed the villages, and murdered the citizens, without regard to sex or age. The ruins that remain bespeak the folly and the crime of the Mohammedan outlaws.

Our progress among these islands was slow, as our little captain obeyed instructions to place a higher value on coal than on time; but this rate of speed was better adapted to careful observation. During our cruise, we ran close to the Great Tomb, an islet three miles long by two and a half miles wide, and on it were a few young trees. Near it is the Little Tomb, barren and without an occupant.

In the early dawn, we anchored in the fine harbor of Lingah, which, seen from the deck of our steamer, presented a pleasant appearance. The white-colored buildings stood amidst palm-groves; and from the residence of the sheikh floated the Persian flag. We landed near a new caravansary, erected for the accommodation of pilgrims and travelers, and sat down in the shade of the palms to enjoy the delicious dates. Each tree was vigorous, and annually yielded fruit to the value of five dollars. The population is estimated at ten thousand, composed of Arabs, Kurds, Persians, Jews, and Armenians. whose costumes bespoke their nationality, and for the support of his creed each was ready to fight. The bazaars are inferior, but contained a supply of Manchester goods. In the rear of the town are mountains high and rugged. Not far from the shore is Mount Bustaneh, whose height is estimated at two thousand feet. Eastward is West Peak, two thousand feet higher. Beyond is Grubbs Notch, three thousand feet above the plain; and further on is Lingah Peak, a thousand feet above the Notch.

Within a few years past, Lingah has had an extensive trade in pearls found along the coast, and which have commanded a high price. But the principal pearl-fisheries in these Persian waters are around the island of Bahrein, three hundred miles diagonally across the Gulf, and on the Arabian side. Thirty miles long and ten miles wide, Bahrein is ninety miles in circumference. One fourth of its area is exceedingly rich, and abounds in date and orange groves. Everywhere are visible the ruins of the forts, the aqueducts, the reservoirs and palaces of the Persians, who formerly possessed this favored island, and under whose prosperous sway three hundred and sixty towns were built. It was known to the ancients as *Tylos*, and is mentioned by Arrian. It has had a checkered and bloody history. The Arabs were driven out by the Persians, the Persians by the Portuguese, the Portuguese by the Persians, and the Persians by the Arabs, who now possess it. Under the miserable rule of the latter, decay has gained the mastery. Of the three hundred and sixty populous villages, a few only remain. Bahrein is the principal town, and has a population of fifty thousand, composed of many nationalities. As there is no sweet water on the island, the people are compelled to resort to a remarkable spring in the sea. Divers attach a bottle to their girdle, descend to within a few feet of the bottom, fill and cork the vessel, pull a signal cord, and are raised by their companions to the surface again. About nine miles in the direction of Katiff is another and larger spring, where the sea is three fathoms deep. A dip-pump is inserted in the bottom of a tub, the tub is placed over the spring, and held in its place by weights. To the pump is connected a hose, through which the sweet water is conducted to the surface, where boats are prepared to receive it.

But the chief interest attached to Bahrein is the pearl trade, which is so extensive that ten thousand persons are engaged therein. Some of the methods adopted to obtain the pearls were practiced by the Romans; but the details of these methods differ with different divers. The pearl-oyster is found in beds like the common oyster, and often in great quantities in certain localities. The most valuable pearls are found in water from six to eight fathoms deep. The diving season usually lasts from June to October. The beds are surveyed, and divided into four parts, and only one part is worked in any one year. This method insures a rest of three years after each fishing season, and has been discovered necessary to the full growth and development of the animal.

When the fishing-time has come, a boat is anchored over a chosen spot, and in it are ten men—five divers and five pullers. The latter remain in the boat, to haul up the divers and receive the oysters; the former strip naked, and dive to the bottom of the sea. The ears of the divers are stuffed with bees-wax, and their nostrils are compressed with a piece of elastic horn; to their waist is fastened a small basket to contain the oysters. When all is ready, they place their foot upon a stone attached to a rope, inhale a long breath, raise their right arm as a signal to pay out the rope, and descend with the stone, holding fast to the rope with the left hand. Having collected as many oysters as he can, the diver pulls the signal cord, and his comrades haul him to the surface again. Some hardy divers can remain under water eighty seconds, and one could remain six minutes; but ordinarily the time is from forty to fifty seconds. They make from twelve to fifteen descents a day, and bring up a hundred oysters each time. Where the water is less deep, a pole is driven into the bottom of the sea, and the divers descend head-first along the pole.

THE PEARL-FISHER.

Having previously filled their mouth with oil, they spirt out the oil as soon as they reach the bottom, which clarifies the shallow water, and enables them to see the oysters. Loaded with the treasures of the sea, they reappear on its surface. But so exhausting are their labors, that divers are short-lived. They rarely attain the prime of life, and in appearance are thin and languid. They are frequently compelled to defend themselves against

the monsters of the deep. They seem not to fear the
shark, but they dread the saw-fish, which has been known
to cut a diver completely in two. Although their labors
are so exhausting, and at times so perilous, yet they are
poorly paid. The proportions of the gains are two to
the diver and four to the master; but the needy fisher-
man is forced in winter to borrow from his banker, and
pay thirty per cent. on the loan; so that at the end of the
fishing season he is as poor as he was at the beginning.
But be he ever so poor, he is in possession of one pearl
with which he will not part. It is an old and universal
custom in the family of the pearl-divers of Lingah and
Bahrein, to bore a pearl on their wedding-day, and to
this they cling as to a sacred charm.

From immemorial time, the pearl has been ranked
among the precious gems, and highly esteemed as one
of woman's chief ornaments. It is the inspired simile of
Divine truth. It is the chosen emblem of good fortune
by poets and romancers. It is numbered among the jewels of royalty. Yet Linnæus has shown that the beautiful pearl is but a slimy excretion developed for the
purpose of covering a grain of sand or some other foreign substance which has accidentally entered between
the delicate mantle and the shell, and, if not thus covered,
would cause irritation to the former. He proved by experiment that, by perforating a living pearl-oyster and
introducing a grain of sand, a nucleus is formed for the
development of a pearl; or, in other words, the natural
accretion of the substance of pearls is always due to some
injury the animal has sustained; and for demonstrating
this fact, Linnæus was knighted. The Chinese are known
to cause the formation of pearls by skillfully introducing
into the shells small beads of mother-of-pearl, which
soon collect an incrustation of calcareous matter; and

the monks in China have imposed on the credulity of the people by securing by this process pearl-coated images of saints and of the Virgin Mary, and exhibiting them as a miracle to confirm their religion. The same animal that yields the precious pearl also produces the mother-of-pearl shells, which are so beautifully carved by the monks of Bethlehem and Jerusalem, illustrative of the holy places.

There are two methods by which the pearl is extracted. In one case the oysters are strewed on the beach, and exposed to the rays of the sun until the animal is dead, and the shells open by relaxation. In the other case an iron instrument is inserted, and the shell of the bivalve is forced open, the gem extracted, and the animal, robbed of its jewel, is thrown into the sea. Many of the oysters brought up by the divers contain no pearls; but frequently in a single shell are found from eight to twelve, and sometimes twenty pearls. Not a few of them are small, and such are called "seed-pearls;" but occasionally one is found so large that it is a fortune in itself. The two famous pearls that Cleopatra proposed to dissolve in vinegar in honor of Mark Antony, at the luxurious banquet to which she had invited him, were valued at $390,000. Napoleon III. possessed an enormous pear-shaped pearl, which he exhibited at the Paris Exposition in 1855. What is known in England as the "Hope pearl" weighs three ounces, and measures four and a half inches in circumference. And while in Russia, I saw among the crown jewels and on the imperial crown thirty-eight vast and perfect pearls, each one a fortune to its possessor.

The annual yield of the pearl-fisheries of Lingah and Bahrein is estimated in value at $2,000,000. And although these Persian pearls are not so white as those of

Ceylon and Japan, yet they are larger than those of the former, and more regular in shape than those of the latter. They are of a yellowish hue, and long retain their golden color; whereas the whiter pearls lose much of their lustre by lapse of time. The uneven specimens are sent to Constantinople for embroidering and head-ornaments; but the perfect and magnificent pearls are sent to India, to Europe, and to America, where they add a fancied grace to the natural charms of woman.

It was midday, and we were again afloat. We were bound for Bushire, on the Persian coast, three hundred and fifteen miles to the north-east. All that afternoon, and till late in the evening, the sea ran with blood. The surface of the deep was of a scarlet color for many miles around us. It was a strange phenomenon, and filled the soul with a sense of horror. "What can it be?" was the spontaneous question of each beholder. Had the fish, small and great, been slain by some unknown power, and their blood come to the surface of the gulf? It seemed the realization of the vision John saw: "And the sea shall be turned into blood." Viewed in the moonlight, and when the phosphorescent waters were disturbed, the spectacle was even more ghastly. Hour after hour we steamed through those reddened waters, and contemplated this wonder of the deep. Some suggested that it was the spawn on which whales feed. Others thought it a mass of young dead fish. But it proved to be a vast quantity of luminous blubber, the mollusca of the medusa species. Its color was intense, and at night it moved in waves of reddened light. It is evidently a characteristic of these waters, as the same had been observed by former travelers.

During the night we passed the large island of Frur, barren and unoccupied. All the next day we ran along the Persian coast, with the high mountains of Persia full in view. Conspicuous among them were Bluff Hill, three thousand six hundred feet high; Barn Hill, a thousand feet higher; and Astuh Notch, the highest of the range. Farther on was the Fall, so called from a sudden depression between two prominent peaks. The pleasure of the prospect was heightened by the many-colored rocks, and the shadows of the clouds on land and sea.

Another night on the gulf had passed. The sun had risen on the towers of Bushire. It was the morning of the third day from Lingah. We were now in the chief sea-port of Persia, in N. lat. 29°, and in E. long. 50° 51'. An English steamer and a few native boats were at anchor in the bay. As the water in the harbor is shallow, we dropped anchor two miles from the shore. The city of Bushire is well located. The mountains around it are picturesque. Bu Reyyal, or the Asses' Ears, is two thousand five hundred feet high. The height of Kuh Khormuj is six thousand five hundred feet. The summit of Roundtop Mountain is ten thousand two hundred feet above the level of the sea. The buildings of the town are constructed of mud and stone, and most of them have three stories. On the roof of each is a tower so arranged as to catch each passing breeze to which there is an allusion in "Lalla Rookh:"

> "The wind-tower on the Emir's dome,
> Can hardly win a breath from heaven."

The streets are narrow, crooked, and unclean. Thirty thousand Persians, Arabs, and Armenians reside within the contracted limits of the place. Neither language can describe, nor can pencil portray, the uncleanliness of the Persian. He is despised by the Arab, who is a cleaner and a nobler animal. When in Peking, I thought it the most foul city I had seen, but Bushire is fouler. At the custom-house sat the Persian officials, who wore high fur hats, carried long swords, and smoked longer pipes.

We were the guests of Mr. Demetrius, an Armenian merchant, engaged in the opium trade. In going to his residence, we found the streets filled with women robed in black, and weeping bitterly. Our landing had occurred on the anniversary of the murder of Hassan and Hassein, sons of Ali, and whose memories are held in veneration next to that of Mohammed. The Persians are their adherents, and are called *Sheeahs*, and differ from the Arabs, who are designated as *Sunnis*. The difference between them relates to the question of succession to the rank and authority of Mohammed the prophet. The Arabs recognize Aboobeker, Omar, and Ottoman as the first three and true successors of the Prophet of Mecca; but the Persians reject these as usurpers, and claim that Ali Hassein and his two sons are the legitimate successors of Mohammed. It was in defense of their asserted rights to the succession that Ali and his sons were slain, and the strife is maintained by their respective followers, and often culminates in violence and death. The anniversary of that sad day is solemnly observed by the Persians. All business is suspended. The mosques are thronged from morning till night. The Mollahs recite the dreadful story of the murder, and with such pathos as to excite the faithful to madness. On that day, and in memory of the martyrs, the women clothe themselves in black, and the "mourners go about the streets." They gather around their mosques, sit upon the ground, smite their breast, and weepingly exclaim, "Why did they die?" From the mosques the faithful march in procession through the streets, with every demonstration of grief. In the afternoon they dramatize the murder scene, and with such effect that the representation seems to them a reality. In a moment of frenzy, they rush upon the men who personate Yezid and Moawziah, the assassins, and beat them in a shocking manner. At such times the fanaticism of the *Sheeahs* is limited by no restraint, and it is dangerous for *Sunnis* and foreigners to appear in the streets.

As the sea-port town of Persia, Bushire has an extensive trade in wool, wheat, opium, and Manchester goods. The articles of export are brought from the interior on the backs of camels, and the imports are conveyed by these beasts of burden, on their return journey, to the inland towns and to the imperial city of the empire. The largest and most elegant dwelling in the city is occupied by the English resident, who is clothed with almost embassadorial power, and is attended by a numerous staff of subordinate officers. A gun-boat awaits his commands, not merely for personal protection, but to enforce the commercial claims of England.

In the beginning of the seventeenth century, Shah Abbas, the Persian emperor, sought an alliance with Great Britain, to expel from the gulf the Europeans then enjoying a lucrative trade at the several ports. As an inducement, he promised to give the English free trade on these waters, and a moiety of the customs collected. The alliance was formed, the other European powers were expelled, and lucky England obtained the lion's share. Her gun-boats are in every port; her consuls exercise a controlling influence on Persian commerce and politics; and her manufactured goods are for sale in every inland village.

By degrees, Persia has lost her supremacy, and her glory has departed. She was once the seat of civilization and political power in the East. For two centuries she was the leading power in the world. Her area was more than four millions of square miles. Her population numbered hundreds of millions. Her victorious arms had carried her mighty sceptre into Media, Babylonia, Assyria, Mesopotamia, Syria, Palestine, Egypt, Northern Africa, and from the banks of the Indus to the palaces of imperial Delhi. Turning to Europe, she measured arms with the Greeks on the plains of Marathon and on the waters of Salamis. But the mighty have fallen. The modern Persians can boast the possession of the tomb of Cyrus the Great, but, like that tomb, their empire is the sepulchre of buried greatness. The fate of Persia was decided on the plains of Naharand in A.D. 641, when one hundred thousand were slain in battle; and when the Arabs compelled the Persians to accept the Moslem faith at the point of the sword, Zoroaster was exchanged for Mohammed, and a great people were forced to abandon a pure and simple religion, and embrace an imposture that has cursed with fanaticism, with bribery, and political decay every nation subject to its power.

With Russia on the north, with Afghanistan and Beloochistan on the east, with Turkey on the west, and bounded on the south and south-west by the gulf, the once vast empire is now but a thousand miles long, six hundred miles wide, and has an area of less than five hundred thousand square miles, and a population of less than ten millions. Ruins, degradation, and misery everywhere abound. The natural resources of Persia are considerable, but, neglected by an ignorant, superstitious, and despotic government, her commerce is insignificant. A majority of her inhabitants are wandering tribes, a little removed from the condition of Mexican Indians. The arts are neglected, the standard of education is low, and the great improvements of modern civilization are treated with contempt. Bribery is prevalent, and poverty is universal. Justice is unknown in the courts, and judicial decisions are purchased by the highest bidder. The Mollahs, or Moslem priests, who administer the local laws, are notoriously corrupt, and to "cheat like a Mollah" is a proverb among the people. Such is Persia of to-day. The only bright spot in all her dominions is where the American missionary is the teacher of childhood and the preacher of a divine religion.

That night the bay of Bushire was brilliant with phosphorescent light. A thick substance floated on the water, and, when disturbed, emitted an emerald light of great brilliancy. An orange thrown into the bay produced a series of the most beautiful illuminated circles. When fish leaped above the surface, they shone resplendent. When eels darted by us, the effect was magical. We dipped up the water, and the light remained. For a rupee the sailors launched a boat, and when it touched the surface of the bay, its sides resembled polished silver. Each lifted oar dripped with glory. The spray that covered the boatmen transformed them into angels of light; and the wake of the boat was a succession of resplendent undulations.

Three days were sufficient for our observations at Bushire. Indeed, the captain and his passengers desired to leave a day earlier than we did; and, had we done so, we should have escaped the most terrific storm we have ever experienced. But time is of the least possible value in the estimation of an Oriental. A day and a thousand years are the same to him. No entreaties can quicken his speed. Money is the only incentive that can induce him to increase his locomotion, and even this is transient in its effects. The traveler from the West, where energy characterizes every movement, and where time is money, is often sorely vexed by the slowness of the people of the East; but he soon learns to suppress his temper, hold his tongue, and permit the Oriental snail to move on apace. The Bushire merchants, both Persians and Europeans, had been preparing their mail, and had been indifferent to our wishes to depart.

It was four o'clock P.M. when the mail-boat came alongside, and in a few minutes thereafter the *Burmah* steamed out of port. Nature had displayed all her storm-signals. The very air felt tempestuous. The wind blew hard, the sea was rough, and at midnight the storm burst upon us in all its fury. Winds howled; rain fell in torrents; lightning flashed and darted through the darkened air; thunder answered thunder; waves broke in madness over us; the *Burmah* rolled fearfully; every thing that had not been made fast dashed with violence against the sides of the steamer; the gloom increased, and the darkness became palpable. It was an awful moment. We were at the mercy of the elements. Our helplessness was apparent. God only could save us. The hours passed wearily. It was now past midnight, and the storm raged with unabated force. The dumb animals gave signs of fear. The poor pilgrims were thoroughly drenched. Every officer was at his post. All hands were called on deck. The stern voice of command resounded through the ship. Our little captain, in his helmet-cap and long coat, was on the bridge thundering out his orders, and enforcing the same by the application of his boot. He was equal to the emergency. The wind came in squalls, sure sign that it had spent its strength. The rain ceased; the thunder died away; the clouds broke; the stars came out; the storm had passed, and we were safe.

The scenes of the night were the subject of conversation the next day. All denied having experienced a sensation of fear. Some claimed to have slept through all that dreadful storm,

"Rocked in the cradle of the deep,"

lulled by the howling winds, and soothed by the deafening thunder. Happy sleepers! Yet their questions as to what had occurred proved that they had been *dreaming* about a storm. We are ashamed of our fears when the danger is over; we are bold when courage has ceased to be a virtue.

But farewell to the Persian Gulf! Early the next morning we were at the mouth of the Shaat-el-Arab, which, in breadth, depth, current, and color, is not unlike the Mississippi. Its chief tributaries are the Euphrates and the Tigris, that have their confluence at Kurnah, the traditional Garden of Eden. At the head of the Persian Gulf and at the mouth of the Shaat-el-Arab is Fao, a telegraph station, and whereat is located a post-office for the accommodation of the few European and Arabian inhabitants. The first indication of our near approach was the yellow color of the water on our starboard side. It was so thick with alluvial matter, and so distinct from the light-green color of the gulf, that, viewed at a distance, it resembled a peninsula of yellow sand. Nor was the illusion dissipated till within a mile of the confluence of the gulf and the river. Our difficulty now was to find the channel. The recent storm had swept away the "Mark"—an immense buoy that had been anchored near the spot. After a fruitless search of four hours, we ventured to enter, and, fortunately, found the channel. Leaving the mail at Fao, we entered the mouth of the Shaat-el-Arab, and steamed against the eight-knot current. At the point of entrance the river is five miles wide, and on either side are low, narrow, alluvial banks, dotted with clumps of bushes. As we ascended, we had Arabia on the west and Persia on the east, not five miles apart. On the Arabian side were tombs and temples; on the Persian shore were beautiful palm-groves. Because the current was so strong we anchored at 6 P.M., and had moonlight on the Shaat-el-Arab.

At an early hour the next morning we resumed our voyage up the noble river. The sun shone with unclouded splendor. The landscape presented a scene of unsurpassed loveliness. On the Persian side were fields of rice and wheat and extensive date-palm groves. From boat and hut the smoke from the fire that cooked the morning meal was floating gently away. On our left and in mid-river was the large island of Mayabich, in whose groves the birds were singing sweetly. On the Arabian side the palms were more numerous, and in the shade of those noble trees were many arcaded buildings. Along the high banks, the people wandered, clad in robes of many colors. In rapid succession we passed village after village, whose happy children shouted us a welcome. Near the margin of a Persian river stood a large town where native boats were at anchor, and beyond it was a smaller hamlet, around which was a cemetery wherein the white tombstones marked the resting-place of prince and peasant.

Eighty miles from Fao is Mahomerah, containing eight hundred houses, the homes of six thousand people. Far from the interior flows the River Karûn, and near it is the Dorak Canal. The Karûn separates Turkey from Persia. The sheikh of Mahomerah is a Turk to-day and a Persian to-morrow. When the Turkish tax-collector comes, the sheikh crosses the river, and claims to be a Persian; when the Persian tax-gatherer arrives, the wily sheikh returns to the other side of the stream, and declares himself a Turk. He maintains an independent sovereignty. His flag is red and white. In front of the palace was his gun-boat, which fired a salute when we dipped our colors, and again when we hoisted them. His palace is ornamented with a pretty colonnade, and surrounded with forts. Adjoining the palace is his harem, wherein is a French lady of much culture, and once of regal beauty. She saw him and loved him; and, dreaming of the splendor and pleasures portrayed in "The Arabian Nights," she entered his harem. Through the latticed window of her cell, she watched us as we passed.

Not far from Mahomerah is the island of Mahasif, and beyond is the crescent-shaped isle of Salihiyah, covered with palms. Boats filled with veiled women glided down the current. Hour after hour we ran along green banks, where the peach, the almond, and the apricot were in blossom. Within the beautiful grove stood an Arab robed in white, and on his brow was a turban of brilliant colors. Here and there, native boats were loaded with dates for a foreign market.

Soon the minarets of Busrah were in sight. We had come a hundred miles from Fao, and nineteen hundred and fifty miles from Bombay. The first stage of our journey was ended. Busrah is the head of navigation for ocean steamers. Four Turkish gun-boats, a transport filled with troops, two or three merchantmen, and many bughalows were at anchor in the harbor. Our coming had been announced by telegraph, and the boatmen, in their small bellems and larger bughalows, clamored for our baggage and for the steamer's freight. They made fast to the *Burmah*, but the powerful current swept them away amidst their loud cursings and bitter complaints.

On going ashore we were welcomed by Dr. Dillion, an

English gentleman of ripe scholarship, and now acting as quarantine physician under the Turkish Government. In his yard was a wild boar of the forest, which was a pet even with the Moslems. The only buildings of note at the landing are the custom-house, the English residency, and the quarters of Dr. Dillion, all located near the jetty for the convenience of commerce. Busrah is the chief distributing port for all the cities, towns, and Arab encampments on the Tigris and the Euphrates, and for a thousand miles inland. To this port are brought, for transshipment to foreign markets, the grain, the wool, and dates raised in the interior; and here the cargoes of the ocean steamers and sailing-vessels are transferred to native boats engaged in the inland trade. For many years the English had the monopoly of this vast trade, but now the French and Germans are competing for commercial supremacy. American vessels occasionally come to Busrah, and load with dates for the United States. Dates are the principal article of export, and it is estimated that not less than ten thousand tons are exported annually. This statement was not difficult to credit after having seen the thriving groves of the date-palm, that extend for a hundred miles on either side of the Shaat-el-Arab.

Entering a bellem, we were rowed up a beautifully embowered stream to the city of Busrah proper. The distance is less than three miles, and the scenery is most enchanting. Along the banks were groves of palms that cast their cooling shadow upon the smooth waters of the rivulet. The air was perfumed with the blossom of the orange, the lemon, the peach, and the apricot. So dense was the foliage in places, as completely to intercept the sun's intense rays. As we ascended, some new object claimed our attention, and only to please. On our left was a garden inclosed, and in the secluded angle of the high walls thereof stood a young man in prayer. Beyond was a tomb shaded by the pomegranate in blossom. Further on, a bughalow was being loaded with henna, wherewith the women of the East color their finger-nails. Down the stream came an ornamented bellem of some opulent Turk. It was pulled by twelve Zanzibar slaves, who sung merrily as they rowed swiftly. Next came a boat filled with beautiful Armenian ladies, richly attired and thinly veiled.

Soon the high walls of the city were in sight, which are eight miles in circumference. The streets are narrow, irregular, and by no means pleasant to the smell. The more pretentious buildings are constructed of brick, and the humbler ones of mud. The bazaars presented a busy scene; horses, camels, donkeys, men, and women jostled each other in the crowded thoroughfares. By the wayside sat a letter-writer, ready to pen a billet-doux for a maiden or a business document for a merchant. Candies, sweetmeats, perfumes, and drugs were displayed for sale. Piece goods from England, silks from France, muslins from Germany, were in the market. Crossing a bridge, we stopped at a Turkish coffee-house. Around the walls were benches of brick-work, three feet high, and covered with matting. On a table were the polished brass coffee-pots and thimble-like cups, together with pipes of every description. On the mats lounged the Arab, the Turk, and the Persian, sipping the delicious Mocha and whiffing the bubble-bubble. In our stroll through the town we passed the post-office, where the Arabs clamored for their mail with the haste and noise characteristic of more civilized people. Further on is the residence of the governor, who, for a Turk, is a person of more than ordinary force of character. Over the imposing portal was the crescent and star, and at the entrance stood the military guard to defend the palace and the harem. Near the residence of his excellency is the office of the British India Steamship Navigation Company. Here we feasted on dates of the most delicious flavor; and here we saw a cheetah,* which has the skin of a leopard, the paws of a dog, and the mouth of a tiger. It is trained to hunt the deer, whose jugular vein it cuts with its razor-like teeth, and sucks its victim's blood. The owner had it for a plaything, but its playfulness is that of the tiger-kitten; for, having teased it above measure, it sprung upon him with glaring eyes, and displayed its terrible teeth.

The population of Busrah is composed of twenty Europeans, and twelve thousand Arabs, Turks, and Persians. Those from Europe are chiefly young men, whose love of adventure or prospects of a speedy fortune induced them to leave Christian homes, and reside in a community destitute of the refinements and happier associations of the West. They are a community within a community. They have nothing in common with the Arabs. Their pastime sports, their literature, their religion, are European. As to morals, the odds are against them, and to practice the better teachings of childhood is a difficult task.

The natives of Busrah are Moslems, with a small body of Armenians. Whatever may be the standard of morals among the latter, they tenaciously adhere to the doctrines of their creed and to the ceremonies of their religion. They are a light-hearted people, and their weddings are celebrated with much pomp and sumptuous entertainments.

But modern Busrah is far inferior in size and elegance

---

* *Felis jubata*, the hunting leopard.

compared with the ancient city. The latter was located about eight miles inland, where are extensive ruins and the remains of once splendid buildings. The prostrate column, the broken arch, the ruined colonnade, are the memorials of a superior architecture. It is the opinion of some that those remains mark the site of the residence of the wealthy Barmecides mentioned in the "Arabian Nights," and the home of Sindbad the Sailor. There is still standing a handsome arch with a lengthened inscription thereon, designating, as some suppose, the tomb of Ali Barmecide. Not far from it is the mausoleum of Zobeir, an Arab chief, one of the earliest followers of Mohammed, and who was slain at the "Battle of the Camel," in A.D. 655, which was fought by the Mohammedans for the attainment of civil power. It is a sacred shrine to the Moslems, who revere the memory of the martyr with undiminished admiration. There are, however, other theories touching the antiquity and historic significance of these ruins. They are supposed by not a few to be the remains of a city occupied by Chaldean astronomers and mathematicians of great repute. And there are others who maintain that there was located the ancient Bussorah, founded by the Emperor Trajan, and rebuilt by the Caliph Omar in the fourteenth year of the Hegira.

Returning to our bellem, we glided down the embowered rivulet, and, waving an adieu to the captain and officers of the *Burmah*, we took passage on the *City of London* for the Garden of Eden.

CHAPTER II.

Historic Lands.—Anticipations and Emotions.—Steamer *City of London*.—The Three Great Rivers.—Confluence of the Tigris and of the Euphrates.—Steaming up the Shaat-el-Arab.—The Floods Prevail.—Shepherds and their Flocks.—The Garden of Eden.—Its Appearance.—Inhabitants and History.—Sail up the Tigris.—Wild Boars of the Forest.—Daring and Successful Lion-hunt.—Tomb of the Prophet Ezra.—Scenes on the Banks of the Tigris.—Grand Mountains.—Arab Villages.—Ruins of Ancient Seleucia and Ctesiphon.—First View of Bagdad.—Guests of Captain Holland.—Wonders of Bagdad.—The People, Bazaars, Mosques, Churches, Tombs, Baths, Jews, and Christians of the City of "The Thousand and One Nights."—Turkish Railroads.—Commerce with the United States.—American Petroleum the Light of the World.

STANDING upon the threshold of the most ancient and celebrated lands known to mankind, it was with no ordinary interest we commenced the second part of our memorable journey. We were within fifty miles of the Garden of Eden, whose bowers of delight invited our presence; whose very name recalled the grandest, saddest memories of our race. Near us flowed the historic Tigris and Euphrates, "whose banks are empires." On our left were the vast ruins of Babylon, the "Golden City," wherein have lived in glory, wherein have died in shame, the greatest of kings and warriors. On our right were the Tomb of Ezra, the Prophet of the Highest; the remains of Seleucia and Ctesiphon, of Greek and Parthian memory; the City of the Caliphs, the "Abode of Peace," the scene of the fascinating legends in "The Thousand and One Nights."

With memories and emotions awakened by such a prospect, we left Busrah amidst the unrivaled splendor of an Arabian sunset. The full-orbed moon rose as the sun declined, and the stars shone with unwonted brilliancy. The evening breeze came softly through the feathery palms, perfumed with the breath of flowery spring. All nature seemed in accord with the sublimity of the thoughts that came trooping through our minds, and of the emotions that animated our souls.

We were passengers on board the *City of London*, a large name for a small steamer; but the Turks, like the French, are pleased with high-sounding titles. A hundred and ninety feet long, twenty-six feet wide, our steamer drew less than four feet of water. Her registered tonnage was ninety and the capacity of her engine was seventy-five horse-power. The main saloon was aft, and therein we ate, and whiled away the hours in useful reading and pleasant conversation. Our state-room was on the port-side, and measured eight by eight. The furniture was neither abundant nor luxuriant. On two sides were wooden bunks. In one corner was a very plain washstand, and over it a small looking-glass. The balance of the furniture consisted of a rickety table and two well-worn mattresses. According to Oriental custom, we were required to provide ourselves with pillows and blankets; for a native of the East never travels without his bedding, and each morning "takes up his bed and walks." It was such a rarity to have seven cabin-passengers on the *City of London*, and three of them ladies, that there was a mutual agreement between passengers and officers to accept the situation, and be agreeable under difficulties. And never was agreement more agreeably kept: the ladies smiled at inconveniences that could not be avoided, and the gentlemen illustrated by their moderation that "man needs but little, and not that little long." Fortunately for our comfort, Captain Cowley proved himself a gentleman whose kindness and politeness knew no cessation; whose intelligent conversation on the history and legends of the Tigris contributed to our entertainment. He had happily married the charming daughter of Captain Holland, who for forty years had sailed between Busrah and Bagdad, and who is called "The Wise Man of the Tigris." In addition to the seven foreigners on board, there were hundreds of Orientals, who occupied every available space on the upper deck, where they spread their beds, cooked and ate, sung and swore, prayed and gambled. Some were merchants from India, some were Banian bankers from Muscat, some were Persian pilgrims from Bushire; and conspicuous among them all was a venerable Jew, bound for the tomb of Ezra the Prophet.

Our progress during the night had been slow, as the current is strong and rapid. The morning light revealed a picturesque but sorry sight. The warm spring rains had melted the snow on the mountains to the east and north, causing the Tigris and the Euphrates to overflow their banks, and the Shaat-el-Arab to flood the country. The scene recalled those plaintive words of the inspired bard: "The floods have lifted up, O Lord, the floods have lifted up their voice; the floods lift up their waves." On either side, the palm-groves were dense, and in their branches the doves had taken refuge. On the summit of a mound above the water stood a solitary Arab, and near him sat the serious pelican. The shepherds had been driven from their folds, and had led their flocks to the higher ground. On our left was a submerged tomb, shaded by three young trees, and near it a deserted village, whose inhabitants had fled to the distant hills. The accumulated waters rushed by with accelerated speed, and against the united force of three rivers we ascended slowly to man's primeval abode.

It was eight o'clock in the morning when we saw for the first time the Garden of Eden. Flowing toward us on our left was the Euphrates, clear and rapid; flowing toward us on our right was the Tigris, muddy and swift. Directly in front of us was the peninsula of Chaldea, at the terminus of which is the confluence of these two historic rivers. On the extreme point of this tongue of land is the Turkish town of Kurnah, with mosque and minaret, with arcaded buildings and huts of the poor, with tall flag-staff and the white tents of the soldiers of the sultan. As we approached, the Euphrates opened wide to our view, while yet the Tigris remained hidden; but in a few minutes the latter was as fully seen. It was, indeed, a grand and never-to-be-forgotten view. The sun shone clear and warm as we neared the Tigris side. Turkish soldiers in blue, and in red fez caps, lined the margin of the river; Arab men in white and Arab women in black gave variety to the scene, and welcomed our approach.

We landed in Eden, and stood upon its sacred soil. Walking to the utmost point of the peninsula, so narrow and dry, I stretched my right hand over the Euphrates and my left hand over the Tigris, while at my feet flowed the Shaat-el-Arab, whose course is to the sea. Returning, we wandered through the palm-groves, crossed the brooklets that flow through the garden, watched the doves as they flew from tree to tree, listened to the birds of paradise carol the melody of their song, read the second chapter of Genesis, and sung the old doxology in the palmy groves of Eden. Ascending to the balcony of an ancient minaret fifty feet high, we looked out on fields green with grass and beautiful with flowers, over an area of many miles whereon are the date-palm and feathery bamboo, and on the four great rivers—the Euphrates, the Tigris, the Jaab, and the Shaat-el-Arab. Oh, what a spot is this for paradise, at the junction of these mighty rivers, in this delightful climate, in this centre of empire!

It is a place of unsurpassed loveliness, where our first parents dwelt in the innocency of their new creation. Its identity has been preserved through the lapse of the centuries, and is the only spot on earth that bears the name of Eden; other places have been designated, but without corresponding proof. Men have sought for the Garden of Eden from China to the Canary Isles, from the Mountains of the Moon to the snows of Northern Russia. Origen and Ambrosius placed it in the third heavens; Moses Bar Cepha, in midair between earth and sky. Reland and Rosenmüller, in Armenia, near the sources of the Euphrates and the Tigris. Some have placed it within the orbit of the moon, others in the moon itself; some on the earth, others under the earth, and others within the earth; some have fixed it at the North Pole, others at the South Pole; some in Tartary, some in China, some on the banks of the Ganges, some in the island of Ceylon; some in Mesopotamia, others in Persia, Babylonia, Assyria, Palestine, and in Arabia; some in Syria, others in Africa, under the equator; some in Scandinavia, others on the shores of the Baltic.* Some, to be doubly sure, have assumed that the whole earth was an Eden, and "eastward was the Garden, forty miles in circumference." Not a few have denied it a terrestrial existence, and asserted that the Biblical account is not historical, but spiritual. Moses, however, is too definite and circumstantial to be understood as dealing in allegory.

But, by common consent, all the theories are reduced to two; and the advocates of both agree that the Gar-

---

* Clark.

den of Eden was somewhere in the valley of the Euphrates, either at the source or at the mouth of that historic river. The distance between the two points is less than two thousand miles. All are in accord that this great valley was the cradle of humanity. Somewhere within its boundaries the primeval man rose at the divine command. Herein was the abode of Noah and his sons, antecedent and subsequent to the Deluge. Herein were the hunting-grounds of Nimrod, whose name is a household word throughout this memorable valley. Herein lived Job and Terah and Abraham, and thence their descendants spread out over all the earth. All the more recent excavations at Babylon and Nineveh confirm this fact. All the cuneiform inscriptions thus far deciphered establish this general belief. All the local traditions of the people, whether Jew, Moslem, or Christian, are in accord with this conclusion.

Those who suppose that Eden was near the sources of the Tigris and the Euphrates hold that the ancient Pison is the modern Phasis, a river of Colchis, which empties into the Euxine Sea, and that the Gihon is the Araxes, which flows into the Caspian Sea. Those who maintain that Eden was at the mouth of the Euphrates have the advantage of a "local habitation and a name," and the greater advantage in the certainty that the ancient Hiddekel is the modern Tigris, and that the Euphrates of the Bible is the Phrat of the Arabs. And some have gone so far as to claim that the River Jaab, which empties into the Tigris near Kurnah, is the Pison of Scripture, and that the Shaat-el-Arab is the Gihon mentioned by Moses. And with the lights we now have, it does no violence to the sacred text to suppose that Eden is descriptive of a vast section of country; that eastward within that section was planted the Garden of Delights, and that through that section flowed a river which parted in its course and formed four rivers.

At present the evidence preponderates in favor of the southern location. Discoveries made within the last decade tend to confirm the supposition that the primeval abode of man was near the confluence of the Euphrates and the Tigris; and it is not too much to anticipate the exhuming of inscribed tablets which will fully establish this belief. And, although after the lapse of so many centuries, exact correspondence in topography is not to be expected, yet, guided by the general features of the scene rather than by the minuter ones, the present traditional Garden of Eden may be accepted until another has been discovered, and its identity more clearly proved. Fully believing in this, I left Eden, singing in mournful numbers, with Mother Eve,

> "Must I leave thee, paradise? thus leave
> Thee, native soil—these happy walks and shades,
> Fit haunt of gods? where I had hoped to spend,
> Quiet though sad, the respite of that day,
> That must be mortal to us both. O flow'rs,
> That never will in other climate grow,
> My early visitation, and my last
> At ev'n, which I bred up with tender hand,
> From the first op'ning bud, and gave ye names,
> Who now shall rear ye to the sun, or rank
> Your tribes, and water from th' ambrosial fount?
> Thee lastly, nuptial bow'r, by me adorn'd
> With what to sight or smell was sweet; from thee
> How shall I part, and whither wander down
> Into a lower world, to this obscure
> And wild? how shall we breathe in other air
> Less pure, accustom'd to immortal fruits?"*

A spot so delightful as this, a site so favorable for a city, did not fail to attract the attention of the royal con-

---

* "Paradise Lost," book ix.

querors of earlier days and allure them to its bowers. On this beautiful peninsula, laved by two majestic rivers, Seleucus Nicator, successor to Alexander the Great, built a city in honor of his queen, and in the ancient annals the city is called *Aspamea*. And from the days of the Macedonian queen, the place has never been uninhabited. It is now called Kurnah, and is not only a large military station held by the Turks, but is the home of two thousand people who represent many nations. And, as a link connecting the present with the past, the telegraph-wires are here stretched across the Euphrates; and from the Garden of Eden I could send a telegram to any part of Christendom.

At no other point in their long and winding course can the two great rivers that meet here be viewed to better advantage. Having their source in the same mountainous region, they flow southward through a valley densely populated, rich in natural productions, and grand in historic associations. With its source in the mountains of Armenia near Ezroom, and not far from the shores of the Euxine, the Euphrates unites three important seas, which, without it, would have no water communication. Seventeen hundred and eighty miles long, its breadth varies from ninety to four hundred yards. In some places it spreads out into a noble lake, but in the Lemlun marshes it is not eighty yards wide. Ordinarily the current is three and a half miles an hour, but in the flood the velocity is increased to six. It abounds in fish, and is so pleasant to the taste that the people fondly call it "The Water of Desire." Boats have ascended ten hundred and thirty miles above its mouth. It is now navigable to Baulus, and the Turks have found it profitable to place thereon a line of steamers. Were it the possession of a Christian nation, it would soon become the channel of an immense trade. Its banks are dotted with towns, among the most important of which is Hillah, in the south, and Birijik, in the north.

The two principal sources of the Tigris are in the southern slopes of the Anti-Taurus range in Northern Armenia. Eleven hundred and forty-six miles in length, its average breadth is six hundred feet, and its average velocity is four and a half miles per hour. It is sometimes navigable for rafts from Diarbekir to Mosul, a distance of two hundred and ninety-six miles, and at all seasons of the year from Mosul to the sea. In the flood-time the distance is made in four days, and the people have christened it "The Cheap Camelier." Vessels drawing from three to four feet of water can ascend as far as Tekrit, and boats properly constructed might reach Mosul, opposite ancient Nineveh. Two lines of steamers are now running from Busrah to Bagdad, a distance of five hundred miles, and connect at the former place with steamers from British India. Chief among its many tributaries are the Jaab, below Kurnah; the Adhuen, above Bagdad; and the Great and Little Zab, near Mosul, all of which are the channels of a large inland trade. The Turkish Government, which neglects every thing but the collection of taxes, has so far neglected to keep the banks in repair that the river has begun to desert its bed, and is now forming vast swamps over the low country, which was formerly rescued by the Babylonians by the construction of immense lakes.

Resuming our voyage, we were now on the Tigris, and had the current of one river less against which to contend. We were bound for Bagdad, the "City of the Caliphs," five hundred miles to the north-east. For two miles we had still in view the groves and tents of Kurnah; but at the end of that distance there is a canal separating Eden from the rest of the peninsula, and uniting the waters of the Tigris with those of the Euphrates. The land north of the canal is a trackless desert of many miles in extent, alluded to by the Prophet Joel: "The land is as the Garden of Eden before them, and behind them a desolate wilderness."*

During the morning we passed vast sections of land covered with water, wherein the cattle stood knee-deep, and from which the shepherds had taken refuge to some high, green knolls. Beyond and on our right were villages surrounded with rice-fields, and rich pastures in which the herds were browsing. On our left was the mud tomb of Abu Khalkhal, shaded by a few palms, and which is a shrine to which the Moslems make an annual pilgrimage. At noon we steamed along a dreary region, dotted with sand-hills, with here and there clumps of thick bushes. Hundreds of jackals were running in every direction, frightened by the whistle of our steamer. Their color is that of the fox; their form is that of the dog. Over and around us flew flocks of crows, with white bodies and black wings. Wild boars were now seen in large numbers—five, six, and ten in a herd—running pell-mell to all points of the compass. Their movement was exceedingly violent, and their motion a tumultuous leap. Armed with rifles, we shot two of one herd —one was shot through the hind-quarters, and sunk down at once; the other was shot through the shoulder, and turned a somersault. The latter rose and ran for a pond of water, on the margin of which he defiantly stood for a few seconds, and then gradually sunk down. A boat was sent ashore to secure the game; but as our men approached the latter, he rose and offered battle, for a

---

* Joel ii., 3.

wounded boar is a desperate antagonist, and will fight to the death. But another shot ended his career, and both were brought on board the steamer. They were enormous creatures; in form like our swine, but larger, stronger, and with coarser bristles of an iron gray. The head of each was elongated, the snout was pointed, the tusks were large, and were a deadly weapon: "The boar out of the wood doth waste it."* That night we had

WILD BOAR OF THE TIGRIS.

boar flesh for dinner, and the roasted spare-ribs were excellent, though the odor was a little strong. As my share of the spoils of the hunt, I claimed the jaws with their enormous tusks, to illustrate the above Psalm, and to adorn my cabinet of Oriental curiosities.

As we advanced, there was on either side a boundless view over rich prairie-lands, whereon were numberless

---

* Psalm lxxxviii., 13.

flocks of sheep, and goats, and black buffaloes, and many reed tents, the dwelling-place of the shepherds. This is one of the richest sections of all the East, abounding in wild and domestic animals, and in a variety of birds. Swans, ducks, geese, snipes, pigeons, bitterns, and birds of the ortolan species, were seen in abundance, while a sight of the flying-fox, of gazelles, of boars, tigers, and lions, was a common occurrence.

Not far from the Tomb of Ezra occurred one of the most daring and successful lion-hunts that have ever taken place on the banks of the Tigris. In the dim twilight of the morning, three full-grown lions were discovered on the eastern bank of the river, and about a mile ahead of the steamer. The alarm was given, and in a moment intense excitement prevailed on board. The captain was notified, the speed of the steamer was lessened, guns and rifles were instantly loaded for the coming encounter. Attracted by the approach of the steamer, the lions had stopped, and one, more daring than the others, with a bound leaped into the river, and attempted to reach the vessel. The sight paralyzed with fear many of the natives on board, but a rifle-shot, fired by the supercargo, proved mortal to the courageous beast, and the launch was immediately sent to secure the carcass. Frightened by the report of the rifle, the other lions turned and ran along the margin of the river. Under a full head of steam, the *City of London* soon came up abreast with the fugitives, who halted, and boldly stood their ground, ready to receive their pursuers. But a shot fired by the captain killed one instantly, and a second shot wounded the other in the leg. With a thundering roar that shook the earth, the wounded beast sprung over the dead body of her companion, and, with open mouth, turned her head toward the boat, and challenged

A LION HUNT.

another onset; but a well-directed shot discharged by the supercargo proved fatal to the proud and defiant creature, who fell near her dead companion. The steamer now ran along the bank, and the prey was brought on board. They were three lionesses, and in one were found four cubs. But the excitement was not to end so suddenly. All agreed that the male lion must be near. Every eye was on the watch. Each inlet and islet was carefully scanned. The glass was brought to bear on each moving object. Nor was the search in vain, for within a mile from the scene of the first encounter, an enormous male lion was seen a thousand yards ahead and two hundred yards inland. He was on a small island, crouching among the bushes. At first he was taken to be a dog, as an Arab encampment was near the spot; but the glass revealed the fact that he was an immense male lion, whose three companions had been slain in his absence. His mane was long and thick, and, when discovered, he was leisurely wagging his bushy tail. A shot aroused him; a second ball, falling near him, made him furious; and, with a thundering roar and a mighty bound, he charged at the ship, and proudly stood at the edge of the islet, as if defying any one to land. His appearance was frightful to behold. A ball struck him on the fore-leg, which caused him to retreat; but on being hit on the hind-quarter by a second shot, he instantly returned to the edge of the bank, and presented an aspect of the utmost rage. There was something grand and terrible in his attitude. He was the impersonation of fury. His eyes glared like balls of fire. He shook his mane in terror, and with his tail he lashed his sides in anger. Frantic from pain, his roar was terrible, and sent a sense of horror to the soul. Though severely wounded, he remained undaunted, and seemed to challenge his pursuers to a closer combat. Had not the water intervened between him and them, some one of their number would have fallen a victim to his infuriated power. As he stood there, he presented a grand sight; but one soon to end. A third ball penetrated his back. It was his death-wound. For a few seconds he maintained his proud and defiant position, as if thinking whether to yield in the unequal contest, or longer resist his foes. But death soon relieved him of pain, and his pursuers of a gallant foe. Sinking slowly to the ground, he uttered one more groan, deep and muffled, and the lion-king of the Tigris was dead.

The captain and his men landed, but, half suspicious that he was not dead, they cautiously approached to ascertain the effect of their well-directed shots. It required five stalwart men to drag the dead lion down to the margin of the river. He weighed four hundred and twenty pounds. His height was three feet and ten inches, and he measured six feet and seven inches in length. His mane was five inches long, and the length of his tail was nearly three feet. He and his companions resembled in color the African lion, and their appearance on the banks of the Tigris is not easy to explain. It is supposed, however, that their lair had been reached by the floods, and having been driven therefrom by the water, they had sought refuge on the higher ground. Had they not been discovered and killed by Captain Cowley and his men, they would have swum the river under cover of the night, and attacked the neighboring shepherds and their flocks.

Having passed a large town of reed huts, where the natives were repairing the levee to prevent an incursion of the waters, we came to the Tomb of Ezra, the Prophet of the Highest. This time-honored mausoleum is an immense structure, crowned with a beautiful dome, which is incased with green porcelain tiles, and surmounted with a gilded circle representing the sun. It is constructed of yellow bricks, and ornamented with arched entrances and balconies, from which the Hebrew children greeted us as we landed. Five noble palms shade the final resting-place of the learned scribe. Over the door-way are two tablets of black marble, whereon are inscriptions in Hebrew. Within and beneath the dome is a carved cenotaph, covered with rich green cloth fringed with gold. On it are white and green banners;

TOMB OF EZRA.

at each corner is a carved urn, emblem of the dead; and near it is a lamp that ever burns. Beneath the cenotaph is the tomb containing the ashes of the holy prophet, and on it are slips of white paper, whereon are written the prayers of Jewish pilgrims. The floor of the mausoleum is paved with blocks of white, black, and green marble. The walls are inlaid with porcelain of many colors, arranged in the form of stars. On the edge of the panels are stars embossed, composed of small mirrors, and high up in the centre of the dome is an immense star similarly made. Here and there on the interior walls are quotations from the Hebrew Scriptures.

In the wall and facing the east is a closet wherein is kept a copy of the Law, and over this Holy of Holies is a representation of the seven-branched gold candlestick of the sanctuary.

It was with no ordinary interest that I stood by the dust of one so deservedly renowned in sacred history. Next to Moses, Ezra is held in the highest esteem by the Hebrew people. In learning he was the equal of the great Jewish Lawgiver, and second only to him in his influence over the religious thought of their nation. To him is ascribed the authorship of the books of the Chronicles, of Ezra, of Nehemiah, and of Esther. He was "a ready scribe of the law of Moses," and rewrote the Old Testament from memory. He restored, corrected, arranged, and settled the canon of the Old Testament Scriptures, and edited the sacred volume, and then wrote the whole in the Chaldaic character, for the use of those of his brethren who refused to return with him from Babylon to Jerusalem. To him belongs the honor of establishing synagogue worship in every town in Jewry, and of introducing the practice of reading therein the Law and the Prophets. And such was his influence with King Artaxerxes Longimanus, that he was permitted to go to Jerusalem with great wealth and power to restore the worship of the true God, and to prepare for the return of his captive countrymen. His first journey occupied four months, and he was everywhere received with the distinction due a royal messenger. After his return to Babylon, he received permission to make a second journey to his beloved Jerusalem, and it was on his return from this second tour that he died at Zamzumu, on the west bank of the Tigris, where his tomb now is. The fact of his burial here is confirmed by the Talmud, and by Rabbi Benjamin of Tudela, who visited his sepulchre in A.D. 1173.

The custodians of the mausoleum are Jews, the descendants of those carried captive into Babylon. In dress and thrift they appeared superior to their Arab neighbors. The Hebrew women are extremely beautiful. There was one whose features were worthy the pencil of Raphael the divine. Hers was a Jewish face, exquisite in outline, lovely in expression, and beaming with intelligence. Hither the Jews make an annual pilgrimage to offer their prayers, and fondly kiss the tomb that contains the dust of him whom they revere. A venerable Jew of three-score years and ten had come with us from Bombay, and approached the shrine with uncovered head and tenderly kissed the cenotaph. Adjoining the tomb is a large caravansary for the accommodation of the Hebrew pilgrims who come from afar. To the north of the mausoleum is a Turkish fort, and the governor in command extorts large sums from the pilgrims who come to worship at the sepulchre of their prophet.

The air grew chilly as the night approached. The Arabs had kindled blazing fires in their encampments, around which they stood in groups. They are nomads, who wander from place to place in quest of pasture. They are poor, and lead a miserable life; yet here their fathers roamed in the centuries by-gone, and here they themselves dwell in the shepherd's rude tent. Their tents are constructed of a large coarse reed, mixed with the tenacious clay of the valley, and covered with the black hides of their native buffalo, or a coarse brown cloth made of camel's hair. Their flocks of sheep, goats, and buffaloes are kept for the milk they yield, and out of it large quantities of butter and cheese are produced. They exchange the produce of their flocks for cloth and other necessary articles, which are brought to their encampments by native merchants who trade along the coast.

A cold rain began to fall, and a stiff north-west wind commenced to blow as the light of day faded from our view. As neither moon nor stars were visible, which are necessary guides to safe navigation on the tortuous Tigris, we were compelled to anchor for the night. Our anchorage was at the "Devil's Elbow," the most difficult and dangerous curve in the river. All felt the chilly air, and the native women and children on the upper deck suffered much during the dreary night. The cold rain continued the next day, and the vast treeless prairies looked desolate enough. Throughout the morning we passed a succession of Bedouin encampments, where were immense herds of horses and yellow cattle, and groups of naked children, who shouted their glee at our approach. At noon we were driven ashore by a powerful current, and so damaged our starboard wheel as to delay us for an hour to make repairs. As we ascended, the Tigris became more tortuous. There were points where we turned at right angles to our course, and at times the curvature was even greater than that. As the crow flies, the distance between Kurnah and Bagdad is less than three hundred miles, but by the sinuous Tigris the distance is nearly doubled. We stopped for an hour at Abu Sijreh, where is a cottage in the midst of a large palm-grove, and where the boys hailed us with merry shouts of laughter. The men of the place were armed with long spears, to defend themselves and their flocks against the wild beasts of the jungle. Later in the day, the Tigris was even with its green banks, while beyond, and as far as the eye could reach, appeared one vast, dreary, watery waste.

Toward evening we anchored opposite the town of

Hud, which is at the junction of the Hud and the Tigris. The scene was exceedingly novel. Naked children rushed to the shore and shouted their merriment. Native women came to the margin of the river, and sat motionless as statues. Native men, poorly clad, but armed to the teeth, watched us as they would an approaching foe. Not far from the river were large date-groves inclosed within high mud-walls. The buildings of the village are composed of mud and stone, and are the homes of two thousand people. The palace of the sheikh is high and imposing. The minaret of the old mosque is inlaid with green, black, and white tiles. The Hud is a large military station, and a place of considerable trade. Along the shore were many burghalows, and two European dredging-machines. The latter, however, are fast going to ruin for lack of knowledge to use them properly. When it became known that the steamer had arrived, a noisy scene followed. Soldiers and civilians lined the shore. Veiled women stood upon the balconies, and others peered through the latticed windows. Some were in black, some in green, some in white. All manifested their curiosity to see the ladies of our party.

Experience had taught the captain to anchor far out in the stream, and not make fast to the shore, as the villagers were accustomed to rush on board in such numbers as to ground his steamer. They would come ostensibly for letters, but rather to pillage. For two hours there were a constant coming and going of boats filled with people. These little boats are more novel than a Yankee notion. They are constructed of a coarse reed, and smeared with naphtha within and without. They resemble in form an acorn-cup, and are called *kooffahs*. Some of them hold a dozen persons. Their motion in the water is that of a spinning-top, and they are propelled by a single paddle, with alternate strokes, first on one side and then on the other; and thus propelled, they go whirling through the water. Many of our native passengers went on shore to purchase food, and their return was the signal of intense excitement. Boats collided, women screamed, men grew pale, and boatmen swore. And such profanity! They swore by their mother; by the wife and sister of the one they cursed. They called each other the "devil's friend."

We were glad when the signal-whistle sounded our departure. Amidst a shout from the shore and a shout from our steamer, we left the Hud, and resumed our voyage. On either side were rich pasture-fields adorned with yellow daisies. Here and there were the pine, the palm, and the bamboo. Far away, grand and gloomy, were the Luristan Mountains. The agricultural wealth of this valley is beyond computation. Forty years ago, when Captain Holland first came up the Tigris, all these river lands were in a high state of cultivation; but the excessive taxes collected by the Turks discouraged the farmers, who abandoned their fields to the wandering Bedouin. The Turk is a consumer, and has never been a producer.

Such was the darkness of the night, that we were compelled to anchor at seven o'clock. In three hours and a half we started again, but in less than an hour we were forced to stop for the night. The morning dawned with brighter prospects. As we advanced, vegetation increased. The grass was thicker and more abundant. Men, in companies of six and twelve, were at work repairing the levees to prevent an overflow. They seemed happy in their work, and shouted to their friends on the steamer. Horsemen appeared along the bank, with saddle-bags filled with produce, and women were seen carrying on their heads baskets of food.

In the afternoon we saw the old and now abandoned fort of Kullah Sultan, which is three hundred feet square, and has a round tower at each angle. Beyond the fort, the west bank is high and bold, and inland is a young forest. The day declined, and the night air was intensely cold. The extreme cold was doubtless due, in part, to the snow-water that came down from the mountains. The next day the Tigris appeared like thin, yellow mud, through which we slowly steamed hour after hour. The quantity of alluvial soil thus carried southward is immense. It is deposited at the mouth of the Shaat-el-Arab, where islands are formed, and whereon cities will be built. We were now in the broadest portion of the Tigris, where the river resembles a lake, and where the current is eight knots an hour.

Happily for our comfort, the morning was glorious. The heavens were clear, and the sun was bright. The air was balmy, and the natural scenery was grand. Forty miles to the east were the Luristan Mountains, whose summits are ten thousand feet above the level of the sea. The higher range was one immense bank of snow, and one head-land peak, boldest of the group, reflected the glories of the rising sun. From the river to the base of the hills, the meadows were clothed with grass and enameled with white daisies. On either side, the banks were high and the soil was rich—a remnant of the better past. It is Pliny who described this section of the valley as the richest portion of the East; and, even now, no one could desire a richer empire than the great peninsula between the Tigris and the Euphrates, and extending from Bagdad to the Garden of Eden.

The pleasures of the day were heightened by the

mountain scenery, ever in view, yet ever changing. The lower range was barren and brown; the higher peaks were white with snow. How grand the view! How pure and calm the vision! At sunset our enjoyment was intensified. The snow-peaks reflected the rosy tints of the declining sun; and when the orb of day had sunk beneath the horizon, the snowy range was colored with a deep, rich blue, that gradually faded into intense blackness. But as the stars came forth, the beautiful snow was visible again. The pointers of Ursa Major, the clustered Pleiades, and the Sword of Orion shone in glory above, and were reflected in the waters beneath.

At seven o'clock that night we were at El-Henna, the "Half-way House," between Busrah and Bagdad; and in six hours thereafter we reached Kût-el-Amârah, a Turkish garrison of fifty men. At this point the river Hye cuts the peninsula, and flows into the Euphrates through six lesser channels. Amârah is the chief coaling station on the Tigris, to which the coal is brought in native boats from Busrah, for the supply of the river steamers.

In the early light of the next morning, we saw two wolves near the shore. They were large, and nearly white. A well-meant shot failed to reach them, and with a bound they were out of sight. An hour later we passed the Turkish steamer *Mosul*, loaded with troops and produce for Busrah. Flags were hoisted in friendly salutation as we passed each other.

At dawn the next day we were at the ruins of Humaniah, and opposite is an old canal cut to avoid a long curve in the river. We could see the river at the other end of the ditch, but there was not water enough therein to float our steamer. The canal is not more than a mile in length, but we were three hours in passing around from one end to the other. Having doubled the cape, we were opposite ancient Babylon, not forty miles to the westward. Beyond, we passed the military station Azzaziah, where there is a well-constructed fort, with central gate-way and four strong bastions. All day long the river continued to be a broad lake, and its rapid current bore southward many native boats loaded with produce. We had left the low country and were now passing through a section of the valley where the river-banks are sixty feet high. The inland plains were covered with grass and bushes. Splendid Arab horses were feeding in the rich pastures. Late in the afternoon we came to Baghdadieh, whereat is a fort, and near which was a large encampment. The half-naked Arabs ran after us and begged for coffee. It was a cruel deception, but one of our native passengers filled a bottle with ashes, and threw it into the river. Quick as thought, an Arab threw off his aba, plunged into the cold stream, clutched the coveted prize, that was to him an Apple of Sodom.

The seventh and last day of our voyage had dawned. Around us were the mighty ruins of the power and glory of Greek and Roman, of Persian and Parthian. Before us lay the battle-field whereon the Roman Severus, the apostate Julian, the Persian Chosroes, and Omar the Saracen had fought for empire. Here the Macedonians had lived in republican freedom; here the Persians had reveled in Oriental splendor; here the Parthian kings had pitched their royal tents, and dwelt therein in pastoral simplicity. On our left were the remains of Seleucia; on our right were the ruins of Ctesiphon, around which cluster the memories of two millenniums.

Seleucia was a republic in the heart of Assyria. Its founder was Seleucus Nicator, the immediate successor of Alexander the Great in the East. To preserve his memory from oblivion, he called it Seleucia. While he survived, it was the imperial city of the Macedonian empire in Upper Asia; and after his death, and long after his empire had ceased to exist, it remained a Grecian colony. Its founder had bestowed upon it the rights and privileges of an independent government. It had a senate of three hundred nobles, a population of six hundred thousand citizens, and a free constitution. It was renowned for its arts, its military power, its love of freedom. Its prosperity continued through centuries, and the fame of its wealth excited the cupidity of the most renowned conquerors of the Christian era. Being less than fifty miles to the north-east, its contiguity and fame had the effect to depopulate ancient Babylon, which verified the predictions of the prophets. When in its glory, the walls of the city resembled an eagle spreading his wings, to illustrate the freedom of its citizens; and such was the strength of its defensive works as to resist an assault of the most powerful enginery of ancient warfare. The city, however, was surrendered to the Romans under the Emperor Trajan, in the year A.D. 116; but after his departure, the citizens revolted and re-asserted their independence. For half a century, Seleucia was free, and was the noblest city on the banks of the Tigris. But its wealth and luxury allured the Emperor Severus to its gates, who sacked and burned the beautiful metropolis, and massacred three hundred thousand of its best citizens. From that day its decline was rapid and certain. In its fall was illustrated the saying, " Measure for measure," for in subsequent years Seleucia suffered from the Parthian kings the same fate she had inflicted on Babylon, as the seat of empire was transferred to the opposite bank of the river, and Ctesiphon became the imperial city; and all that now remains of the Greek colony are fragments of porcelain, pieces of pottery, and immense shapeless mounds of broken bricks. Out of the ruins the Arabs have built a square fort, with a round tower at each angle. Near the fortress were a few tents, and along the shore a few native boats were at anchor.

On the eastern bank of the Tigris are the more definite and more imposing remains of Ctesiphon, whose history is written in blood. At first the capital of the kings of Parthia, it became the winter residence of the Persian monarchs, who, having enjoyed the cool breezes of the mountains of Media at Ecbatana during the summer months, came hither in winter to enjoy the milder climate of Ctesiphon. In subsequent centuries, it contained the "white palace of Chosroes," the most wonderful and magnificent structure in the valley of the Euphrates. Around its walls were fought the most bloody battles known to history. In thirty-three years after its capture by Trajan, it had recovered its former greatness; but, in the middle of the second century, it was captured by the Emperor Severus, whose soldiers carried away immense treasures of gold and silver, and who led forth a hundred thousand captives to grace the conqueror's triumph. Yet it survived the plunder of its palaces, and the captivity of so many of its noblest citizens, and for two hundred years was the seat of Persian royalty. It was in the year A.D. 363 that Julian the Apostate, with sixty thousand Roman soldiers, demanded its unconditional surrender. He had marched down the peninsula, and fixed his camp on the west bank of the Tigris amidst the ruins of Seleucia. To bring his fleet of twelve hundred boats from the Euphrates to the Tigris, he reopened the old canal that Trajan had made, and which now remains a little to the north. Crossing the Tigris at dead of night, Julian opened the battle at early dawn, and which lasted for twelve consecutive hours. The Romans were victorious on the plains, but the Persians were victorious in the city. The proud walls of Ctesiphon bade defiance to the assaults of the Roman legions. Unable to take the city, Julian burned eleven hundred of his boats, the brilliant conflagration of which transformed night into day; and, marching northward and inland east of

ANCIENT CTESIPHON.

the river, he was overtaken by the Persians; and in the battle of Samara, not far from Bagdad, Julian was slain by a javelin that penetrated his liver.

Ctesiphon remained the seat of Persian luxury and power down to the seventh century, when it was sacked and destroyed by the Saracens. And when the victors entered the gates and beheld the palace, they shouted, "This is the white palace of Chosroes; this is the promise of the apostle of God." The spoils of the victors were immense. It required a mule to carry away the tiara and cuirass, the belt and bracelets, of Chosroes. This gorgeous trophy was presented to Omar, the commander of the faithful; and the gravest of his companions condescended to smile when they beheld the white beard, the hairy arms, and uncouth figure of the veteran who appeared before them wearing the royal ornaments of the great king. But of all the trophies, the most magnificent was a carpet of silk, ninety feet in length and as many in breadth, which decorated one of the apartments of the palace. It was a piece of tapestry of the most extraordinary workmanship. A paradise, or garden, was depictured on the ground; the flowers, fruits, and shrubs were imitated by the figures of the gold embroidery and the colors of the precious stones; and the ample square was encircled by a variegated and verdant border. The Arabian general persuaded the soldiers to relinquish their claim, in the reasonable hope that the eye of the caliph would be delighted with the splendid workmanship of native industry. But, regardless of the merit of art and the pomp of royalty, the rigid Omar divided the prize among his brethren of Medina. The picture was destroyed; but such was the intrinsic value of the materials, that the share of Ali alone was sold for twenty thousand drachmas.*

The sack of Ctesiphon by the Saracens was followed by its gradual decay and final desertion. Covering an area of many miles are mounds of moderate height, of a light color, and strewed with fragments of pottery and porcelain. They extend eastward in a semicircular range, and their continued line and form indicate the circuit of the city walls. But the most conspicuous and interest-

---

* Gibbon.

ing object is the ruin of the "white palace of Chosroes." We had seen it from earliest dawn, and by the higher refracting atmosphere of the East it towered in all its grand proportions. When viewed from our steamer, it reminded me of Westminster Abbey. It is less than half a mile from the margin of the river. It is composed of two wings, and a central hall that extends the whole length of the palace. It is constructed of fine burned bricks, each twelve inches square and three inches thick, covered with a superior cement. Its eastern front is three hundred feet in length, and in the centre is a noble arch, one hundred and twenty-eight feet high, and with a span of ninety feet. The walls are sixteen feet thick. The face of the front is ornamented with four rows of arched recesses, each one the miniature of the great arch, and all of the most delicate and exquisite workmanship. The wings have their front divided into two stories, the lower one of which has large arched niches and an arched door-way, each separated from the other by convex pilasters, going up half way the height of the building. In the second story there is a succession of concave arched recesses, divided from each other by semi-columns, and diminishing in proportion to the top of the remaining portion of the front wall. In its ruins the great structure is grand to contemplate, but when perfect its appearance must have been superb. The magnificent banqueting-hall extends a hundred and sixty feet east and west. At the eastern end is a wall wherein is a door-way twelve feet wide and twenty-four feet high. The imagination can scarcely realize the grandeur of this apartment, resplendent with Oriental ornamentation, and brilliant with the gorgeous display of Persian royalty.

Near the eastern bank of the Tigris, and opposite the

two cities, are the remains of a brick bridge that once spanned the river. The portion that we saw just above the water is seventeen feet wide and sixty feet long; and the height of the most perfect remaining pier is eight feet.

Not far from the palace is the tomb of Suliman the Pure, who was Mohammed's barber, and who became a convert under the persuasive eloquence of the prophet himself. Hither the barbers of Bagdad come in annual procession, in the month of April, to do homage to the memory of a fellow-craftsman. The tomb consists of a domed sanctuary, a vaulted piazza, and to it is attached a caravansary for the accommodation of the pilgrim barbers. Over the sepulchre are three tall palms, and hence it is sometimes called the "Tomb of the Three Palms." Near it are the urned ashes of another of even greater distinction. They are the dust of Hadhaifah, who was secretary to the prophet. And in a third tomb are the remains of the Caliph Moostasem Billah, who was slain by Heslakoo, grandson of the famous Genghis Khan, the founder of the Mogul dynasty in Persia.

Once more afloat, we soon came to the river Dialah, which runs inland many miles, and which is the channel of an extensive trade with the encampments and villages that line its banks. A solitary tree marks the spot where it pours its clear, sweet waters into the Tigris. It is half the breadth of the latter stream, and its current does not exceed two miles an hour. On the northern bank were a few grass huts, whose occupants earn a living by transporting travelers across the stream, and near them were a few tents of Arab shepherds. This Dialah is mentioned by Xenophon, and somewhere on its banks, and near the Tigris, stood the populous and flourishing city of Sitace; and not far from it was a bridge of thirty-seven boats. But town and bridge have long since ceased to exist, and there is to-day no trace of their existence. The river is now famous for an enormous fish, so large as to form a good load for a donkey. These large fish are taken to Bagdad, where they are sold at a moderate price to the poorer classes.

It was midday when we had our first view of Bagdad, the renowned "City of the Caliphs." So sudden was the view, and so brief withal, that it seemed like an enchanted vision. Dome and minaret, tower and mausoleum, rose above the dense groves of the royal palm. Away to the north-west were the golden pinnacles of Kathimain and the unique monument to the beautiful Zobeida; while on our right were the green-tiled and swelling domes, the graceful minarets, towering above the pine and cypress, and the massive walls of the "City of Peace." But the gorgeous vision lasted only for a moment, and then disappeared for an hour, while we followed the sinuous channel of the Tigris. All around us were the unmistakable signs that we were near a great city. Village succeeded village; plantation touched plantation; men in white, women closely veiled, and children innocent of a rag, were chatting, laughing, and wondering how we could steam against wind and current.

Soon the vision re-appeared, enlarged, diversified, and rendered more beautiful by a thousand new objects, thrilling us with delight, dimpling with smiles the cheeks of our fair ones, and provoking heartier laughter from those made of sterner stuff.

A voyage of twenty-five hundred miles is ended. All is well. We now pass the English residency, with its high walls, and orange-groves, and lofty flag-staff, bearing on high Briton's proud banner. Saluting the English gun-boat *Comet* as we pass, we dropped anchor in front of the Turkish custom-house, whose officials rushed on board to examine baggage and passports. Soon the river was covered with kooffahs, those acorn-shaped boats, whose owners screamed and clamored in frantic tones to induce us to employ them. The excitement was no less intense on shore, for the arrival of the *City of London* was a great event to the people of Bagdad. Merchants expected their goods from Manchester and Bombay; bankers were anxious to receive remittances, while all anticipated the coming of the mail from Europe, from India, from the shores of Persia and Arabia.

Colonel C. Herbert, her Britannic majesty's political resident and consul-general, sent his boat, with a polite invitation for us to be his guests; but Captain Cowley's invitation had been accepted, and we were to be the guests of Captain Holland, whose amiable daughter Mr. Cowley had married. It required some skill and no little care to jump into a kooffah, for, like a wooden bowl on the water, it bobbed and dipped where the weight happened to be greatest; and the only position of safety was to sit down like a Turk on the bottom of the boat. All in, seven in number, and away we went twirling through the water like a boy's top, laughing at our fears, and more at our novel navigation. We landed in the mud, but were soon on the high terrace, and, passing through a vaulted passage-way, we entered a spacious court, where we were received with generous hospitality.

We had to regret the absence of Captain Holland, whom we left at Busrah. Forty years ago, he made an expedition up the Tigris, and since then he has been a resident of Bagdad. In all respects a worthy representative of Great Britain, he is esteemed for his intelligence, his moral worth, and his high social character.

He loved and married a native Christian lady, who is the mother of his thirteen children, and who is still in the freshness of her womanhood. Queenly in her appearance, womanly in her address, generous in her hospitality, entertaining in conversation, she is gifted with a mind quick to perceive, nice to discriminate, impartial to judge, and candid to decide. Her home is the abode of peace. Love reigns in the household. Her children and children's children are happiest when in each other's society. Her daughters are amiable and engaging; her son, educated in England, is a noble specimen of maturing manhood.

The Holland mansion is on the bank of the river, built of brick, two stories high, and within is a large courtyard, wherein palms are growing. On the ground-floor are the cool apartments occupied by the family in the day-time, during the intense heat of midsummer; while on the house-top are the spacious platforms whereon the family sleep in the hot nights of summer. The apartments assigned us were all that we could wish for comfort and for pleasure. The sumptuous Oriental dinners, the well-stored library, the drawing-room entertainments, the evening devotions, united to complete the circle of our daily delights. For more than a week we were the welcome guests of this happy family, whose kindness anticipated every want, whose pleasure was supreme when their guests were happiest. To them were we indebted for practical suggestions as to traveling in the East. They thought it no annoyance to aid us to employ servants, to make contracts, to purchase our necessary outfit for our long inland journey. And when the "elect lady" of our party was ill, each one was a ministering angel unto her. All this was the realization of our dream of Oriental hospitality. It was more: for the boasted hos-

CAPTAIN BOLLAND'S HOUSE, WITH MODERN STEAMER AND KUFA.

pitality of the Turk is a hospitality of equivalents. The guest is expected to return in kind equal to what he has received. It is gift for gift; dollar for dollar. To be well thought of among the Turks, the traveler's donations should be princely. They estimate him not by what he is, but by what he gives. But not so at Captain Holland's. That queenly wife and mother would not allow child or domestic to receive the gifts in gold which we felt it a privilege to offer; and even the servants who had received presents were required by their mistress to return the same. She thought such gifts demoralizing to those who received them. She would have her children unselfish in their entertainment of strangers, and her servants unselfish in their attention to her guests. Such hospitality is so rare in the East, especially outside of Christian society, that I mention it here with no ordinary pleasure.

The enchanting stories of "The Thousand and One Nights" had excited our expectation as to the Oriental magnificence of Bagdad, but the reality was not a realization of our fondly cherished dreams. The changes wrought by time, and by the rise and fall of dynasties, are more apparent in the "City of the Caliphs" than in Cairo or Damascus. But the past is not to be inferred from the present. Six centuries ago, Bagdad was the proud capital of the caliphs, whose empire extended from the Pillars of Hercules to the Wall of China, and from the Indian Ocean to the Frozen Sea. It was then an emporium of wealth and magnificence. It was the royal abode of the Abbassides, chief of the family of the prophet, and was held in veneration by all the kings of the desert Arabs as the seat of power and glory. The great palace was three miles in circumference, and embowered in a forest of fruit-trees. Within the inclosure was a lake, formed by the waters of the Tigris; and within the spacious park were kept a multitude of birds and animals, so that hunting and fishing could be enjoyed as constant diversions. The space inclosed was equal in extent to that occupied by the castellated palace and hanging gardens of ancient Babylon.* The founder of the city was Al Mansour, second caliph of the Abbasside dynasty, who called it the "Abode of Peace," a title still used in official documents from the Sublime Porte. Its history dates from the year 762 of our era. With the resources of a vast and rich empire at his command, its founder lavished his wealth and displayed his taste to make it a city of extraordinary magnificence. And such was his wealth at the time of his death, that he left to his successor $150,000,000 in gold. His son Al Mamoun excelled his father in the splendor and luxury of his reign. On his bridal-day, he showered on the head of his beautiful bride a thousand pearls of the largest size and of the most exquisite hue. His palace was adorned with thirty-eight thousand pieces of tapestry, twelve thousand of which were of silk embroidered with gold. In the royal gardens were gold and silver trees, each with eighteen branches, and in them were birds of gold, who warbled their melody by the action of ingenious machinery. In his hunting-grounds, a hundred lions were kept for his sport. Superb barges, elegant as the gondolas of Venice, floated on the Tigris. The high officers of his court, and the eunuchs who held the keys of his harem, were gorgeously attired; their buttons were of gold and costly gems. Nor was he unmindful of learning and culture. The college of Bagdad cost two hundred thousand pieces of gold, and could boast of more

---

* Benjamin of Tudela.

than six thousand disciples. A hundred thousand manuscripts, beautifully translated and elegantly bound, adorned the library. It was the seat of Arabian learning. Astronomy was studied with assiduity and success. The first arc of the meridian was measured in the "College of the Learned," and water-clocks were there successfully invented. Such was the extent of a physician's library, that he informed the Sultan of Bokhara that it would require four hundred camels to transport his books. Some idea of the vastness of the population may be formed from the statements of historians, that eighty thousand men, sixty thousand women, and twenty thousand slaves formed the funeral procession of Ibn Hanbal, a distinguished Moslem sage.*

Bagdad attained the height of its power in A.D. 786, under the reign of Haroun-al-Raschid, and his charming Scheherzade of "The Thousand and One Nights." He carried his victorious banners to the gates of Byzantium when Irene was on the throne, with the infant Constantine in her arms; and, returning to the "Abode of Peace," he ruled his empire with prudence, and treated his enemies with contempt. In the height of his glory, he inscribed a letter to the Emperor Nicephorus, calling him a "Roman dog."

His name recalls those charming entertainments so vividly depicted in "The Arabian Nights," and of which his capital was so largely the scene of the stories therein told. Whoever was their author, those stories have an immortality. The time and place of their composition, and whether the characters therein delineated are real or fancied, are disputed points; yet their influence is world-wide, and the pleasure they afford is immense.

---

* Gibbon.

The best of the "Entertainments" may have come from India, the cradle of story and fable; the most tender and sentimental love-tales may be of Persian inspiration, but the life-like pictures and witty anecdotes are purely Arabian. The passion for adventure, for love and revenge; the craft and successful plots of womankind; the hypocrisy of priests; the corruptibility of judges; the gilded palaces, the charming women, the lovely gardens, the exquisite repasts, are no less true now of town-life in the Mohammedan East than centuries ago. These same stories, which captivate and transport even Christian minds by the splendor of their pageantry, the variety and boldness of incident, and the fervid expression of natural desires, are the familiar stories nightly related in the coffee-houses and harems of Bagdad. The story of Zobeida and her two Sisters, and the petrified city of the Indes, of Sindbad the Sailor, of The Three Calenders, Sons of Sultans, and the Five Ladies of Bagdad, are now the entertaining tales of every-day life. And whether from the educational effect of these "Entertainments" on the common mind of the East, or from a natural genius inherited, the love of story-telling is universal in the Orient, and a master in the art is a favorite with all.

A city like Bagdad, so celebrated for its wealth and splendor, was a tempting prize to ambitious conquerors. The Tartar hordes sought its treasures in A.D. 1251; and their leader, Hulaku Khan, put to a cruel death Mostazem, the last of the caliphs, and massacred three hundred thousand of its citizens. One hundred and fifty years thereafter, it was besieged and captured by Tamerlane, the Mogul; and the place is pointed out on the western bank of the Tigris where he caused to be erected two pyramids, composed of ninety thousand skulls of the most influential citizens, whom he had cruelly slain. Since then the city has gradually decreased in wealth, power, and population. The Turks came in A.D. 1638, who are now masters of the situation. Since their advent, it has been a place of contention between them and the Persians. Within the last half century, its population has been reduced from one hundred and ten thousand to less than seventy thousand. The great empire of the caliphs has been divided and subdivided, to augment the revenues demanded by the Sublime Porte. Thirty-five years ago, the pashalic of Bagdad was one of the most important and wealthy in the Turkish empire, and was the first in rank. Its jurisdiction then extended from the shores of the Persian Gulf up the Euphrates to Anah, where the Aleppo District commenced; thence across Mesopotamia to the Hamreen Hills and the great plains of Kerkha; and thence to the junction of the Shaat-el-Arab and the Mahomerah, with Kurdistan on the north; but to-day the authority of its pasha is limited to the districts surrounding the city, inclusive of the Arab tribes that encamp in the neighborhood, while Busrah and Diarbekir are placed under independent pashas.

Yet Bagdad is still beautiful for situation, though not the joy of the whole earth. It is divided by the Tigris into two parts, the smaller quarter being a suburb on the western bank. The two portions are connected by a bridge of boats a thousand feet long, but such a bridge as only Turks would suffer to remain a day. Its present condition indicates their disregard for the safety of human life, and is one of the many proofs that they have the least public spirit of any people on the globe. Situated on a plain, the principal part of the city is on the eastern bank of the Tigris, and the buildings along the river abut the water's edge. The high walls of the town are both old and new, constructed of bricks of different kinds, chiefly gathered from the once stately structures of ancient Babylon. The older sections of the wall indicate superior workmanship, while the modern portions are in keeping with the dilapidated condition of the Turkish empire. At the principal angles of the wall are large round towers, on which are mounted batteries to salute the pasha and frighten the Arabs. Two of the larger and older towers are grand and gloomy. They were constructed by the caliph Nasr, in A.D. 1221, as announced by an inscription thereon, executed in the best style of the old Arabic sculpture. The three gates of the city are massive and imposing. They are the gathering-places of merchants who trade in cotton; of venders of things new and old; of magicians performing magic tricks; of story-tellers convulsing with laughter the listening crowd; of Jewish money-changers, ever willing to turn an honest penny; of mule-owners, always anxious to transport the traveler; of soldiers strutting in their little brief authority; of beggars, whose persistent importunities, if directed to the right place, would open the pearly gates of paradise.

Nearly half the space included within the walls is covered with the ruins of better days; and in the other half are gardens, wherein are the orange, the fig, the pomegranate, the apricot, and the palm. The streets are narrow, crooked, unpaved, and, on rainy days, impassable for pedestrians. No people in the world bathe half so often as the Turks, yet no people are half so indifferent to offensive odors. Whatever is within, the outside of the platter is never clean. They are passionately fond of perfumes, and are partial to the oil of roses; yet there is not a street in Bagdad that is not a sink of deadly vapors.

MARKET-PLACE OF BAGDAD.

The gloom of the principal thoroughfares is increased by the construction and the materials of the buildings. Most of the houses are composed of a pale-yellow brick, and on either side of the street are blank walls, penetrated by a low, narrow door-way, with here and there a small latticed window. The entrance is secured by a heavy door of planks, fastened by strong iron clamps, and, when closed, is an effectual barrier to all intruders. This low portal leads to a spacious court-yard, opening into which are ranges of apartments furnished and ornamented according to the wealth and taste of the occupants. Connected with all the better class of private residences in Bagdad are subterranean rooms, called *serdaubs*, which are a cool retreat in the day-time from the intense heat of summer. The flat roofs of the dwellings are so many unroofed chambers, wherein the family take the evening meal and sleep during the heated season. And, as may be readily imagined, the early dawn presents to the traveler a novel sight, when, on a thousand housetops, the sleepers awake from their dreams and begin to shake dull slumber from their souls.

The public buildings of Bagdad have the enchantment that distance lends to the view. The palace of the pasha is more noticeable for its extent than for its magnificence. Viewed from an eminence, the swelling domes and lofty minarets of a hundred mosques, rising above the palm and orange groves, present to the eye of the beholder a pleasing landscape. Some of the mosques are old and grand. That of the vizier, which abuts the Tigris, and is near the bridge, has a noble dome and a graceful minaret, but is less attractive than the one near the Maidan, whose rich arabesque-work, imposing entrance, lofty pointed arch, sculptured bands, and beautifully wrought inscription, are not altogether unworthy the "City of the

Caliphs." The mosque of the pasha is distinguished by the lamps on its exterior gallery that burn throughout the night, but is not so large and grand as that of Abbas-el-Kaddr. Most of these mosques are surmounted with Persian domes, whose height is greater than their diameter. The exterior of the dome and minaret is incased with glazed tiles of green and white, and the body of the mosque is streaked with vermilion.

On a sunny day, the streets of Bagdad presented a picturesque and lively scene. Richly caparisoned horses, and white asses fantastically marked with henna, each led by a turbaned groom on foot, bore some "prince of the blood" or high official from palace to palace; Turks in flowing robes and broad white turbans; Persians in high black caps and closely-fitting tunics; the Bokhara pilgrim in white head-dress and wayworn garments; the Bedouin chief in his tasseled keffieh and striped aba: Bagdad ladies in white and scarlet draperies, fretted with threads of gold, and black horse-hair veils concealing wanton eyes; Persian women wrapped in shapeless garments, and Arab girls wearing a single blue skirt, mingled in one motley throng in the merry bazaars.

The creed, the nationality, the trade, the station in life, are indicated by the dress worn in the street. The Jew and Christian are known by their dark robes and turbans, formed of blue muslin or Cashmere shawls. The Persian is recognized by his tight tunic and rimless hat. The desert Arab is distinguished by his silk head-dress, his woolen cloak, and curved dagger. The Moslem proclaims his faith by his clean white turban, and the Mohammedan mollah by his turban of green. And the Government official, whether civil or military, is known by his European costume and red fez.

Such is the cosmopolitan character of the population

of this city, that St. Peter could have an audience representing all nations to hear another pentecostal sermon. Khoords, Persians, and Arabs, Turks, Hindoos, and Africans, French, Germans, and English, Spaniards and Italians, Jews and Christians, dwell within the city walls. Of the sixty-eight thousand inhabitants, fifty-five thousand are Moslems, ten thousand are Jews, two thousand are native Christians, and the balance are from all nations under heaven, except America.

The Jews are by far the most interesting portion of the population. They claim to be the descendants of the captives carried into Babylon. Some boast of a pedigree from King David, and recite the melodies once sung in the Temple at Jerusalem. Among the most distinguished of their number was Eliezer Ben Isamah, known as the President of the Fifth Class, who traced his descent from the prophet Samuel, and who performed on the harp in the exact manner that was in use in the days of the royal David. But one greater than he was called Daniel, the son of Hasdai, and "Conductor of the Captivity," who had preserved a book of his genealogy in direct descent from David. His brethren recognized him as their leader, nor was the caliph slow to accord to him the honor. By order of the Government, all classes of the citizens were commanded to show him due respect. When he went on a visit to the caliph, he was attended by horsemen, and preceded by a crier, who proclaimed, "Prepare ye the way of the Lord; make his paths straight." He was another Daniel in the realm. He was attired in robes of silk ornamented with Phrygian embroidery. He wore a splendid tiara, encircled with a white veil, held in its place by a chain of gold, and he rode in the second chariot of the kingdom.*

---

* Benjamin of Tudela.

Bagdad is now the head-quarters of the Hebrews for all parts of the valley of the Euphrates, from Hillah to Mosul. The ancestors of some of them settled here two hundred and fifty years ago, having come from Anah, on the Euphrates, where the captives were colonized after the destruction of Jerusalem. At present the Jews have fourteen synagogues, and ten schools for the education of their children. Here the Hebrews assemble annually from all the neighboring cities, to keep the Passover. Hither all letters are directed and thence remailed to their owners. As a class, the Hebrews are rich and intelligent. Some are bankers, some are merchants, some are goldsmiths. The latter are the jewelers of Bagdad, and their bazaar is the most interesting portion of the city. True to their religious faith, they intermarry, and are a nation within a nation. The chief rabbi is in the prime of life, and of rare attainments. I sought an interview, and he complied with my request. He expects the restoration of his people to the Promised Land, and is living in daily expectation of the Messiah's advent.

On the Jewish Sabbath I visited five of their synagogues. All are inferior structures. The largest and best is a court fifty feet square; and on each side are alcoves, wherein are seats covered with Persian carpets. In the east side is the Holy of Holies. In the centre is a square canopy supported by twelve pillars, and from the roof lamps depend. On the platform beneath the canopy stood the officiating priests, who chanted the Psalms of David and selections from the Law and the Prophets. Near the entrance to the court is a miniature temple, whereon is an inscription in Hebrew, which the people fondly kissed as they departed from the sacred place. Above the lateral alcoves are the latticed apartments for the women. Some of the Hebrew ladies were extremely beautiful, and their appearance indicated that they loved their ornaments as did their mothers in the days of Isaiah. All were well and some were richly attired, indicating their thrift and worldly prosperity. While I was in the city the whole Jewish community was greatly excited. One of their merchants had sworn on the Holy Book that he was worth less than his assets justified, and this he had done to avoid a financial obligation. A new disease had broken out among the Jews, and seemed incurable. The priests regarded it as a judgment from the Lord to punish this act of perjury; and, to appease the Almighty's wrath and check the disease, they declared that the perjurer must confess, or be excommunicated.

On a beautiful Sabbath morning I visited the several Christian churches of the city, and witnessed their form of worship. The Christian community, of two thousand souls, is composed of five distinct sects. In accordance with an old usage and mutual consent, the members of four of these denominations intermarry. In the marriage-contract it is stipulated that the wife may choose her own church, but the children must be baptized in the church of the father. The Monophysite Armenians, however, are averse to this arrangement, and decline to marry those not of their communion.

The Christians of Bagdad are natives, and form part of the great Eastern Church, as distinguished from the Church of the West. The Armenians are divided into two branches, the Papists and the Monophysites. The church of the Papal Armenians is a small and inferior building. On the high altar is the picture of the Assumption of the Virgin, and before it the native priest was celebrating mass, for the benefit of the few females who compose his flock. The church of the Monophysitic

Armenians is a low, plain edifice. A robed priest and two deacons were officiating at the high altar. The services consisted in intoning selections from the Psalms and the Gospels, and a sermon on repentance, which was more brief than pointed. A silk curtain extends across the chancel, behind which the venerable priest retired, as into the Holy of Holies, and responded to the chant by the deacons. At the close of the service, bread was blessed, and all the people partook. During the ceremony, one of the deacons *incensed* each worshiper, except the women. According to custom, the men sat on the floor, and in front; while the women sat in the rear, and behind a latticed frame. As each worshiper entered the sacred edifice, and also when he retired, he made the sign of the cross thrice, and thrice he bowed his head to the floor. While the Armenian ladies adhere to the Eastern style of dress, the gentlemen have donned the costume of the West, except the hat, in place of which they wear the red fez.

From the Armenian I wended my way through crooked lanes to the Syrian church, which is a more pretentious structure. The Syrian Christians are papal in creed and in ritual, but not subject to the jurisdiction of the pope. On the walls of their church are some excellent pictures illustrative of Scriptural scenes and of pious legends. Clad in elegant robes, the bishop officiated; and, at the conclusion of the mass, he blessed a crucifix, which he presented to be touched by the layman nearest the altar. Having touched the sacred emblem, he extended his hand to the person sitting next to him, and thus the blessing was communicated to all the people. An old man insisted on giving me the blessing, but I thought it had become too diluted to possess any virtue. I subsequently had an interview with the bishop in his episcopal residence. He was robed in purple, and from a heavy gold chain depended a jeweled crucifix. In the course of our conversation, he expressed the opinion that it would be difficult to convert the Moslems to the Christian faith. He recognized the pope as head of the Church, but declared himself independent of the jurisdiction of the Holy See. The interview was interrupted by the incoming of the bishop's sister, who seemed more interested in showing me the elegant robes she had embroidered for the priests than in conversing on the state of the Church.

The Chaldean Catholics have a larger community. The walls of their spacious church are adorned with pictures, and over the altar is one representing the Trinity. Not less than two hundred persons were present at the service. Having left their shoes at the door, the men sat on the carpeted floor in front, and the women sat behind a screen in the rear. Two priests were confessing those who approached them for that purpose.

The French Roman Catholic church is a new and handsome structure. The altar-piece is a noble picture representing Mary standing beneath the Cross. A hundred persons were present at mass, and among the number were several Europeans. Here the women were in front, sitting on Persian rugs, and the men sat on benches in the rear of the spacious *auditorium*.

Although these several churches differ in creed and polity, yet in their ritual they are not unlike. Robed priests celebrated mass; clouds of incense perfumed the air; the confessional was conspicuous in each; and Mary was prominent in all. Priests and people are the representatives of a perverted Christianity.

In my wanderings among the churches I had the opportunity to see the Christians of Bagdad, observe their manners, and note their style of dress. As in more civilized countries, the ladies appear at church attired in their richest and most showy apparel. Only a few of the Christian women wear the veil; but, as a custom and an ornament, they envelop themselves in the elegant silk *izar*, which is held together at the chin by the thumb and forefinger of the right hand, so as quite to cover the face. Their fondness for jewelry is displayed in the excess of their ornaments, which are numerous and showy. But in nothing more are the Christian women distinguished from their sisters of the Moslem faith than in their dress and ornaments. The street attire of Moslem women is extremely plain, and never attractive. The veil is universal with them, and constantly worn when in public. Those of the poorer class wear the *yasmak*, made of stiff black horse-hair, which imparts an air of poverty and gloom. And so completely are the rich and the poor disguised by the veil, that a husband can not recognize his wife on the street. Those who are allied to the Arab race, whether by blood or habits of long intercourse, have a passion for adorning their persons with blue stains, that are not only indelible, but most forbidding in appearance. They stain their lower lip with the deadly hue, their ankles with anklets, their wrists with bracelets, their breasts with wreaths of flowers, and their necks with a zone, in imitation of some beautiful necklace. And this work of decorating the female form in the latest approved style is performed by professional artists in Bagdad.

But there is one ornament worn by both men and women of which none are proud. It is to them what the "Aleppo button" and the "Delhi boil" are to the people of those more distant cities. It is a frightful ulcer that appears on the lip, on the nose, on the chin, or on the

NATIVE CHRISTIAN WOMEN.

forehead, and the scar left is carried through life. I did not see a native man or woman of Bagdad who had not this ornamental mark. It appears on every child born in the city some time between the sixth and twelfth month after birth, and lasts for one year. It is generally superficial, but sometimes it sloughs to the bone. The natives divide it into the "male," which is superficial, and into the "female," which is the sloughing ulcer. There is no known remedy, either to prevent or to cure. The Jews tried inoculation, but without success. Foreigners and strangers are subject to it, and have it on the ankle, the wrist, or the nose; and it has made its appearance on them long after they have left the city. Nor is the brute exempt from the malady, as it attacks dogs, and terminates frequently in their death. Dr. Colville, the learned and distinguished English surgeon and physician of the city, has given the subject long and careful study, and to him I am indebted for the above facts.

During my sojourn of ten days in Bagdad, I frequently strolled through the bazaars, which never failed to excite my curiosity and afford me the pleasure of novelty. Some of these bazaars are long, straight, and wide, vaulted with brick, with circular openings in the ceiling for air and light; while others are covered with a roof of reed-mats, supported by a wooden frame-work. The shops are stalls arranged on either side, and therein are displayed for sale the luscious fruits of the East, rich confectioneries, the clothing worn by all classes and both sexes, the swords, daggers, guns, and pistols carried by the Bedouins, the gay trappings for the Arab horse, the tapestry from Persia, silks from Aleppo, pearls from Bahrein, merchandise from England, and petroleum from America.

Commercially and politically, Bagdad is the most important city in the Turkish empire east of the Euphrates. The pasha is usually a high dignitary, and his power is correspondingly great. It is a large military station, and in connection therewith are extensive and well-constructed barracks and a flourishing military school. It is the residence of an English, French, German, and Russian consul, who vie with each other in their vigilance in behalf of their respective governments. The English political resident and consul-general has a jurisdiction to Mosul, three hundred miles to the north-west, and is supported in a princely manner. A gun-boat is at anchor before his residence, and awaits his commands. The present incumbent is a gentleman of culture and refinement. In the absence of a clergyman of the English Church, Colonel Herbert performs the ritualistic service in the residency on each Sabbath morning, for the religious benefit of his family and those of the European population who wish to attend. But, unlike his most gracious sovereign, Queen Victoria, who esteems it a privilege to commune in a Dissenters' chapel; unlike the Archbishop of Canterbury, who sends his dean to the meeting of the Evangelical Alliance, largely composed of Dissenters; unlike Dean Stanley, whose Christian liberality prompted him to invite a Dissenting clergyman to preach in Westminster Abbey, Colonel Herbert could not so far overcome his sectarian prejudice as to invite to officiate in the residency a Dissenting minister who might by chance spend a Sabbath in Bagdad.

The banking capital of Bagdad is in the hands of the Jews; the foreign trade of the city is controlled by Europeans. The custom-house is the most extensive building of the kind north-east of Bombay. But the extent and value of the trade can not be easily ascertained. All parties regard secrecy as essential to success. The custom-house officials decline to furnish the consuls with trade statistics; and the agents of the steamship companies refuse to communicate the value of the exports and imports carried in their vessels, lest such information might lead to the organization of rival companies. But the large number of revenue officials employed by the Government, the number of steam and sailing vessels that are entered and cleared at the port, and the wealth of the steamship companies engaged in the trade, suggest an approximate estimate of the business done. In 1873, ten thousand tons of wheat were shipped from this port to India, and the present trade of the city is ten times larger than it was five years ago. Caravans are daily arriving from Persia, from Damascus, and from the Mediterranean, *viâ* Aleppo and Mosul, loaded with goods for the Bagdad market; and, on their return, are loaded with goods brought from India and the Persian Gulf, to be distributed in all the intermediate inland towns.

And Bagdad is rapidly becoming a railroad centre. A road is now in operation on the west bank of the Tigris, extending from the city to Kathimain, a distance of six miles, and the dividends of which are ten per cent. per annum. At present there is but a single track, but with frequent cut-offs. The cars are of English manufacture, constructed with seats within and on the top, and are now drawn by horse-power. Three cars leave simultaneously from each end of the road, at regular intervals of fifteen minutes, and meet midway, where there is a long cut-off. There is a conductor on each car, and the fare is six cents. The road was built by the Turkish Government; but the officials stole so much that it was sold to a company of natives and foreigners, and now pays ten per cent. There are three brick dépôts for the accommodation of passengers who travel on business, for pleasure, or to worship at the sacred shrines of Kathimain. And a route is now being surveyed for a road to extend from Kermanshah, on the Persian frontier, through Bagdad to Kerbulle, near Khan-el-Haswa, within a day's ride of the Tower of Babel. And the day is in the near future when the Euphrates Valley Railroad will be an accomplished fact, connecting, as it will, the Mediterranean with the Persian Gulf; and the child is now in its cradle who will hear the conductor shout, "Change cars for Babylon!" "All aboard for the Garden of Eden!"

The only article imported from the United States and sold in the bazaars of Bagdad is American petroleum. It is entered at the port of Alexandretta, on the Mediterranean, and transported a thousand miles on the back of camels. It is one of the marvels of this marvelous age, that our petroleum is everywhere to be found in the Levant and the Orient. It lights the dwellings, the temples, and mosques amidst the ruins of ancient Babylon and Nineveh. It is the light of Bagdad, the City of the Thousand and One Nights; of Orfah, the birthplace of Abraham; of Mardeen, the *Macius* of the Romans; and of Damascus, the "Gem of the Orient." It burns in the Grotto of the Nativity at Bethlehem, in the Church of the Holy Sepulchre in Jerusalem, amidst the pyramids of Egypt, on the Acropolis of Athens, on the Plains of Troy, and in cottage and palace on the banks of the Bosphorus and the Golden Horn.

It is the opinion of good judges that a lucrative trade might be established between the United States and the port of Bagdad *via* the Persian Gulf. Were the price lessened by a cheaper transportation, American petroleum would find a ready market in the towns on the Persian frontier, and would be thence carried to the villages and cities in the interior of the empire; it would be in general demand in the towns on the Tigris and Euphrates; and the quantity consumed in Bagdad and the adjacent country would be incalculably increased. And, were the proper measures adopted, American agricultural implements might be introduced to supersede the rude implements that have been in use since the days of Adam. The valleys of the Euphrates and of the Tigris are among the richest and most magnificent grain and pasture lands in the world, and the produce thereof might be indefinitely increased by the introduction of improved implements of tillage. Other products of the creative genius of our country have found a market in the East.

The American sewing-machine is used by the natives in Beirut, in Damascus, in Jerusalem, and would command a high price in the valley of the Euphrates; and the return trade in dates, in wool, in Persian carpets, in Aleppo silks, would be correspondingly large. The richest dates grow here. The largest flocks of sheep and goats are to be found in this section of Turkey, and the quantity of wool produced is immense. A better quality, and at lower prices, can be obtained here than that which is now shipped to the United States from ports on the Mediterranean. The Persian carpets would not only be an ornament, but a serviceable article, and would be in demand were they largely introduced into the American market; and the native silks, especially those embroidered with gold and silver thread, and made up into divan-covers, opera-cloaks, sacks, and jackets, would be exceedingly pleasing to our American ladies.

CHAPTER III.

Five Days among the Ruins of Ancient Babylon.—Preparations for the Journey.—Early Start.—Bridge of Boats.—Crowd of People.—Celebrated Tombs.—Raising Water.—Luncheon by the Way-side.—First View of the Ancient Ruins.—The Pilgrim's Khan.—First Night among the Ruins.—Again in the Saddle.—Ancient Walls.—Arab Villages.—Telegraph Poles.—The Old Canals.—Remains of Belshazzar's Palace.—The Famous Hanging Gardens.—Daniel's Lion's Den.—Harps on the Willows.—Rivers of Babylon.—The Euphrates.—Immense Palm-groves.—Bridge of Boats.—Modern Hillah.—Our Khan.—American Petroleum.—Telegraph Station.—Call upon the Pasha.—Playing with a Lion.—Sail on the Euphrates.—A Night in Hillah.—Start for the Tower of Babel.—Dangers in the Way.—Wonderful Ruins.—Ascend the Tower of Babel.—The Fiery Furnace.—The Glory of Babylon.—Progress of its Decline.—Prophecy Fulfilled.—The Warriors of the Desert.—Return to Bagdad.

The central ruins of ancient Babylon are sixty miles to the south-west from Bagdad. The renowned city occupied a portion of the peninsula formed by the Tigris and the Euphrates. The length of that peninsula from Bagdad to the Garden of Eden is three hundred miles, and its average breadth is less than thirty miles. It is narrowest opposite Seleucia and Ctesiphon, and broadest south of Babylon, between Al-Khuidr and El-Shib. Upon this "narrow neck of land" are those mighty ruins which we were now to explore, and thereon occurred those great events that have made the name of Babylon imperishable in the annals of time, and the scene of which we were now to visit.

The road thither was rough, the fatigue was excessive, and the dangers were great, but the compensation outweighed them all. The mode of traveling is by horse, or camel, or mule, or *khajawah*, or *tukhteravan*, or on foot, as wealth may permit or taste incline. We chose horses, which are kept for hire at Bagdad for something more than a dollar per day. Through the kindness of Captain Cowley, we had secured a servant who could speak enough English to be a medium of communication, but who had such extravagant notions of an American's wealth as to demand three dollars a day. The British consul-general had commissioned his cawass, Ashur, to accompany us as guide and for military protection. To him was intrusted an order from the Pasha of Bagdad to the Governor of Hillah, informing the latter that we were American travelers to the ruins of Babylon; that we were peaceable and honorable persons; and that he should receive us with all proper attention, and protect us to the extent of his power. We were to mount horses that were small, tough, and swift. We were to lodge in khans, more remarkable for their size than they are for their cleanness; and we were to eat the food of the Arabs, more luscious to the taste than pleasing to the sight.

At seven in the morning, all were ready. Mounting our horses, we rode slowly through the narrow streets of the city to the great gate that opens to the bridge of boats which spans the Tigris. The roar of the current, the dilapidated condition of the bridge, the multitude of persons and animals thereon, caused our horses to shy and caper, no little to our annoyance. Only Turks would tolerate such a bridge, and collect toll for the danger of crossing thereon. Safely over, we entered the bazaars on the western bank, filled with people purchasing food for the morning meal. Ashur led the caravan, and the people opened ranks sufficiently to allow us to pass single file. Our "elect lady" was the absorbing object of attraction to men and women, who laughed and chatted as she passed in review before them; and, had she been a visitant from the moon, she could not have excited greater wonder. After passing through noble palm-groves, we were on a vast plain dotted with tombs, huts, and statelier structures. Near us and on our right was the tomb of the beautiful Zobeida, the favorite wife of Haroun-al-Raschid, celebrated in "The Arabian Nights;" and beyond were the golden domes and lofty minarets of Kathimain, where sleep in death the descendants of the ill-fated Hosien-Ali. As we advanced, we passed caravans of camels, trains of donkeys, and processions of pilgrims to some Mohammedan shrine. In one hour we reached the Tigris, which bends to the westward in a long and sweeping curve, where many native boats were at anchor awaiting a favorable wind to waft them against the powerful current. Near the curve were a few Arab huts, where fruit and other refreshments were for sale. Around the village were pretty gardens and fields of grain, which men were irrigating in the following novel manner. A semicircular recess twenty feet in diameter had been made in the bank of the river; over this a frame-work had been erected, composed of the trunks of the date-tree, and consisting of two upright posts and a transverse bar. On the transverse bar were rollers, and over the rollers traversed a rope. To one end of the rope was attached a large leather bucket, which descended to the river by its own weight and soon filled; the other end of the rope was fastened to an ox, which was driven over a steep artificial slope at an angle of forty-five degrees, and, thus uniting its weight with its strength, raised the heavy bucket. The water was then poured into a small conduit, and conveyed to the gardens and fields through little canals that ran in every direction. It was altogether a primitive and clumsy method of irrigation, and indicated the absence of mechanical skill among the Arab farmers.

We were now on the great plain of Chaldea, bleak and barren as a desert. The mirage was frequent and illusive as ever. Out of the apparent water rose the tall palm-trees, too tempting to weary travelers. In two hours we were at Khan Cheqwah, where were mounds of buried ruins. The great plain was covered with a perfect net-work of ancient canals and water-courses; but a "drought is upon her waters, and they shall be dried up."* Their lofty embankments, stretching far away in long lines till lost in the hazy distance, or magnified by the mirage into mountains, still defy the hand of time, and seem rather the work of nature than of man. For two hours we rode through a scene of solitude and desolation to Khan Azaad, where we were only too glad to dismount from our hard Arab saddle, and refresh ourselves with *lebben*, or sour milk, and eat the coarse bread of the desert. Here the Arab men and women gathered around us in wild wonderment, examined our cloths, and made remarks which we were fortunate enough not to understand. The Arab's sense of the ludicrous is quick and keen, and what to us is the most fashionable is to him the most ridiculous. He can be as grave as a gravestone, and as merry as a clown. Their criticisms on our dress, on our mode of eating, on our intonations, excited roars of laughter among the admiring crowd.

Again in the saddle, we passed Khan Mahmoodich in two hours, and an hour later we were opposite the unoccupied Khan-el-Beer. We all felt the fatigue of the ride, but there was no help for us. No traveler accustomed

---

* Jeremiah l., 38.

to the roomy, elegant saddle of the West should attempt to use the narrow saddle of the Arab; if he does, he will pay a penalty of indescribable pain. Onward we rode for two and a half hours, which seemed as many days. Owing to the illusive atmosphere of Chaldea, the great Khan-el-Haswah seemed "near, yet so far." It was now five o'clock. We had come just half-way, or a distance of twenty-seven miles. The sun was declining; the air was growing chilly, and safety required us to halt for the night. Reining our jaded horses up to the great khan, we gladly dismounted, and prepared for a night's lodgings with the "beasts of the stall."

THE KHAN.

But what a place to sleep in, especially for a lady! As the pencil is more effective than the pen in conveying an idea of a khan, the accompanying sketch, from a photograph taken on the spot, will enable you to conceive the more readily the appearance of a hotel on the desert plains of Chaldea. The Khan-el-Haswah is an immense inclosure, with a wall eighty feet square and twenty feet high, and built of ancient bricks dug up from the ruins of nobler structures. Its corners are truncated. The entrance is a high, semi-cupola; along the front wall is a brick terrace four feet high and as many wide, for travelers to rest on during the day. Within the entrance is an alcove at each of the four corners, with a brick platform four feet high, and sufficiently spacious for three persons to sleep thereon. From these alcoves there extends a covered arched passage-way around the four sides of the building, with recesses on the inner side ten feet high, with a platform three feet from the ground, and six by six in area. On the outside of this covered passage, and fronting the interior court, are similar chambers, open to the air, yet sufficiently sheltered from the sun in all his points of bearing during all the hours of the day. There are twelve of these recesses on each side of the square; and in the centre of the interior court are raised platforms of brick-work, for travelers to sleep on during the summer, when the heat is so intense. Towering high above the wall is the minaret, from whose balcony the Moslem traveler is called to prayers. These great khans are about six miles apart, extending the whole distance between Bagdad and Babylon. They were built by Persian kings, or wealthy and pious men of the same nation, for the accommodation of pilgrims to the sacred shrines. But they are more generally used as a place of safety from the midnight depredations of thieving Arabs, who roam over these Chaldean plains in quest of plunder, and from the wild beasts of the desert, who seek their prey under cover of the night. Pilgrim and traveler so time their journey as to reach one of these caravansaries ere the sun sets, and hither the shepherd leads his flock of sheep and goats for shelter and protection. When all are in, and while yet the twilight lingers, the great doors are shut and bolted, nor are they opened again till the morning light appears. These caravansaries are free to all, without money and without price, and are the cheapest and filthiest hotels known to mankind. We occupied a series of alcoves north of the main entrance. The floor was covered with fine straw, dust, and fleas. In all the adjoining recesses were Arabs—some smoking, some eating, some sleeping. From the women of the village we bought eggs, milk, bread, and pomegranates, and, after our frugal repast, we spread our rugs and blankets on the brick platform, and lay down to pleasant slumber. But sleep was impossible; for at our feet horses neighed, sheep bleated, donkeys brayed; and to these harmonies the Moslem added his humdrum chant, and the shepherd the rude music of his cracked flute. It was a free concert. And when beast and shepherd grew weary of their own familiar tones, then we were assailed front and rear, right and left, feet and head, by the "*fleaing* artillery," whose thirst for blood was insatiable. And so passed our first night among the ruins of Babylon.

At five the next morning the great doors of Khan-el-Haswah were opened, and we gladly resumed our journey. Weary of my Arab saddle, I joined a procession of pilgrims, and walked two miles. But the constant danger of being surprised by marauding Bedouins compelled me to mount. On our right, and near the Euphrates, was the great khan of Hadjee Suliman, where the pilgrims stop *en route* for the tomb of the Prophet Ezekiel, which is beyond the river. We soon came to an extensive circular ridge, that may be part of an old wall, or the embankment of an ancient canal, against the sides of which the sands of the desert had been driven by the winds. Over all that plain, as far as the eye could reach, are ancient mounds, remains of old canals, fragments of furnace-baked bricks, of fine red pottery glazed in red and green and blue colors, and heaps of the ruins of once proud structures. In four hours we reached the Khan Mohaweel, where we lunched on eggs, *cubis*, *lebben*, dates, oranges, and wheat-cakes a foot in diameter. These refreshments were bought from the women of the desert, whose lower lips were colored with a blue stain, whose faces were otherwise tattooed with blue and red colors, the palms of whose hands were stained with the yellow henna, who had rings on their toes, and huge rings in their noses. Around the khan are a few mud-huts, constructed in the form of a bee-hive, in the top of which is an aperture for the smoke to go out and for the light to enter. A few paces to the south of the village is the largest canal we had yet seen, and filled with water from the Euphrates. On measuring it, I found it to be forty feet from bank to bank, and fifteen feet from the top of the bridge to the surface of the water. The bridge is sixty feet long, constructed of ancient bricks, and at its south end are two rough conical brick pillars. The water is four feet deep, and men were at work dipping it up and pouring it into small canals for irrigation. Women and girls descended the steep bank of the main canal, filled their large earthen jars with the water for household uses, and, like the Jewish maidens, placed the jar upon the shoulder, and gracefully bore it to their homes. The women are the water-carriers in the East, and in every village and encampment I visited I saw them at the spring or well or river filling their pitchers, as of old. Not far from the bridge was a grain-field of twenty acres, and on it was a cluster of date-palms, which looked beautiful in contrast with the arid desert around me. This oasis owed its life and beauty to the neighboring canal, whose waters came from the Euphrates, which was ten miles to the eastward. Indeed, water is the chief requisite to make the "desert rejoice, and blossom as the rose."* The fertility of the

---

* Isaiah xxxv., 1.

plains of Chaldea would be restored were its numerous canals once more in existence. There is now on these great plains what the Arab calls a "jungle," consisting of a bush a foot high, and hither the shepherds lead their flocks during the day, but return with them to the khan at night, to escape the robbers and the beasts of prey. The flocks were in good condition; the fleece was long and thick. As we advanced, we saw herds of camels feeding in the jungle, and by them stood their keepers, armed to the teeth, and prepared to protect their herds from the clutch of the thief or the jaws of the wild beast.

All around us were mounds of ruins, the sad remains of Babylon's departed greatness. I wandered on purpose from the party, and sought solitude. Thoughts of the mighty past filled my mind. I dismounted, and walked over the great plains of Chaldea, and recalled the historic past, when Nabopolassar and Nebuchadnezzar, Belshazzar and Cyrus, Darius and Xerxes, Alexander and his generals, were the mighty actors on this great stage of the world's history; when Daniel and his brethren were captives by its classic waters; when Greek met Assyrian, and Roman met Persian in the battle array, to fight for empire and renown; when palace and castle, tower and temple, massive walls and brazen gates, stood in their glory, where now their remains are strewed; when gardens bloomed, and fountains played, and millions of people lived in pride and luxury. But, alas! how unlike the past is the present! The Lord of hosts hath spoken: "And Babylon shall become heaps, a dwelling-place for dragons, an astonishment, and a hissing."* The renowned king and mighty warrior are no more; the

---

* Jeremiah li., 37.

great empire has ceased to be; palaces and towers are heaps of ruins.

But the sadness of such reflections was relieved by a sublime fact. The telegraph extends from Bagdad to Babylon, and all along our weary path it had been to me the promise of a better future. The poles are of iron, to prevent injury from beast or Bedouin, and are constructed, like a telescope, for easy transportation. There are two wires, and the sighing of the winds thereon was like the mournful music of the winds on the Hebrew harps that hung upon the willows. As I wandered over the dreary plains, I placed my right hand on one of the poles, and felt that I grasped one of the pillars of our modern civilization.

Not far from the large canal of Mohaweel was a long line of earthen ramparts, which doubtless were a part of the great wall of Babylon, and which now mark the northern remains of the ancient city. Ascending their summit, we obtained a view of the boundless plain, through which, and on our right, flowed the Euphrates, with its dark belt of evergreen palms. Around us were low mounds, covered in part by the drifted sands, and beneath which are the walls and foundations of former buildings. As we rode onward, it was not difficult to trace the lines of the ancient streets, and the once beautiful squares of the city. On every hand were the proofs that the Babylonians did not neglect the advantages bestowed upon them by nature. By a system of navigable canals, that may well excite the admiration of even the modern engineer, they connected the Tigris and the Euphrates, those great arteries of commerce. With a skill showing no common knowledge of the art of surveying, and of the principles of hydraulics, they took advantage of the different levels in the plains, and of the periodical overflow of the two rivers, to complete the water communication between all parts of the province, and to fertilize, by artificial irrigation, the otherwise barren and unproductive soil. So thoroughly impressed was Alexander the Great with the importance of these works, that he ordered the canals cleansed and repaired, and superintended the work in person, steering his boat with his own hand through the channels.* During our

ANCIENT BABYLONIAN CANALS.

morning ride we crossed five of the larger of these canals, two of which were dry. At one place the natives were at work digging a canal to irrigate their gardens and grain-fields. But it was apparent that they worked on a different plan from that adopted by the Babylonians. The bottom of the ancient canals was on a level

---

* Layard.

with the ground, and the material for the embankments was brought to the spot; but the modern canal is dug, and its banks consist of the dirt thrown up.

At eleven o'clock we gained our first view of Mujelibe, where stood the magnificent palace of Nebuchadnezzar. The sight was an inspiration, and onward we rode. In a direct line it seemed not far, but between us and it there was a deep canal hidden from our view. So exciting was the prospect that I rode directly for the great mound, but found the canal impassable. It required an hour to reach the bridge, on whose southern end were two conical brick columns. When on the bridge, we were to the south of the mound. But, turning abruptly, and following the south bank of the canal, we were soon on the ruins of the palace of Babylon's great king.

Called by the Arabs Mujelibe—"the overturned"—and identified by Rich, by Buckingham, by Layard, as the remains of the great palace of Nebuchadnezzar, the mound is an oblong square, whose sides face the four cardinal points, whose circumference is twenty-one hundred and eleven feet, and whose highest point is one hundred and forty feet above the surrounding plain. The western face presents the appearance of a building, and near the summit are the remains of a low wall, composed of unburned bricks, cemented with clay-mortar of great thickness. On the south-west corner of the summit are the ruins of one of the four towers which ornamented the once grand structure. Over all its sides and summit were fragments of pottery, vitrified bricks, glass vessels and ornaments of mother-of-pearl. In the northern side I entered a recess, high enough to stand in, and on two sides are brick walls of superior construction, and from the recess ran a passage to the right, entering the very heart of the mound. Near this passage-way a quantity of marble had been discovered, and, subsequently, a coffin of mulberry-wood, containing a human body, inclosed in a light wrapper, and partially covered with bitumen, which crumbled into dust when exposed to the air. And in another narrow passage nearly ten feet high, and originally lined with finely burned brick, on which were inscriptions, a second wooden coffin was found, containing a skeleton in a good state of preservation. Under the head of the coffin was a round stone, and attached to the outside of the coffin was a brass bird, and inside was an ornament of the same material, which had been suspended to some part of the skeleton. Near this was also found the skeleton of a child. The brass ornaments indicated a high antiquity, but whose are the remains it was impossible to tell. These excavated recesses are now the dens of wild beasts, as in them are the bones of sheep and of other animals, together with a large quantity of porcupine quills, and from them came a smell like that of a lion. In all those cavities are owls and bats, foretold by Isaiah: "Wild beasts of the desert shall be there; their houses shall be full of doleful creatures; and owls shall dwell there, and satyrs shall dance there."*

As we wandered over this great mound, penetrating its recesses, threading its narrow, winding ravines, clambering its steep, rugged sides, we were convinced that it is composed of the remains of many different edifices, such as belonged to a great palace. Not a hundred and fifty feet from its base, on the northern and western sides, are low mounds, the traces of the triple walls which once inclosed the royal palace of Nebuchadnezzar, king of Babylon. The view from the summit of the mound was exceedingly impressive, and filled the mind with thoughts

---

* Rich.

of the mighty past. On our right, and not far away, the Euphrates flowed majestically through verdant banks, until lost to sight amidst the palm-groves of Hillah, whose mosques and minarets were seen five miles to the southward; while six miles beyond appeared the Tower of Babel, now a fragment of one of the greatest structures reared by the hand of man. A mile to the south of us were the remains of the once beautiful Hanging Gardens, constructed to please the Median queen, and

BELSHAZZAR'S PALACE.

justly considered one of the Seven Wonders of the World. Before us, stretching far away to the northward and to the southward, were lofty banks of ancient canals that fret the country like natural ridges; and here, there, and everywhere were shapeless mounds, covered with fragments of glass, marble, pottery, and inscribed bricks, mingled with a white nitrous soil, whose blanched appearance completed the picture of desolation.

We were standing on the platform, on which stood the superb palace of Nebuchadnezzar, the magnificence of which excited the admiration of all who beheld it. At once a castle and a palace, it was surrounded by a triple wall, whose inner gates were made of the brass taken from Jerusalem, and once composed the sacred vessels in the Temple of Solomon.* The outer wall was high and stately, six miles in circumference, and constructed of well-burned bricks. Within the third was the second wall, four miles in circuit, upon which were portrayed all kinds of living animals, and wrought in curious colors. Within the second, and immediately surrounding the palace, was the first wall, whose circuit was over three miles, whose height and thickness were greater than either of the others, and on whose interior face were delineations of hunting-scenes, representing the queen on horseback striking a leopard through with a dart; and near her the king, in close fight with a lion, piercing him with a lance. Within the triple inclosure, and on this platform, rose the palace, which far excelled in magnificence any other in the empire, and wherein the walls were varnished; the wood-work was gilded and silvered, and the saloons and halls and chambers were ornamented with representations of the sun, moon, and stars, of birds and beasts, of kings and queens in the resplendent robes of royalty, the work of artists who understood the use of color, and who displayed such a taste in its combination in ornamental designs as to greatly excite the admiration of the strangers who came to Babylon.† The walls of the banqueting-hall were coated with mortar and plaster of the finest quality, and upon the plaster of the wall of the king's palace the fingers of a man's hand came forth and wrote, " MENE, MENE, TEKEL UPHARSIN."‡ Here Belshazzar gave that memorable feast

---

* 2 Kings xxv., 13. † Layard. ‡ Daniel v., 25.

to a thousand of his lords, whereat he and his princes, his wives and his concubines, drank wine from the golden and silver vessels which Nebuchadnezzar had taken out of the temple at Jerusalem, and which feast was terminated so abruptly by a ghastly apparition, and so disastrously, by the murder of the king and royal guard. Here Daniel, an eye-witness to both, reproved kings, defended his captive brethren, and displayed a devotion to his God which power could not intimidate, nor royal favors corrupt.

Descending from the summit of the mound, and remounting our horses, we rode for a mile across a valley covered with rank grass, and crossed by a line of low ridges composed of brick and mortar. We were now on the margin of the river, and found it delightful to wander along its palm-grove banks, and perhaps near where the Hebrew captives hung their harps upon the willows and wept when they remembered Zion. A little to the south, and near the river, were what seemed to be the remains of an embankment, which was about twenty-two hundred feet long, nine hundred feet broad at its base, and forty feet perpendicular in its greatest elevation. This, doubtless, was in part the ruins of the quay which the king built to prevent the overflowing of the river, and which was eighty feet thick and fifteen miles long, the distance from the north to the south wall of the city. From this embankment steps descended to the edge of the water, and at the bottom of each flight of steps were brass gates, which were opened during the day and closed at night. On the bottom of the river, near the spot where we stood, are a quantity of bricks, that are, no doubt, the remains of the beautiful quays, from which extended a bridge that here spanned the Euphrates, and which connected the two parts of the city. The bridge was constructed by much labor and at a prodigious expense. To accomplish this, it was necessary to divert the river from its accustomed channel. To effect this, a reservoir was dug on the western bank, thirty feet deep, and one hundred and forty miles in circumference, into which the waters of the Euphrates were conducted through large canals. Stone piers were then built on the bottom of the river, and planks of wood were extended from pier to pier, which formed a pathway. When all was finished, the waters were restored to their ancient channel, but the great lake remained full for the use of the western section of the city. Some of the old writers refer to a tunnel, constructed of brick, which was twelve feet high from the springing of the arch, and five hundred feet long, and at either end of which was a gate of brass. Through that tunnel the queen was wont to pass from her palace on the east bank to the one which stood on the west. And they also mention an obelisk five feet square and one hundred and twenty-five feet high, cut in the mountains of Armenia, and erected here to commemorate the completion of the tunnel and the bridge. But all these monuments of the past have been swept away, and not a vestige remains to honor the king or immortalize the builder.

Our presence had attracted the Arabs, who had left their miserable huts to watch our movements, to gratify their curiosity in looking at the strangers, and to obtain, if possible, a backsheesh, which their modesty will never allow them to decline. Yet their coming was an advantage rather than an annoyance. From childhood they had been familiar with these ancient mounds, and knew every spot of special interest. Taking the most intelligent one as a guide, we crossed the lower slopes of the embankment, and were soon among the ruins of the fa-

HANGING GARDENS.

mous Hanging Gardens. These gardens covered three and a half acres, and were the work of Nebuchadnezzar, to delight his queen, Amytis, a native of Ecbatana, in the mountain regions of Persia, and who, weary of the monotonous plains of Babylonia, longed for the mountain scenery of her native land. To realize her wishes, he caused to be built a structure of brick-work four hundred feet high, which, when finished, resembled a mountain covered with trees and adorned with flowers. The whole consisted of a series of terraces, rising in graceful gradations from the margin of the river to the summit of the artificial mountain. The outer wall was twenty-two feet thick, and a thousand feet long on each of its four sides. Each terrace was supported by arches, and the ascent from terrace to terrace was by marble steps ten feet wide. On the top of the arches were laid large flat stones, sixteen feet long and four feet broad; over these were layers of reeds, covered with bitumen, upon which were two rows of bricks cemented together with plaster; on the plaster were placed thick sheets of lead to prevent the moisture from injuring the foundations. Upon all this extensive floorage of lead was strewed the rich mold sufficiently deep to allow the plants and trees to take root therein. To furnish a greater depth of soil for the roots of the largest trees, vast hollow piers of brick were constructed at agreeable points and filled with earth. The soil of the whole garden was kept moist by means of a machine, placed on the highest terrace, which drew up the water from the Euphrates, and distributed it by means of small conduits to all parts of each successive terrace. In the spaces between the several arches were magnificent apartments, whose walls were encased with glazed bricks, colored with a brilliant blue, red, and yellow, and wherein the queen and her maidens were wont to recline in the heat of the day. Around the walls of the highest terrace were battlements, and at the angles were lofty towers commanding a view of Babylon, then in all its magnificence.

With an Arab for a guide, we wandered over the immense ruins of this stupendous structure, justly considered one of the "Seven Wonders of the World," whose massiveness and beauty excited the admiration of all beholders, whose memory has been cherished through all the centuries of subsequent time. As it was the joy of the queen, and the pride of the king, its immense height and vast proportions justified the bold symbolic language of the prophet: "Behold, I am against thee, O destroying mountain, saith the Lord: and I will stretch out mine hand upon thee, and roll thee down from the rocks, and will make thee a burnt mountain."* This vast ruin is over two thousand feet in length and breadth, and more than forty feet high. It consists of walls eight feet thick, ornamented with niches, supported by pilasters and buttresses, built of the finest brick, still clean and sharp, laid in cement still bright and tenacious. Upon nearly every brick are clearly and deeply stamped the name and titles of Nebuchadnezzar, and, as a peculiarity, the inscribed face of the brick is always placed downward, as if the better to preserve the name of the great king. High upon one of the terraces is a solitary tree, called by the natives "Athelo," and who maintain that it flourished in ancient Babylon. Only one side of its trunk remains, yet the branches at the top are still green, and, gently waving in the wind, produced a melancholy rustling sound. It is an evergreen, and of a species not common in this section of the East. Its trunk is large; its height is fifteen feet; its great age is beyond question. Standing as it does on the very summit of the mound, it was not planted there, amidst a heap of ruins, by any subsequent hand, and is, therefore, esteemed the last of the beautiful trees which once adorned the Hanging Gardens.

But our Arab guide knew of a greater wonder than that solitary tree. His excited manner indicated an object of greater interest. Agile as a gazelle, he leaped from mound to mound, and bade us follow him. In a depression four feet deep, we found a lion, of dark-gray

---

* Jeremiah li., 25.

granite, ten feet long and as many high, standing over a man with outstretched arms. The discovery was won-

DANIEL'S LIONS' DEN.

derful. Our party felt the excitement of the moment. Here, no doubt, was the lion's den into which Daniel was thrown; and this sculptured lion, with a man beneath him unharmed, was to commemorate the miraculous deliverance of the prophet, who from the den of lions replied to the king: "My God hath sent his angel, and hath shut the lions' mouths, that they have not hurt me."*

Ascending the highest mound, the eye swept over a scene of utter desolation. A little to the south were ruins of even greater extent than any we had yet examined. They are called by the Arabs Amran Ben Ali, as they are crowned by the tomb of a Moslem saint, known as the son of Ali; and near the tomb is the small village of Jumjuma, which means Calvary—the place of a skull. This great mass, the remains of some grand palace, is over three thousand feet in length, more than two thousand feet in its greatest breadth, sixty feet high above the level of the plain, and resembles in form a quadrangle. Whether this is the ruin of a royal palace which stood near the Hanging Gardens, or was the residence of some prince of the blood, is now unknown. That it was a vast and magnificent structure, is evident from the extent and superior character of the remains. It may have been the abode of Daniel when president of the Imperial Council under Darius, and where "he went into his house; and, his windows being open in his chamber toward Je-

---

* Daniel vi., 22.

rusalem, he kneeled upon his knees three times a day, and prayed, and gave thanks before his God, as he did aforetime."* For it is a curious confirmation of this supposition, that Layard here discovered several terra-cotta bowls, covered on the inner surface with Hebrew letters written in ink, which may have belonged to the Jewish servants of Daniel's household. The inscription has been

THE CHARM-BOWL.

translated by Mr. Ellis, of the British Museum, who confirms the opinion that the writers were Jews. As the Hebrew captives were corrupted to believe in the divination practiced by the Chaldeans, inscriptions were writ-

---

* Daniel vi. 10.

ten in ink on the inner surface of bowls; the writing was then dissolved in water, to be drank as a cure against disease, or as a precaution against the arts of witchcraft and magic. But as the writing on these bowls remains fresh and distinct to this day, it is evident that they had been prepared and laid aside against the coming of the evil day. The inscription on one of the bowls, which I subsequently examined in the British Museum, purports to be a letter of dismissal or of divorce to Satan and other evil spirits. It runs thus: "This is a bill of divorce to the Devil, to Satan, to Nerig, to Zachiah, and to Abitur of the mountain, and to the night-monsters, commanding them to cease from Beheran in Batnaiun, and from the country of the North, and from all who are tormented by them therein. Behold, I make the counsels of these devils of no effect, and annul the power of the ruler of the night-monsters. I conjure you all, monsters, both male and female, to go forth; I conjure you by the sceptre of the powerful One, who has power over the devils, and over the night-monsters, to quit these habitations. Behold, I now make you cease from troubling them, and make the influence of your presence cease in Beheran of Batnaiun, and in their fields. In the same manner as the devils write bills of divorce and give them to their wives, and return not unto them again, receive ye your bill of divorce, and take this written authority, and go forth, leave quickly, flee, and depart from Beheran in Batnaiun, in the name of the living, by the seal of the powerful One, and by the signet of authority. Then will there flow rivers of water in that land, and there the parched ground will be watered. Amen. Amen. Amen. Selah."

As intimated in this curious inscription, the ancient Jews believed that evil spirits married, that they quarreled with their wives, and that they divorced them. And they also believed in the existence of night-monsters, who appeared in the form of a beautiful female, who surrounded human habitations, where they lay in wait for children in the darkness of the night.

The day was fast declining, and we had five miles yet to ride to a place of safety for the night. We tried in vain to hire a boat to convey us down the Euphrates, to the town of Hillah; but the Arabs in charge of our horses feared that the sum paid for the boat would be deducted from the amount due them, and to all our inquiries we were answered, "No boat can get;" or, "Boat have bad leak;" or, "River go too fast for little boat." So, resigning ourselves to the fate of an Arab saddle, we turned to the south-east, keeping our eye steadily on an immense palm-grove in that direction. We were soon on the caravan road, which runs from Bagdad to Hillah, and which crosses old canals and low ridges, once the inclosure of stately buildings. Trains of donkeys, caravans of camels, soldiers on horseback, men and women on foot, were hastening to Hillah to find a safe refuge for the night. Within an hour we reached the northern edge of the great date palm-groves, inclosed within low mud-walls, and which cover many acres of land on the eastern bank of the Euphrates. As the crow flies, the distance yet to be made could not have been more than two miles: but we were compelled to follow the road, which turned to every point of the compass, winding around the mud-walls that inclosed a small plantation of palms here, and a larger one there, so that hour after hour passed ere we reached the bridge of boats over the Euphrates. Yet the weary hours were somewhat relieved by the sight and shade of the beautiful palm, chosen emblem of peace and plenty. As we approached the town, the schoolboys were engaged in mimic warfare, armed with bamboo poles, with which they fenced in a furious manner. Our coming was the signal for a truce, and the combatants surveyed our party with curious delight. Many of them had never before seen an American lady, and she was to them the greatest of curiosities. Passing through a narrow gloomy street, we soon reached the bridge of boats, which was thronged with people, horses, asses, and camels, going and coming, and crowding against each other with such force as to threaten some with a bath, if not a grave, in the Euphrates. Our Bagdad horses behaved badly in the confusion, and had to be led by our attendants. Crowds of natives lined the opposite bank of the river, dressed in robes of many colors, and gathered around us in wild excitement, wondering at our advent in their midst, and clamoring to know where we were going, and what the object of our coming. Finding it impossible to pass, we ordered Ashur to clear the way, who, with drawn sword and prancing steed, opened a path for us to escape, without harm to ourselves or those who pressed against us. Passing slowly through the thronged bazaars, and turning southward, we stopped at the pasha's khan, and requested entertainment during our stay in Hillah. The proprietor was a tall, well-dressed Arab, who received us with Oriental salutations. His khan is large and clean for an Arab abode. It was a two-storied brick structure, with open alcoves below, fronting a spacious court, and arched rooms above, opening on a broad wooden balcony. Our room was twelve by twenty, and ten feet high, ornamented with two arches, black with the smoke of former pilgrims, ventilated by a hole in the rear wall, and the only means by which daylight could enter the apartment. The door was huge, roughly made, hung on wooden hinges, and so broken at the bottom as to allow the night-monsters of Old Babylon to enter and take us unawares. On the broken brick floor we spread our mats and made our beds. Our keen appetites were soon satisfied with a dinner of boiled chicken, fresh bread, eggs and milk, with plenty of dates, oranges, and pomegranates bought in the well-supplied bazaars. The sun had gone down, the moon and stars shone brightly in a clear Eastern sky; the air was chilly, and the voice of nature called us to repose. But sleep came not. Jackals barked, cats crept beneath the door, and leaped through the hole in the wall; rats fed on our eggs; fleas assailed us; a drunken Moslem pilgrim in an adjoining room chanted his Koran in humdrum tones half the night; and from a near minaret an old muezzin called the faithful to prayers, chanting that "prayer is better than sleep."

Hillah is a Moslem town of ten thousand inhabitants, who are Arabs, Jews, and Christians. The Euphrates flows through the village, and is here something less than five hundred feet wide, about fifteen feet deep, and has a current of two and a half knots an hour when the water is low, and flows a knot faster when the water is high. The two parts of the town are connected by a bridge of boats four hundred and fifty feet long. Nine-tenths of the population live on the western side. The old mudwall, which incloses the place on three sides, is scarcely sufficient to resist an assault by Bedouins, armed with swords and lances. The brick towers are more ornamental than useful. The three gates are more noticeable for their dimensions than for their strength. According to an Eastern custom, they are named after the principal place to which they lead. The one on the north is called Hussein; the one in the centre, Tahmasia; and the one on the south, Iman Ali. Only one of the two mosques is within the inclosure. The one which stands beyond the walls is the larger. It is called Mesjid-el-Shems, and is said to contain the tomb of Joshua! The dome is supported by Gothic arches, which rest on brick pillars three feet in diameter. The dome is like a pineapple in form and appearance. On the top of a pole, which is higher than the dome, is a liberty-cap of mud, and is said to turn with the sun, in honor of Joshua. Within the town, and far beyond the walls, are extensive gardens and palm-groves. The bazaars are on the main street which leads to the bridge, and were well supplied with dates, rice, Manchester goods, and American petroleum.

Hillah is said to have been built in the year 1102 of our era, by Bene Mozeid, and the materials for its building were taken from the ruins of Babylon. The present governor is subject to the Pasha of Bagdad, and has a jurisdiction from the canal Husseinia, on the north, to the village of Hasca, on the south. After wandering through the bazaars, we called upon his Excellency, who subsequently sent us an invitation to dinner, but which pleasure we were compelled to forego for lack of time. While we chatted with the gentlemen of the court, our "elect lady" was escorted into the harem, and was there received with much attention by the several wives of Shibli Pasha. The youngest and most beautiful of the wives was the mother of a son only a few days old. All the ladies of the harem were richly attired, and shone resplendent in their costly gems. Coffee, preserves, and the fragrant narguileh were passed to the visitor; and she added to their pleasure by allowing the ladies to examine minutely all parts of her costume.

In the pasha's yard was a young lion chained, but so tame that a child played with it. This was the realization of the promised millennium: "The wolf also shall dwell with the lamb, and the leopard shall lie down with the kid; and the calf and the young lion and the fatling together; and a little child shall lead them."* Lions are common in Hillah, and have been allowed to roam through the streets unmolested. One was a daily customer to the stalls of the butchers, who, on his approach, made a hasty retreat, leaving him in undisputed possession. Having satisfied his hunger, the lion would depart to some pleasant spot, stretch himself in the sun, and allow the Arab boys to take such liberties with him as their mischief might suggest.

The attention we had received from the pasha was soon noised abroad, and our presence in the streets excited the populace. Crowds followed us wherever we went, wondering at the strangers who had come so far. To escape the annoyance, we took a boat and glided gently down the classic Euphrates. On leaving the boat, we wandered along the embowered shores. It was the evening hour. Memories of the mighty past came trooping through the mind. From the one hundred and thirty-seventh Psalm we read those melancholy lines: "By the rivers of Babylon, there we sat down, yea, we wept, when we remembered Zion. We hanged our harps upon the willows in the midst thereof. For there they that carried us away captive required of us a song; and they that wasted us required of us mirth, saying, Sing us one of the songs of Zion. How shall we sing the Lord's song in a strange land? If I forget thee, O Jerusalem, let my right hand forget her cunning. If I do not remember thee, let my tongue cleave to the roof of my mouth; if I prefer not Jerusalem above my chief joy."

---

* Isaiah xi., 6.

The descendants of some of these captives reside in Hillah. They have a synagogue, and strictly observe their Sabbath. They have preserved their pedigrees, and trace their lineage to the princes and prophets of Judah. Many of them came to our khan, and in appearance were the finest-looking men in Hillah. They are merchants and bankers, who control the principal trade and money transactions of the place. They believe that the ashes of their prophet Ezekiel are entombed in Kifil, twelve miles to the south-west over the desert. Hither the Hebrew pilgrims annually go in thousands, from Hillah and Bagdad and other Chaldean cities; and thither

TOMB OF EZEKIEL.

they have gone from a very early period. So large is their assembly to this shrine, that their temporary abodes cover twenty miles of open ground. The mausoleum of the prophet is worthy the greatness of his name. The façade of the imposing structure consists of sixty towers; the space between every other tower is a place of prayer. Within a spacious court is a model of the Ark of the Covenant, and behind the ark is the sepulchre of Ezekiel, the son of Buzi. Surmounting the edifice is a noble dome, seen from afar to guide the pilgrim to the holy shrine. According to the Rabbi Benjamin of Tudela, the mausoleum was erected by Jeconiah, king of Judah,

and thirty-five thousand Jews, who were released from
captivity by Evil-merodach, king of Babylon; and, to
commemorate their appreciation of the character and services of the eminent prophet, the names of the founders
of the monument were inscribed on the walls of the sepulchre. At the head of the long list was the name of
the king, Jeconiah, and at the foot was the name of Ezekiel. On the Day of Atonement, the lesson is read from
a very large manuscript Pentateuch transcribed by the
prophet himself. A lamp burns night and day over the
tomb of the holy seer. In an adjoining house is a large
collection of books, some of them as old as the second,
some coeval with the first, Temple. And it is customary,
even at the present day, for the Jews who die childless
to bequeath their books and manuscripts to this library.
Of the ten thousand inhabitants of Kifil, not a few of
them are Jews, the descendants of the captives who built
the sepulchre of the prophet, and who now cling to it
with melancholy affection. Whether his sacred dust is
therein enshrined or not, his residence in Babylon with
the other captives is a fact recorded by himself, in these
modest words: "In the fifth day of the month, which
was the fifth year of King Jehoiachin's captivity, the
word of the Lord came expressly unto Ezekiel the priest,
the son of Buzi, in the land of the Chaldeans by the
river Chebar; and the hand of the Lord was there upon
him."[*]

At an early hour the next morning, with a Turkish
soldier for guide and escort, furnished by the governor
of Hillah, we started for Birs Nimroud, the Tower of
Babel. The site of this renowned tower is six miles to
the south-west from Hillah, on the west bank of the Eu-

---

[*] Ezekiel i., 2, 3.

phrates, and six miles from the river. Passing out of the Iman Ali gate, where soldiers were receiving their rations for the day, we crossed the ditch which surrounds the walls of the city, and rode for half an hour through palm-groves and beside fields of rice and corn. We were now on the plain of Shinar, vast and barren, dotted with patches of jungle, and white with a nitrous soil. Our guide seemed nervous, and we were ordered to keep close together. His practiced eye discerned dangers of which we were ignorant. It was no less bold than hazardous for us to attempt the tour, especially with a lady, whose charms might tempt the chieftains of the desert, or who might at least demand a large ransom for her safe return. We could observe horsemen in the distance, and smoke ascending from behind a mound, where the lawless Bedouins of the desert had made their camp. For some reason, which was never explained to us, our guide made a most fatiguing détour to the eastward. We had been riding along the direct road to the tower, with every prospect of reaching it in a little more than an hour, but a remark from an old man, whom we chanced to pass on the road, induced the guide to turn eastward through a section of the desert soft and rough like a newly plowed field. His excuse was that there were marshes to the west of us; but something more than marshes were the motive for the détour, as, on our return to Hillah, he followed the path which he now declined to pursue. But our anxiety was allayed, and our fears forgotten, by the prospect before us. Like the approach to the pyramids of Egypt, the approach to the Tower of Babel is intensely exciting. Rising suddenly out of the desert plain, a riven, fragmentary, blasted pile, and standing out against the sky, without another prominent object near to relieve the view, its solitary appearance was strangely impressive. Nor did distance lend enchantment to the view. The nearer the approach, the more impressive the sight. Such was the enchanting power of the vision, that the eye was transfixed, and the spell of history was upon the soul. Before us was the oldest historic monument known to man. Its form assumed a new outline with each curve in our devious path. Now it resembled a fallen pyramid with a portion of a tower remaining on the summit; now it appeared like a truncated cone, abruptly broken by some Titan's power; anon, it loomed up a

TOWER OF BABEL.

vast mass of shapeless ruins, as when, by some mighty convulsion of nature, temples are thrown on temples, and towers are piled on towers. We had seen nothing like it on all the plains of Babylon.

In two hours we had reached its base, and immediately ascended to its summit. Its sides are rent, and its crest is broken. Two thousand three hundred feet in circumference, the great mound is two hundred and fifty feet high.* Its summit is covered with immense frag-

---

* In the "Remains of Lost Empires," and in the "Assyrian Discoveries," it is given as 150 feet. But Rich, Layard, and Buckingham make it 250 feet.

ments of brick-work, and solid, vitrified masses of brick and mortar. Some of these masses resemble huge black rocks, fifty feet in circumference, thrown together in the utmost confusion; but, upon a closer inspection, they appeared to be, what they really are, portions of great walls, in which the brick and mortar are still visible, but bearing the marks of the action of the fiercest fire, as if blown up by gunpowder, or scathed with the lightning of the heavens. On the western side of the summit is a solid pile of brick, fifty feet high by twenty-eight feet in breadth, diminishing in thickness to the top, which is

BRICK FROM THE TOWER OF BABEL.

broken and irregular, and rent by a large fissure running through a third of its height. Extending through it from side to side are holes nine inches square, designed, no doubt, for ventilation. It is composed of the finest burned bricks, with inscriptions on them. The admirable cement by which the layers are held together is almost invisible, yet so tenacious that it is nearly impossible to separate one brick from another. On the northeast side is a wall of small bricks of the finest quality, and is as firm to-day as when laid by the hand of the master-builder thousands of years ago. The weather has channeled deep ravines in the sides of the mound, revealing here and there a mass of yellow bricks laid in white mortar, and which are evidently sun-dried, and not kiln-burned. They are not less than twelve inches square, and four inches thick. They all bear the name and titles of King Nebuchadnezzar. The translation of the inscription on the one I brought away, to be placed in my cabinet of curiosities, is as follows: "Nebuchadnezzar, King of Babylon; preserver of Bit-Saggal and Bit-Sidda; eldest son of Nabopolassar, King of Babylon."

The most eminent antiquarians in Babylonian researches regard this ruin as the remains of the Tower of Babel. For the history and description of that celebrated tower we are indebted to Moses, to Herodotus, to Diodorus, to Strabo, to Pliny and Quintus Curtius, whose account has been confirmed, in later times, by Rabbi Benjamin of Tudela, and by Rich, Buckingham, and Layard, the most distinguished explorers of our own day. The statement by Moses is brief and definite: "And it came to pass, as they journeyed from the east, that they found a plain in the land of Shinar; and they dwelt there. And they said one to another, Go to, let us make brick, and burn them thoroughly. And they had brick for stone, and slime had they for mortar. And they said, Go to, let us build us a city, and a tower, whose top may reach unto heaven; and let us make us a name, lest we be scattered abroad upon the face of the whole earth."* These additional facts are elsewhere given by the inspired historian: "Nimrod was a mighty hunter before the Lord. And the beginning of his kingdom was Babel." "So the Lord scattered them abroad from thence upon the face of all the earth: and they left

---

* Genesis xi., 2-4.

off to build the city. Therefore is the name of it called Babel."

These brief but comprehensive allusions seem well sustained by a number of very important facts. It is an opinion now generally received that the plain of Shinar is all that section of country between the Tigris and the Euphrates extending southward to the confluence of those two rivers. It is also curious to observe that, while there are no stone-quarries in this section of the peninsula, yet the soil around Babylon is of a fine clay mixed with sand, and, when dried in the sun, becomes hard and solid, and forms the finest material for beautiful bricks, which, when exposed to the sun for half an hour, become hard as stone. But, whether baked in the sun or burned in a kiln, the bricks which compose the tower are exceedingly hard, and illustrate the proposition of the builders—"Let us make brick, and burn them *thoroughly*." And it is no less interesting to observe that, while they had "brick for stone," so they also had "slime for mortar," which was bitumen collected from the immediate neighborhood, that furnished them an excellent cement, and so tenacious that it requires a greater force to separate two bricks thus cemented than to break the brick itself. Nor should it escape our attention that "Nimrod" and "Babel" are terms which have always been, and are to-day, as familiar to the natives of this great peninsula as household words. "Nimrod, the mighty hunter before the Lord," is a great personage with them, and to him they ascribe whatever is wonderful and mighty. They apply the term "Babel" to any remarkable mound of ruins, as significant of historic greatness. It is now generally conceded that Nimrod and his contemporaries commenced to build this tower, confirming the sacred text: "And the beginning of his kingdom was Babel;" and historians and explorers also agree, "that they left off to build the city."

With these historic facts apparently so clearly confirmed, it was with no ordinary interest that I sat down amidst the ruins on the summit of this mound, and read the inspired words of Moses. What memories they recalled! The wanderings of the descendants of Noah; the ambition and kingship of Nimrod; the high resolve to build a tower which no flood could submerge; the displeasure of the Lord; the confusion of tongues; the dispersion of the people; the lapse of the ages which followed; the completion of the tower by Nebuchadnezzar; its vast proportions and unrivaled magnificence; its destruction by Xerxes; the desire of Alexander to restore it to its former glory; its subsequent desolation for two thousand years, a lair for the lion and a den for the leopard; and its present imposing aspect, seen by the traveler of to-day, as seen by Alexander and Xerxes three hundred years before the Christian era.

And whoever was its builder, at whatever time it was constructed, and for whatever purpose it was reared, two facts are significant: *There is no other such ruin in the land of Shinar;* and, if this is not the Tower of Babel, *it is a ruin without a name!* At its base, along its sides, on its summit, are the indications of an immense structure. On the north and west, a part of a quadrangular inclosure can be readily traced. At its base, the first step of the ascent can be distinctly observed. At the north-east angle, the second stage of the great structure is apparent; above it is the third, which recedes within the second; and on the third is the fourth, a solid wall, fifty feet high, twenty-eight feet broad, and fifteen feet thick, pierced longitudinally and transversely with small channels for the free circulation of air, and being less in dimensions at the top than at its base. Upon this were other sections, whose total height was six hundred feet.

How grand must have been that tower, when seen in the vastness of its proportions and the fullness of its glory. Commenced by Nimrod, continued by Semiramis, completed by Nebuchadnezzar—it was at once a sanctuary, a mausoleum, and an observatory. It was inclosed by a wall four thousand feet in circumference, a fragment of which remains. The base of the tower was a square, five hundred feet on each side, or two thousand feet in all. Its form was that of a pyramid, composed of eight separate stories, rising in symmetrical proportions, and receding within each other to the enormous height of five hundred feet, and crowned with a statue of Belus, forty feet high, and placed in an upright posture. The ascent was on the exterior, and consisted of broad flights of steps, extending from terrace to terrace. Midway the ascent was a resting-place, furnished with easy-chairs for the repose of those who made the ascent. The uppermost story was the sanctuary, beautifully adorned, and in it was a golden table.

Near the tower, and within the sacred inclosure, was a smaller structure, wherein was a golden statue of Belus in a sitting posture, around which were large tables and chairs of gold. Without the temple was a golden altar whereon were offered sucklings, while near it was a larger altar for the sacrifice of full-grown animals; and adjoining this temple were the apartments for the accommodation of the priests and their attendants. The site of this temple was probably the mound, three hundred feet to the west, fifty-five feet high, and fourteen hundred feet wide, now crowned with the tomb of Makam Ibrahim Khalil, and said to have been the spot where the three Hebrew worthies were thrown into the fiery furnace.

What memories cluster around this ruin! Of its identity with the Tower of Babel there is scarcely ground for a reasonable doubt. The present dimensions and structural appearance of the mound so nearly correspond with the descriptions of the tower by Herodotus, Strabo, and Pliny, as to justify this opinion. Its location on the west side of the Euphrates is not at variance with the *positive* statement to the contrary of any of the ancient writers. The Arabs call it "El Birs," and "Birs Nimroud;" the former by way of brevity, and the latter in honor of the "mighty hunter before the Lord." "Birs" may be a corruption of *Berus*, and *Berus* of *Belus*, which would not be considered remarkable changes in any of the Semitic languages.

If the original purpose of the tower was to be a place of refuge and safety in case another flood came upon the earth, it subsequently served the threefold purpose of mausoleum, where kings were enshrined; of temple, where Belus was worshiped; and of observatory, where the Chaldean astronomers observed the rising and the setting of the stars. In two of these objects it corresponds with the pyramids of Egypt, where royalty was entombed, and astronomical observations were made. As the temple of the god Belus, it was the place where were deposited the "gold and silver vessels which Nebuchadnezzar had taken out of the temple which was in Jerusalem."[*] On its summit were probably made, at least in part, those astronomical records, dating back nineteen hundred years before our era, and which Calisthenes found in Babylon when Alexander the Great captured the city, and which Calisthenes transcribed, and sent a copy thereof to Aristotle. And the Jews have a tradition that here was

---

[*] Daniel v., 2.

imprisoned their king, Zedekiah, of whom it is written: "And they slew the sons of Zedekiah before his eyes, and put out the eyes of Zedekiah, and bound him with fetters of brass, and carried him to Babylon."* And, also, that here Nebuchadnezzar was confined within the spacious grounds of the temple when bereft of his reason, and when he "did eat grass as oxen, and his body was wet with the dew of heaven, till his hairs were grown like eagles' feathers, and his nails like birds' claws."†

Some are disposed to condemn the description of this renowned tower by Herodotus and others, as extravagant, but a few comparisons with well-known structures will suffice to show their probable accuracy. The base of the tower was 2000 feet in circumference, and its height was 500 feet. Its form was that of a pyramid, and consisted of eight stories, each succeeding section being less in dimension than the preceding one, and on the top of the highest was a statue of Belus 40 feet high; so that the whole was but a little less than 600 feet in its extreme height. The great Pyramid of Cheops is 480 feet high, and the circumference of its base is 2292 feet.

The Coliseum of Vespasian covers six acres; its height is 157 feet; and its larger diameter, including thickness of walls, is 584 feet.

The length of St. Peter's, in Rome, is 613½ feet; its height, from the pavement to the top of the cross, is 448 feet; and the diameter of its great dome is 195½ feet.

The circumference of St. Paul's Cathedral, in London, is 2292 feet, or within 343 feet of half a mile. From east to west it measures 510 feet, and 282 feet from north to south; and the elevation of the cross from the foundation of the church is 404 feet.

---

* 2 Kings xxv., 7. † Daniel iv., 33.

The magnificent tower of the Strasburg Cathedral is 461 feet in height, 13 feet higher than the cross on the dome of St. Peter's, in Rome.

The celebrated pillar near Delhi, India, called the *Kootub Minar*, is now 242 feet high, with a base diameter of less than 50 feet; but in its completeness, its height was 300 feet, and consisted of seven stories, most of which remain.

The Capitol at Washington, unrivaled in all the earth for grandeur, covers three and a half acres, has a length of 752 feet, a depth of 342 feet, and a height of 350 feet.

In the light of these well-ascertained facts, we can very readily believe the statements of the ancient writers as to the grand proportions of the Tower of Babel; and its subsequent history seems to confirm what we have read as to its immense treasures and costly furniture. Darius Hystaspes would fain have taken away the massive statue of gold, but could not execute his wishes; but his son, Xerxes, not only stripped the tower of all its treasures, statues, and ornaments, but plundered the Tomb of Belus, put the priests of the temple to death, and then reduced the splendid tower and its adjacent buildings to their present condition. And we have Strabo and Arrian for our authority, that when the city was surrendered to Alexander, he commanded ten thousand men to remove the rubbish, preparatory to the rebuilding of the tower; but after working two months, they were ordered to desist, as the workmen made less progress than their general had anticipated.

There is an apparent extravagance of language on the part of the Bible writers in their descriptions of the greatness and glory of Babylon. Their words seem more picturesque than true. They speak of it as "the glory of kingdoms, the beauty of the Chaldees' excellency;"* "the golden city;"† "the lady of kingdoms;"‡ "abundant in treasures;"§ "the praise of the whole earth;"‖ and "great Babylon that I have built."¶ But these praises, uttered in prophetic vision, are fully sustained by historic facts; and these words of eulogy are more true than picturesque, if we may rely on the testimony of profane writers. Herodotus, who was an extensive traveler, who had seen all the great monuments of the age in which he lived, has said of Babylon: "Its extent, its beauty, and its magnificence surpass all that has come within my knowledge." And no less eulogistic is the language of Diodorus Siculus, of Quintus Curtius, of Strabo, and of Pliny, who describe it as one of the wonders of the world, and the admiration of mankind. It had a glory of walls, of palaces, of temples, of hanging gardens, of canals, of quays, of tunnels, of bridges, of commerce, of treasures, of armies, and of dominion. The great empire of which Babylon was the imperial city included an area of a 1000 miles in length, 250 miles in breadth, and a superficial area of 250,000 square miles. Within this was Babylonia *proper*, which was 320 miles long, and from 20 to 100 miles wide on the east of the Euphrates, and west of the river its length was 350 miles, and its breadth was from 25 to 30 miles. In the eastern section there were 18,000 square miles, and in the section west of the Euphrates there were 9000 square miles, making a total of 27,000 square miles. Six hundred years before our era, and during the reign of Nebuchadnezzar, the kingdom was in the fullness of its power, wealth, and glory. That greatest of all the Babylonian kings built or enlarged the cities of

---

* Isaiah xiii., 19.   † Isaiah xiv., 4.   ‡ Isaiah xlvii., 5.
§ Jeremiah li., 13.   ‖ Jeremiah li., 41.   ¶ Daniel iv., 30.

Sippara, Barsippa, Cutha, Chilmad, and Teredon. With the resources of an empire subject to his command, he constructed a canal 500 miles long, extending from Hit to the Bubian creek, on the Persian Gulf, through which the commerce of India was brought to his dominions. But his ambition was to make Babylon the grandest city in the world.

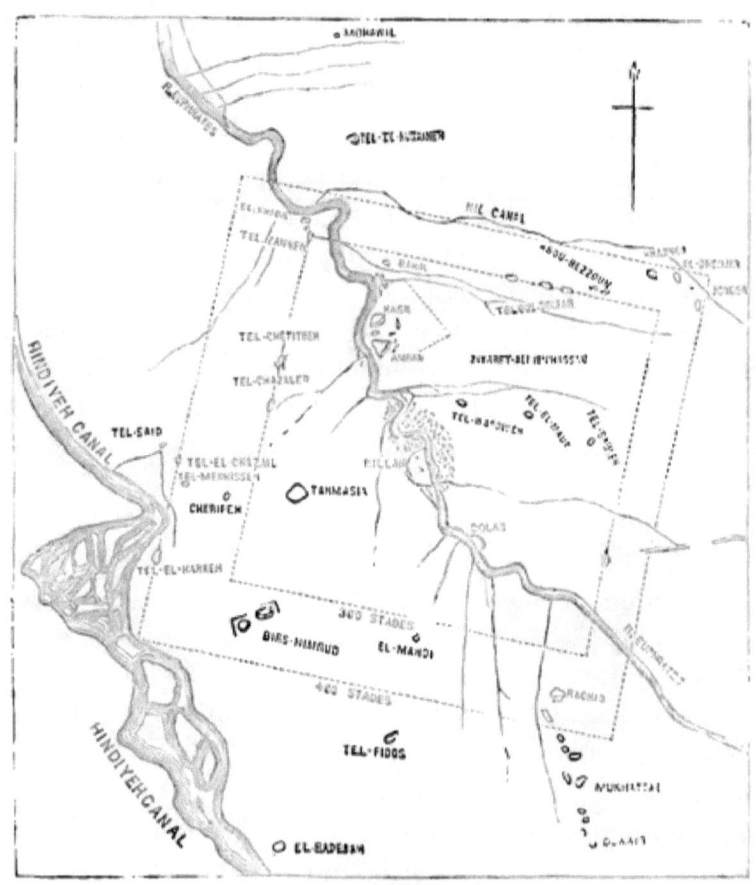

PLAN OF ANCIENT BABYLON.

And how magnificent must have been the "golden city," the "beauty of the Chaldees' excellency," when complete in all its vast proportions! Sixty miles in circuit, the great city was in the form of a square, each of its four sides fifteen miles long, and surrounded with a trench, deep and wide, and filled with water. From the margin of the moat rose the great wall, containing 200,000,000 yards of solid masonry, or nearly twice the cubic contents of the great wall of China, composed of the earth thrown up from the trench, and faced with sun-dried brick, each stamped with the name of the proud king. The great wall was eighty-seven feet thick, so wide as to allow four chariots to move abreast thereon, and, from the bottom of the moat to the top of the parapet, three hundred and fifty feet high. Two hundred and fifty towers, each ten feet high, rose above the parapet. One hundred gates of brass opened to as many noble avenues; and between every two gates were four of the towers, with other towers at the angles of the wall. Each of the fifty streets was fifteen miles long and one hundred and fifty feet broad, which crossed each other at right angles. Then there were half streets, with houses on one side and the wall of the city on the other, each two hundred feet broad. These avenues, crossing each other as they did, divided the city into six hundred and seventy-six squares, each square two and a half miles in circuit. Around these squares, and facing the streets, were the buildings, three and four stories high, while the centre of each square was a beautiful garden, irrigated from the numberless canals which conveyed the waters of the Euphrates to the palace of the king and the cottage of the peasant. Spanning the river, and connecting the two parts of the city, was a bridge five hundred feet long and thirty feet wide. Down the brick embankment, broad steps led to the water's edge. Above the bridge and embankment rose an obelisk one hundred and twenty-five feet high, to commemorate the completion of works so great. Along the banks of the river were the Hanging Gardens, blooming with fragrant flowers, shaded by a thousand trees, cooled by fountains whose jeweled waters sparkled in the sunlight. Surrounded by a triple wall, and guarded by gates of brass, rose the royal palace, whose walls were adorned with pictures of the chase, of martial processions, and festive scenes; whose apartments were furnished with the carpets of Persia, the silks of Damascus, the jewels of Bokhara; whose imperial occupant was at once the dread and the admiration of all nations. Rising above all the other structures was the Tower of Babel, six hundred feet high, crowned with a statue of Belus, made of the finest gold, which shone resplendent in the morning and evening sunlight. Into the city flowed the wealth of all nations. Merchants came from afar. Caravans came from Egypt, Idumea, Syria, Sardis, and Susa. The highways across the desert, from the plains of Palestine and the hills of Arabia, were protected by fortified stations; walled cities served as resting-places and store-houses; and wells, at regular intervals, gave an abundant supply of water during the hottest season of the year. Other causeways led from Mesopotamia and Persia and Media, on which were caravansaries for the accommodation of man and beast. Up the Persian Gulf came vessels freighted with frankincense, precious stones, ivory, ebony, dyes, spices, and silks from Ceylon and India; down the Tigris and the Euphrates came rafts of inflated skins, loaded with goods from Armenia and Kurdistan; while in the marts of commerce in the city were offered to the foreign merchant Babylonian carpets, silks, woolen fabrics, embroidered with figures of mystic animals and with exquisite designs, which were not less famous for the beauty of their texture and workmanship than for the richness and variety of their colors.* Around each palace and temple, in the great castle, at the hundred gates of brass, in the two hundred and fifty towers on the walls, were stationed that army of warriors who had plundered Egypt, who had sacked Jerusalem, and subdued Mesopotamia. And by the "rivers of Babylon" sat king, priest, and prophet, captives from the Holy Land; while from conquered province and kingdom was brought the annual tribute of gold and silver, of horses and camels, of young men for the army and maidens for the palace, the spoils of war. Great, indeed, was Babylon! Great in all that men considered greatness. Proud of his magnificent city, vain of his success, forgetful of One higher than he, "The king spake, and said, Is not this great Babylon, that I have built for the house of the kingdom by the might of my power, and for the honor of my majesty?"†

But how a city so populous, so wealthy, so magnificent, could become a desolation, is a fact as interesting as it is true. The period of its might and glory was less than a hundred years. Prior to the sixth century before the Christian era, Babylonia was a province of the Assyrian empire, and its vassal king was Nabopolassar, father of Nebuchadnezzar. But when, about six hundred and twenty-five years before our era, the empire of Assyria gave signs of decay, Nabopolassar joined the allied armies of Media and Persia under Cyaxares, to throw off the Assyrian yoke, and, being successful, received, as his share of the spoils of war, Nineveh and the whole valley of the Euphrates. His reign was long and prosperous, and, at his death, was succeeded to the throne of the great empire by his son Nebuchadnezzar,

---

* Layard. † Daniel iv., 30.

who reigned forty-four years, and died at the advanced age of eighty, justly renowned the greatest monarch of the Eastern world. At the death of Nebuchadnezzar, his son, Evil-merodach, came to the throne, whose brief and quiet reign did not exceed two years. Conspiracies followed. Usurpers sought the crown and sceptre of Babylon. But the right of succession prevailed, and Belshazzar ascended the throne of his fathers. Unfortunately for him and his kingdom, he incurred the displeasure of Cyrus, who marched his victorious armies against the imperial city, and, having captured it by stratagem, reduced Babylonia to a province of Persia. And thus, after an existence of eighty-eight years, from 625 to 538 B.C., the great empire of Babylon was numbered with the things of the past.

So long accustomed to their freedom, to a life of luxury, and the splendors of a proud and powerful court, the Babylonians revolted, and struggled hard to regain their ancient independence. They maintained themselves in a siege of twenty months against Darius, the son of Hystaspes, whom Cyrus had commissioned to retake the city: but their long endurance was unavailing, for Darius was triumphant, and, to prevent another revolt, ordered his soldiers to demolish the great wall, which had been the pride of Babylon, and the admiration of the world. This memorable event occurred in the year 510 B.C., and was but the fulfillment of a prophetic denunciation uttered two centuries before. A greater calamity, however, awaited the "golden city." Just twenty-nine years thereafter, Xerxes returned from his disastrous campaign against the Greeks, and, to replenish his exhausted means, plundered the city, demolished the Temple of Belus, and carried off the gods of gold and the rich ornaments belonging to that noble structure. Conqueror succeeded conqueror. There was no power that could avert the final ruin of "Babylon, the glory of kingdoms." After the defeat of Darius, and the overthrow of the Persian supremacy, Alexander the Great gave it the final blow, in 325 B.C. Three years thereafter, his successor, Seleucus Nicator, laid the foundations of Seleucia, less than fifty miles to the north-east, on the banks of the Tigris, and thither he compelled the inhabitants of Babylon to go in large numbers, to augment the population of his new imperial city. Nor was this the last vial of wrath to be poured upon the devoted city. The end was not yet. One woe had passed; another was yet to come. The Parthians had succeeded the Macedonians, and the kings of Parthia caused, in the year 127 B.C., another emigration. Some had ventured to return to their miserable homes, and were clinging with fondness to the ruins of happier days, when the plague sent many to their graves. As evils never come solitary, but rather in rapid succession, so, about this time, the embankments which had prevented an overflow of the river, but which had been so long neglected, gave way, and the waters of the Euphrates flooded the city.

The destruction of a great city is not easy to accomplish. It is not the work of a day. Its final abandonment and utter desolation require the vicissitudes of centuries. A thousand years elapsed from the death of Belshazzar, the last king of Babylon, to the time when the city became a "desolation, a dry land, and a wilderness." Neither plague, nor flood, nor deportation, could exhaust completely the population. The Christian era was ushered in by the birth of a Saviour, and a remnant of Jews and Chaldeans still clung to the seat of departed greatness. And Babylon might have lingered in her reduced condition, had not religious intolerance provoked a civil war, the cause of which was the devotedness of the Jews to their religion, a large number of whom perished in the persecution; and those who escaped the sword fled for refuge to Seleucia. To punish the remnant of the inhabitants for a revolt, which occurred in the early part of the second century of our era, the Parthian king, Evemerus, deported numerous families into Media, where they were sold as slaves, and burned many beautiful edifices, which had escaped the torch of preceding conquerors. But the work of utter destruction was not completed, for, at a later period, the Emperor Trajan visited the house in Babylon in which Alexander the Great had died, and performed religious ceremonies to the memory of that great warrior. But the beginning of the end had come. Lucian of Samosata, a town not far from the Euphrates, who wrote during the reign of Marcus Aurelius, refers to Babylon as a "city that had been remarkable for its numerous towers and vast circumference, but which would soon disappear, as Nineveh had done." This was the condition of the "beauty of the Chaldees' excellency" at the close of the second century of the Christian era. In two hundred years thereafter, the canals which led from the Euphrates became obstructed by the alluvial deposits, and Babylon was converted into a vast marsh; and fifty years later, the river changed its course, leaving only a small channel to mark its ancient bed. And from the fifth century to the present time, all writers, whether secular or ecclesiastical, who refer to the subject, describe Babylon as destroyed, forsaken, and a desolation.

It was with no ordinary interest that I sat amidst these ancient ruins, and read from the Bible those prophetic denunciations against the "golden city," which had been uttered prior to and while yet Babylon was in her strength and glory, and the exact fulfillment of which it was my privilege to witness. The past returned with the reality of the present. Twenty-five centuries passed in review before me. The voice of Isaiah was heard in sublime apostrophe: "Come down, and sit in the dust, O virgin daughter of Babylon, sit on the ground: there is no throne, O daughter of the Chaldeans: for thou shalt no more be called tender and delicate. Sit thou silent, and get thee into darkness, O daughter of the Chaldeans: for thou shalt no more be called The lady of kingdoms."[*] On my right were the plains and mountains of those conquering hosts whom the prophet summoned to battle: "Go up, O Elam: besiege, O Media."[†] "Make bright the arrows; gather the shields: the Lord hath raised up the spirit of the kings of the Medes: for his device is against Babylon, to destroy it."[‡] "Thus saith the Lord to his anointed, to Cyrus, whose right hand I have holden, to subdue nations before him; and I will loose the loins of kings, to open before him the two-leaved gates, and the gates shall not be shut."[§] Around me lay the ruins of that proud city whose terrified inhabitants refused to fight, and whose king Cyrus challenged to a duel: "The mighty men of Babylon have forborne to fight, they have remained in their holds: their might hath failed."[‖] Before me flowed the ancient Euphrates, whose waters Cyrus diverted on the night he took the city: "That saith to the deep, Be dry, and I will dry up thy rivers."[¶] On its margin lay the remains of the great embankment, down whose side broad steps were laid to the water's edge, where were the "two-leaved gates," which a drunken guard had left open: "And the gates shall not be shut."[**] Through those twenty-five un-

---

[*] Isaiah xlvii., 1, 5.   [†] Isaiah xxi., 2.   [‡] Jeremiah li., 11.
[§] Isaiah xlv., 1.   [‖] Jeremiah li., 30.   [¶] Isaiah xliv., 27.
[**] Isaiah xlv., 1.

guarded gates, which opened to as many avenues in the city, Mede and Persian passed at dead of night, to surprise a city abandoned to feasting and revelry: "In their heat I will make their feasts, and I will make them drunken."* "Prepare the table, watch in the watch-tower, eat, drink: arise, ye princes, and anoint the shield."† "I have laid a snare for thee, and thou art also taken, O Babylon, and thou wast not aware: thou art found, and also caught, because thou hast striven against the Lord."‡ In the confusion that prevailed, herald met herald, bearing dispatches to the king: "One post shall run to meet another, and one messenger to meet another, to show the king of Babylon that his city is taken at one end."§ "The king of Babylon hath heard the report of them, and his hands waxed feeble."|| Not far from that high embankment lay the ruins of Belshazzar's palace, wherein, on that dreadful night, the king had made a great feast to a thousand of his lords, and at his command were brought the gold and silver vessels that were taken out of the house of God, which was at Jerusalem, from which he, his princes, wives, and concubines drank wine, and praised the gods of gold, of silver, of brass, of iron, of wood and stone; when suddenly, amidst the scene of revelry and blasphemy, came forth fingers of a man's hand and wrote on the plaster of the wall, "Thy kingdom is divided, and given to the Medes and Persians." "In that night was Belshazzar, the king of the Chaldeans, slain;" and, by appointment by Cyrus, "Darius the Median took the kingdom."¶ From palace and castle, from gate and tower, through the broad avenues, along the by-ways, a surprised and terrified people fled, but only to be over-

---

* Jeremiah li., 39.   † Isaiah xxi., 5.   ‡ Jeremiah l., 24.
§ Jeremiah li., 31. || Jeremiah l., 43.   ¶ Daniel v., 1–31.

taken and slain by their cruel pursuers: "Every one that is found shall be thrust through; and every one that is joined unto them shall fall by the sword."* "Therefore shall her young men fall in the streets, and all her men of war shall be cut off in that day, saith the Lord."† To this indiscriminate slaughter of the inhabitants Xenophon testifies; and, to restrain his soldiers therein, Cyrus commanded his cavalry to massacre only those found in the streets; while to the people he issued an order to remain within their houses.

On the mound where I sat, and on the plain below, were the scattered vitrified remains of that proud temple wherein Bel was worshiped and Nebo received Divine honors, but which Xerxes destroyed, and plundered of its gods and treasures: "Bel boweth down, Nebo stoopeth; their idols were upon the beasts, and upon the cattle."‡ "Declare ye among the nations, and publish, and set up a standard; publish, and conceal not: say Babylon is taken, Bel is confounded, Merodach is broken in pieces; her idols are confounded, her images are broken in pieces."§ Nowhere on the vast, dreary plain around me, within a circuit of sixty miles square (the assigned limits of "Great Babylon") could be seen in its ancient glory the great wall of the city, with its gates and equidistant towers, all of stupendous height and thickness, which once existed: "Shout against her round about:..... her foundations are fallen, her walls are thrown down."∥ "Thus saith the Lord of hosts; The broad walls of Babylon shall be utterly broken, and her high gates shall be burned with fire."¶ The destruction of such vast fortifications is no less a won-

---

* Isaiah xiii., 15. † Jeremiah l., 30. ‡ Isaiah xlvi., 1.
§ Jeremiah l., 2. ∥ Jeremiah l., 15. ¶ Jeremiah li., 58.

der than were their enormous dimensions. Cyrus commanded the destruction, and Darius Hystaspes executed the order in part. Subsequent conquerors demolished what Darius had left, aided by the winds and rains of the ages; so that to-day can be seen, and only here and there, low, shapeless, detached mounds, where once the proud walls stood. From the summit of Babel, I looked out upon a vast sheet of water, the overflow of the Euphrates, whose embankments, utterly neglected, had broken away, and "The sea is come up upon Babylon: she is covered with the multitude of the waves thereof."*

How strangely, grandly true seemed these prophetic utterances, as I read them amidst the scene of their fulfillment! They were predictions by Isaiah and Jeremiah, and the facts therein announced are confirmed by Herodotus and Xenophon, by Diodorus and Strabo, by Arrian and Quintus Curtius, by Benjamin of Tudela and Beauchamp, by Rich and Layard. Isaiah lived two hundred and fifty years before Herodotus, and three hundred years before Xenophon. He prophesied one hundred and fifty years before Nebuchadnezzar came to the throne, and over two hundred years before Cyrus took the city. Jeremiah lived one hundred and fifty years before Herodotus, and two hundred years before Xenophon, and prophesied nearly one hundred years before the city was taken by the Medes and Persians. Prophecy is history foretold; history is prophecy fulfilled. Isaiah and Jeremiah were the prophets; Herodotus and Xenophon were the historians. The correspondence between the predictions and the historic facts is no less marvelous than true. It is scarcely probable that the historians were aware of the prophecies of the Hebrew

---

* Jeremiah li., 42.

seers, and, had they been, we have no reason to suppose that they had any interest in making good the predictions. There are, however, some prophecies which required a thousand years for their fulfillment, and of which the traveler of to-day is the living witness. Sublime in language, definite in statement, minute in description, Isaiah foretold the utter desolation of the once proud city: "And Babylon, the glory of kingdoms, the beauty of the Chaldees' excellency, shall be as when God overthrew Sodom and Gomorrah. It shall never be inhabited, neither shall it be dwelt in from generation to generation: neither shall the Arabian pitch tent there; neither shall the shepherds make their fold there. But wild beasts of the desert shall lie there; and their houses shall be full of doleful creatures; and owls shall dwell there, and satyrs shall dance there. And the wild beasts of the islands shall cry in their desolate houses, and dragons in their pleasant palaces."* It was, indeed, bold in the prophet to predict that a city so vast and grand as Babylon "shall never be inhabited." It stood on a peninsular plain between two noble rivers, and, by irrigation, the soil was rich and productive, while by means of those rivers an extensive commerce was carried on with Mesopotamia, Arabia, Persia, and India. But all attempts to perpetuate the existence of the city have signally failed. It is a well-known fact that Alexander the Great determined to make Babylon the seat of his empire. He commanded the people to rebuild the portions which had been destroyed. He ordered ten thousand of his soldiers to clear away the rubbish, that the Temple of Belus might be restored to its former splendor. He hastened his return from India, that he might

---

* Isaiah xiii., 19-22.

accelerate the work of restoration; but he returned to Babylon, not to reign, but to die. His indomitable will, his vast resources, his pride and ambition to be sovereign monarch of the East, his delight in the noble city whose gates had been opened to receive him, whose priests and chief men had greeted him with royal gifts, all seemed to conspire to prove the oracles of God a failure. But no device against the Lord shall prosper. Man proposes; God disposes. In his thirty-second year, Alexander is smitten with fever, and dies on the very scene of his triumph. His great empire is divided by his generals; and Seleucus Nicator builds Seleucia, to be the new capital of the East, and thither departed the citizens of Babylon.* At a subsequent period, the Parthian kings made Babylon a hunting-park for royal sports, which promised to last long; but the Divine decree had gone forth, and another human purpose failed. Again and again, both Chaldeans and Jews returned, and fondly clung to the seat of ancient empire; but fire and sword, plague and the floods, drove them thence.† Out of the ruins of the "golden city," the materials were taken wherewith to build Seleucia and Ctesiphon, Bagdad and Hillah, and other cities of less renown. In no sense is the Moslem town of Hillah, with its ten thousand inhabitants, the restoration of the ancient city. The walls, the temples, the palaces, the dwellings of Babylon, have not been rebuilt. The once proud city is a desolation without an inhabitant.

"Neither shall the Arabian pitch his tent there," is as true to-day as ever in the past. On the plains of Arabia, in the valleys of Syria, from Bagdad to Mosul, the Arab spreads his tent wherever night overtakes him.

---

* Arrian. † Jerome.

and lies down therein confident of safety; but when traveling between Bagdad and Hillah, he times his journey to be at a khan at the close of each day. And when the daring European traveler presumes to encamp amidst the ruins of Babylon, he does so under the protection of a strong military force, who stand guard the live-long night; and even he does so at his peril from Bedouin robbers and wild beasts of the desert. And the shepherd is no less fearful of danger than the Arabian. At sunrise, the shepherds lead their flocks of sheep and goats to feed during the day in the jungle, but return therewith to the fortified khan ere the sun goes down. They never fold their flocks in the jungle or on the plain, so that Isaiah's prophetic words are still true: "Neither shall the shepherds make their fold there."

Isaiah's menagerie offers more difficulties to the interpreter of his prophecies, and the beasts and birds he specifies may not be identified with certainty. But that the ruins of Babylon have been and are now, together with all that section of the peninsula, the resort of wild beasts, of poisonous reptiles, and "doleful creatures," is a fact mentioned by the most intelligent and reliable travelers. The Parthian kings were not aware that they were fulfilling an ancient prophecy when they converted a portion of the space within the walls into a hunting park, in which they kept many wild animals for their royal sport. Rauwolff, a German traveler, who visited the ruined city in the sixteenth century, says of the Temple of Belus: "This tower is so full of venomous animals that it can only be approached during two months in the winter, when they do not leave their holes." In the year 1657, a Carmelite monk passed up the Euphrates *en route* for Bagdad, and, when near Hillah, he "heard the roaring of the lions, who from time to time answered one another from the opposite shores of the river, to our no small terror." In December, 1811, Mr. Claudius James Rich, then English consul at Bagdad, made excavations among the ruins of Belshazzar's palace, and says: "There are many dens of wild beasts in various parts, in one of which I found the bones of sheep and other animals, and perceived a strong smell, like that of a lion. I also found quantities of porcupine quills; and in most of the cavities are numbers of bats and owls. It is a curious coincidence that I here first heard the Oriental account of satyrs. I had always imagined the belief of their existence confined to the mythology of the West; but a native, who was with me when I examined the ruins, mentioned by accident that in this desert an animal is found resembling a man from the head to the waist, but having the thighs and legs of a sheep or goat; that the Arabs hunt it with dogs, and eat the lower parts, abstaining from the upper on account of their resemblance to those of the human species." Of the ruins of the Hanging Gardens, he observes: "All the people of the country assert that it is extremely dangerous to approach this mound after nightfall, on account of the multitude of evil spirits by which it is haunted." In speaking of the neighboring section of country, inhabited by the Afaij Arabs, Layard notes the fact: "In the jungles are found leopards, lynxes, wild cats, wolves, hyenas, jackals, deer, porcupines, boars in vast numbers, and other animals." Lions walk about the streets of Hillah, and in the governor's yard I saw one chained, and with it men and boys were playing. A large lion was in the habit of coming regularly every evening from the Euphrates to a canal, which I crossed on my way to Babylon, and which repeated his visits in search of prey till shot by one of the Arabs. Captain Cowley, of the steamer on which I came up the Tigris, shot three lions, which had their lair on an island nearly opposite the ruined city; while on almost every day of the voyage we saw wolves, wild boars, and other dangerous animals.

Such is the remarkable fulfillment of the extraordinary predictions of the Hebrew prophets. What they foretold has become historic. The prophet of the future is now the historian of the past. And the coming ages are to testify to the inspiration of the Sacred Record. "It shall never be inhabited," is a prediction for all future time. What the future may bring forth is known only to the Omniscient. Great changes are impending in the East. A railroad will yet traverse the whole valley of the Euphrates. In the application of projected improvements, the Euphrates and Tigris will be navigable for hundreds of miles inland. Commercial communication by steamer and locomotive will be established between the Mediterranean and the Indian Ocean. The great peninsula of Babylonia is too important in location and resources not to be affected by the coming changes. Yet the purpose of God shall stand, and his word shall not fail. "The Lord hath opened his armory, and hath brought forth the weapons of his indignation: for this is the work of the Lord God of hosts in the land of the Chaldeans."* His armory is full of all weapons necessary for the defense of his word. Beneath the ruins of Babylon are inscribed tablets which will be brought to light when needed to vindicate the prediction of the seer and the record of the historian. Thus far the excavations at Babylon have been limited, and the discoveries have been few; but the discoveries thus far made have sustained the Bible writers in the most extraordinary man-

---

* Jeremiah l., 25.

ner. Daniel's account of the insanity of Nebuchadnezzar has been called in question; but medical science has designated the king's mental malady as *lycanthropy*, during which the patient imagines himself to be an animal, and for the time assumes the habits of the animal he fancies himself to be. Nebuchadnezzar imagined himself to be an ox, and like an ox he ate grass; and the fact is no less curious than interesting, that in the valley of the Euphrates there is a grass which is succulent, has a mild peppery taste, is eaten by the natives, and is called "Nebuchadnezzar's grass." And recently a large tablet was discovered, on which were inscribed the reign, the madness, and death of Nebuchadnezzar. For a long time, the opinion prevailed that Daniel had made a mistake in naming Belshazzar as one of the kings of Babylon. It was stated that no such king had existed, as his name could not be found in the annals of the kingdom; but in due time a tablet was exhumed bearing the name of "Belshazzar, King of Babylon." Such illustrations are sufficient to show how hazardous it is to assail the truthfulness of the Divine Record, for the evidences thereof lie buried in the earth.

Descending from the summit of Babel, and crossing the intervening valley, we ascended the companion mound on which tradition locates the "fiery furnace of Shadrach, Meshach, and Abed-nego." Around us were heaps of brick and mortar which had undergone the action of fire. The tomb of a Moslem saint now crowns the summit, and adjoining it is a small mosque, wherein we might have remained all night, had not our soldier-guide protested, and warned us of the danger from wild beasts and Bedouin robbers.

In less than three hours we were again at Hillah, and at sunrise the next morning we started on our return journey to Bagdad. The day was delightful; the skies were bright, the air was balmy, and the vernal sun shone genially upon us. Crossing the boat-bridge over the Euphrates, and wending our way through the palm-groves on the opposite bank, we soon passed the "lions' den," looked for the last time on the Hanging Gardens, waved an adieu to Belshazzar's palace, and then rode rapidly to Khan Mohaweel, where we rested for two hours. At 4 P.M. that day, we reached the miserable Khan-el-Haswa, where personal safety compelled us to remain for the night. But sleep was impossible. At two the next morning I called the party, and within an hour thereafter we were on our way. A train of pack-donkeys had preceded us, but we soon passed them on the road. The darkness was sensible, and it was not easy to keep the narrow paths, and we were as "those that watch for the morning." A chilly wind was blowing from the south-east. In two and a half hours we passed Khan-el-Beer. The light now began to appear. The stars melted. Jupiter held his own to the last. The crescent of the old moon rose first; an hour later, the sun came up. The only cheering object around us was the telegraph, that reminded us of home, and of the sublime fact that I could send a telegram from old Babylon to any part of Christendom. I was, however, recalled from the pleasing contemplation by the indications of approaching danger. Our soldiers halted; they shouted, "Keep together!" In a moment, as if they had sprung from the ground, sixty armed Arabs issued from the khan. As they approached us, they began their war-dance to the music of a wild song. Now they fenced in mimic warfare; now they marched at quick-step; now they clapped their hands, and yelled like demons. They were ready for mischief, but were deterred by the com-

FIGHTING PILGRIMS.

ing daylight and the brave words of our soldiers. They proved to be a company of pilgrims on their way to some distant Moslem shrine, and who defray the expenses of their pilgrimage by plundering caravans and unprotected travelers. They are the descendants of Ishmael, " whose hand is against every man, and every man's hand against him." They are the freemen of the desert who have never been enslaved. They were the neighbors of the Assyrians and Egyptians, but never their subjects. Neither Cyrus nor the Parthians reduced them, as a body, to subjection. Phœnicia, Palestine, and Syria were taxed by their conquerors, but those same conquerors did not tax the Arabs. Alexander the Great overran Asia, but the Arabs took no notice of his authority. He was provoked, but could not subdue them. Antigonus made two attempts to compel them to submit to his dictation, but signally failed in both. Always acting like a free people, they were friends to-day, and enemies to-morrow. The Romans desired, but never succeeded, to make Arabia a Roman province. Pompey and Augustus entered their country and left it again. Nor did Trajan and Severus do more. But under their prophet, as Saracens, they were the masters for three centuries of the most important portions of the earth. They have defied Tartar, Mameluke, and Turk, and are still the freemen of the desert.*

At eight o'clock we were half-way. The hours seemed long. Many were on the road coming and going. We met two funeral processions on the desert. The body of the dead was resting on a wooden frame placed crosswise on a mule: the female mourners were mounted on donkeys; the men followed on foot. One was the fu-

---

* Newton.

neral of a poor peasant; the other, the funeral of a rich man, whom we had passed when on our way to Hillah. He was then in a *tukhteravan*, on his way to Bagdad for his health; he was now on his way to the grave.

At length the domes and minarets of Bagdad were in view. Never were weary travelers happier than we. Wearily we crossed the long bridge of boats and entered the "Abode of Peace," where a cordial reception awaited us in the hospitable home of our host, and where we gave expression to the gratitude of our hearts to Him whose goodness had been over us during the most interesting and perilous journey of our life.

CHAPTER IV.

Sail on the Tigris.—Perilous Situation.—Shrines of Kathimain.—Modes of Traveling.—Making a Bargain.—Departure from Bagdad.—First Night's Experience.—Half-way House.—Delli Abbass.—Adam's Fleas.—Den of Robbers.—Hills of Hamreen.—Beautiful Flowers.—Karateppeh.—Storks, and their Habits.—Jebarah Portrayed.—War of Words.—Walking Qualities of the Arab.—Town of Kifri.—Turkish Soldiers.—Day of Rest.—Storm on the Desert.—Crossing the Dreaded Dooz.—Dooz Khurmuttee.—Changeless East.—Conscripts.—Dandy Officer.—Village of Tavok.—Singing Dervish.—Robbers.—American Songs.—City of Kerkook.—Traveling with the Pasha's Wives.—Excitement in the Hills.—Altoon Kupri.—Remarkable Bridge.—Ancient Arbela.—Battle between Darius and Alexander the Great.—Greater Zab.—A Night with the Shepherds.—Habits and Customs of the Bedouins.—Eleventh Day Out.—Domes of Mosul, and Gates of Nineveh.—Crossing the River.—Mine Host.—Mr. Rassam.—Splendid Residence.—City of Mosul.—Mosques, Churches, and Bazaars.—Easter-Sunday.—Elegant Ladies.

AFTER tiffin, on a sunny day in March, we made an excursion to the shrines of Kathimain and the tomb of Zobeida. The captain of the English gun-boat *Comet* offered one of his large boats to convey us up the Tigris to the railway-station. In our party were five ladies, two gentlemen, three children, and one servant. The boat was manned with four oarsmen and a coxswain. The river was high, the current strong, and the boat heavily loaded. By keeping along the eastern shore, we escaped the full force of the powerful current. But we had to pass under the bridge, through a narrow passage, through which the river rushed with unwonted force. I had watched our approach to the point of entrance with no little anxiety, but hoped for the best. Our boatmen were no less anxious. It required all their strength to pull up to the point, but the counter force of the current was too much for them, and, dropping their oars, they caught hold of the under beams of the bridge and pulled us through. But, before they could get their oars in the water again, the tremendous current swept us sidewise against one of the boats that floated the bridge, and we were at the mercy of the maddened, tumultuous, rushing river. Apparently there was no hope for us. Some of the ladies screamed, and the children cried aloud. A watery grave opened its portals to receive us. Our boatmen lost their presence of mind; our coxswain trembled with fear; our end had come. The people crowded the bridge, and shouted all manner of advice to our terrified seamen; while the more thoughtful got into their small boats to pick us up after we had capsized. It was an awful moment. The memories of a life came rushing through the mind. God only could save us. Inspired with superhuman strength, our servant, two of the boatmen, and one of the gentlemen seized the bridge, and held fast till the oars were placed in the water. Then came the struggle. After a most determined effort, we succeeded in gaining on the current, and pulled toward the shore. How the seamen struggled, sweat, panted for breath! Had one failed, we were all gone. But there was one in the boat whose presence of mind did not forsake her for a moment. When the danger was most imminent, Mrs. Holland kept the other ladies from any sudden movement, and spoke "brave words" to the coxswain, who shook like an aspen-leaf. The captain of the *Comet* had been watching us through his glass, and, blaming his men for their stupidity, he punished them on their return. By a bold dash they should have shot through the narrow, dangerous passage-way beneath the bridge; and this he com-

BRIDGE OF BOATS AT BAGDAD.

pelled them to do, by way of discipline for the future. While I thought them to blame, yet they had worked so hard, and I was so grateful to the kind Providence that had saved us, that I interceded for their pardon.

At the landing, we chartered the inside of a horse-railway car for Kathimain, which was six miles to the northwest. The top of the car was crowded with natives, who smoked, chanted, and chatted, to their amusement and to our annoyance. The usual fare is sixpence, but we paid double that, for the privilege of having the inside of the car to ourselves. This is the first railroad built in Southern Babylonia, and has thus far proved a financial success. The contrast between traveling by rail and by camel, horse, or donkey, is fully appreciated by the natives. The cars are like those used in New York, with additional seats on the top. The track is laid along the bank of the river, and the view of the Tigris and its green islands was exceedingly picturesque. The town of Kathimain is small and filthy, and the people are fanatical to violence; but it contains a shrine most sacred to the Sheeahs of the Moslem faith. Here is the tomb of Imaum Musa-el-Kathem, the great-great-grandson of the ill-fated Husseyan, the second son of Ali, who was son-in-law to Mohammed; and beneath the same mosque is the tomb of his grandson, Mohammed Taki. Both fill a martyr's grave. The former was poisoned by Haroun-al-Raschid, and the latter by the relatives of the Caliph Mamun. Over their tomb is a grand mosque, surmounted with two domes completely covered with beaten gold, the gift of the great Nadir Shah. The four tall and graceful minarets, ornamented with colored tiles inlaid on their surface, form, with the golden domes, a group of imposing splendor. The exterior of the walls of the mosque is covered with sayings from the Koran, inlaid in mosaic work. From the entrance to the spacious court to the grand portal of the mosque is a tesselated pavement; and around this court a bazaar was held, furnished with chaplets, rosaries, and other trinkets, to aid the faithful in their devotions. The narrow streets leading to the mosque were thronged with pilgrims from Thibet, Cashmere, Afghanistan, and Persia, who were soldier-saints, and as ready to draw their splendid swords to spread their

TOMBS OF KATHIMAIN.

faith as were their fathers. They watched our movements with a hateful eye, and made remarks calculated to provoke a quarrel. Theirs is a militant, but not a triumphant, faith. Their weapons are carnal, but not mighty. To kill a Christian is the most acceptable act of worship they can perform. They are most fanatical and violent when on a religious pilgrimage, or near a sacred shrine. As there were unmistakable signs of an outburst of their fanaticism, we deemed it the better part of valor to visit the bazaars, where the love of money is mightier than the love of religion, and where a Christian feels himself comparatively safe, even among fanatical Moslems, while he has money to spend.

On our return, we passed the tomb of Zobeida, the favorite wife of the Caliph Haroun-el-Raschid, whose name

TOMB OF ZOBEIDA.

recalls the tales of "The Thousand and One Nights." This charming woman died in the year 831 of our era, and was here buried with every demonstration of grief characteristic of the Orient. The tomb has an octagonal base, whereon is a pointed dome seventy feet high, the inner surface of which is covered with small concave niches, which form the Arabic frieze. Beneath the dome lies the beautiful Zobeida, and near her is the body of Ayeshah, wife of Hassan Pasha, who died at a subsequent period. And just beyond the tomb, we passed the spot where the cruel Tamerlane erected his pyramids of human skulls.

Once more in Bagdad, it required nearly a week to complete the needful preparations for our overland journey of a thousand miles, from the "City of the Caliphs," *viâ* Nineveh, through Mesopotamia, across Syria, to Iskenderoon, on the Mediterranean. There is a shorter route to the sea, which is across the desert, and by way of Damascus; and there is a longer route, which includes Armenia, and terminates at Samsoon, on the Black Sea. Whichever route is selected, the journey is performed either by caravan or by post-horses, and the difference between the two consists in the time required and the money demanded. I had intended to take the desert route to Damascus, a distance of six hundred miles, but was dissuaded therefrom by the certainty of being plundered by the Bedouins. An English courier leaves Bagdad once each week with official dispatches and the ordinary mail, which he delivers at Damascus, to be forwarded by *diligence* to Beirut, and thence by steamer to England. He is mounted on a swift dromedary, travels from forty to sixty miles a day, and performs the journey in ten days. In taking this route, the traveler must reduce his luggage to the smallest possible compass, and must be content with such fare as he can carry with him, as nothing in the shape of food can be procured after he leaves Hit, on the Euphrates; nor will he find shelter, save by chance, under the hair-tent of some Bedouin. As he is constantly liable to be plundered, he must take with him no valuables whatever. There is no fear of bodily harm from the Arabs when no resistance is offered. The most favorable season on the desert is spring or autumn. During the winter, when pools of water are frequent, the stages of rest may be multiplied; but from June to November, a supply of water must be carried for two intermediate stages. If the traveler has no luggage, and is unattended by guide or servant, he pays fifty dollars in gold for the use of a dromedary, and flies over the plains with the mail-courier at the rate of sixty miles a day. For each additional dromedary, for guide, servant, or luggage, the amount will be about forty dollars.

The other routes are through thickly settled sections of Mesopotamia, and are as old as the commerce of the world. They are the old post-roads of the east, over which the couriers fly as on the wings of the wind. If the traveler is so inclined, and is at home in the saddle, he can travel with the mail-carriers, who urge on their horses to the top of their speed, and who have frequent relays; or he may proceed only one stage a day, and occupy as many days as it suits his convenience. Distance in the East is measured by the hours, and not by the miles. It is one hundred hours from Bagdad to Nineveh; and from there to the sea, at Iskenderoon, it is two hundred and six hours, or three hundred and six hours in all. From Nineveh to Samsoon, on the Black Sea, it is two hundred and thirty-four hours; or to Scutari, on the Bosphorus, it is three hundred and seventy-six hours. The hour is generally considered the equivalent of three miles. But this is a rule with a sliding scale. Where the road is smooth and level, the hour is equal to from four to five miles; where rough and mountainous, from two to two and a half miles. For the camel, the donkey, and the man, it rarely exceeds two miles and a half; but for the horse, it is equivalent to an additional mile.

The post-routes are merely tracks, impracticable for

wheels, and so difficult at the mountain-passes as to necessitate a slow walking pace. The Turkish post-stations, or rest-houses, are hovels, gloomy and filthy, and occasionally the stable is the only shelter for the traveler. The tourist must not expect to find on any part of the journey a first-class hotel, or a second-class inn, or a third-class tavern. Nor will he find a lunch-room, or restaurant, or saloon of any description known to civilized man. The Turkish coffee-houses are not for the entertainment of travelers, but are resorts frequented by smokers, gamblers, and idlers. At each stopping-place there is a caravansary for the accommodation of man and beast; and for the privilege of resting therein all night a small sum is given to the custodian. At nearly all these caravansaries there are hucksters, who sell eggs and milk, fruit and fowls, and a coarse bread, made of unbolted flour, and formed in thin cakes, two feet in diameter.

Traveling with the post is the cheaper. The hire of a post-horse is about three and a half piastres per hour, or something less than fifteen cents. But whether the number of horses engaged be one or more, the traveler must be accompanied by a *driver*, for whose services, beyond the hire of his horse, there is no charge, save in the form of the customary baksheesh of from twelve to twenty-four cents per stage. When the country is disturbed, horsemen, stationed along the line, escort the post or travelers. Their services are gratuitous; but their attendance necessitates a slower speed, and a small gratuity is expected and generally given.

In traveling by caravan, the saddle-horses and baggage-mules are engaged for the whole journey, and at a price on which their owner and the traveler can mutually agree. As in the East every thing is done by proxy, so, in arranging for a tour, the preliminary bargain is made through "a go-between," who demands a commission from the party employed, and expects a present from the party who employs. When it was known in Bagdad that we intended to make an overland tour to the sea by caravan, a large, well-dressed Oriental, with an earnest, business-like air, called to inform us that he knew just what we needed for the journey, and could recommend good horses, mules, and attendants. As we had had a very sore experience in the Arab saddle to Babylon and return, we had determined to get a *tukhteravan* for our "elect lady," and *khajawahs* for ourselves, together with two saddle-horses for a change. The *tukhteravan* is not unlike a palanquin, high enough for a person to sit in, long enough for a person to lie down in, with glass windows, and wooden shades at the ends and sides, with a double door on either side, and with shafts in front and shafts behind. It is borne by two mules or horses, and is the most pleasant mode of conveyance in the East. It has its drawbacks, as when the mules stumble, or shake themselves, or when, in crossing a ditch, the front mule leaps and the hind mule does not leap, causing a very serious drawback to the occupant. But on a smooth and level road the motion is agreeable; and in a well-made *tukhteravan* the traveler is protected from the rain and the sun. It is the aristocratic mode of traveling among the Orientals, and is a luxury indulged in only by the rich and the ladies of a pasha's harem.

The *khajawah* is far more democratic, less expensive, and less comfortable. A pair of *khajawahs* resemble a pair of pannier-baskets carried on the back of a horse or a mule. The cheaper kind are simply a pair of strong wooden boxes, each large enough to accommodate an adult person; but the better kind are covered with an

A KHAJAWAH.

awning of oil-cloth, supported by a light frame-work of wood, with curtains of cotton cloth on the back and sides, and in appearance resemble a large-sized dog-kennel. They are united by a strong band of leather, and so placed on the mule as to balance each other. A girdle is then passed under the animal, which is drawn sufficiently tight to hold the *khajawahs* in their place. When all is ready, you mount by means of a ladder, and sit on a matting of straw. You are required to sit on the side next the animal, to keep your legs well up, or sit *à la turque*. The motion is not pleasant, yet the fatigue is less than on horseback. But you are constantly liable to mishaps, as when, in a moment of forgetfulness, your companion leaps out of the other side, or the mule stumbles, or, in coming to a ditch, the mule leaps, and leaves you and the *khajawahs* on this side of Jordan. Occasionally, *tukhteravans* and *khajawahs* can be hired for a journey, but we are compelled to purchase. Our Oriental " go-between" informed us that a *tukhteravan* would cost fifty dollars in gold, would require two mules, three attendants, and would accommodate but one person; while a pair of *khajawahs* would cost twenty-five dollars, would require but one mule, and would accommodate two persons. *Khajawahs* were, therefore, ordered. He then brought to our lodgings Hadji Jebarah, the owner of a hundred mules, valued at twenty thousand dollars, which constituted him a rich man in the estimation of his neighbors. A single glance at his strongly marked features convinced me that Jebarah was a character, and so he proved himself to be. He was elegantly attired, and as affable as a Chesterfield. He swore by his right eye, by his beard, by the crown of his head, that he would deal justly by us, and would prove true to the last. When pronouncing such solemn asseverations, he would close his eyes, clasp his hands, and sigh gently as a saint in prayer. He agreed to furnish three mules and two saddle-horses, and take us to Aleppo for one hundred and twenty dollars in gold. He was to accompany us, and be attended by a servant. The contract was drawn in the English consulate; and by its terms we were to advance seventy-five dollars, and pay the balance at the end of the journey. In our verbal agreement, Jebarah was to furnish three mules and two horses, but in the contract it was specified that we were to pay for double the number. This seemed like sharp practice, and we demurred. It was, however, an Eastern custom, and there was no alternative. The object of the custom is to secure the owner of the animals against loss if a mule or horse dies, and is a modest way to get a double price for the services rendered.

Having completed our contract with Jebarah and advanced him fifteen pounds, we had to employ two drivers, a dragoman, and purchase the necessary outfit for the journey. Our "go-between" Oriental brought us two Arabs of Bagdad, athletic, familiar with the road, and to whom we became very much attached. One was Hadji Flash, and the other was Hadji Merridj. They were to lead the mules which carried the *khajawahs*, and each was to receive forty-five dollars in gold for the tour. It was not, however, so easy to secure a good dragoman, and we were obliged to take Fatoheh, a Chaldean Christian, a native of Bagdad, who spoke bad English, who had high notions of an American's wealth, who demanded three dollars per day, a horse to ride, and all incidental expenses paid, but who was neither remarkable as a cook nor tidy as a servant. But he knew the road, was a man of courage, and did us good service. To him was intrusted the purchase of our outfit, such as cooking-utensils, table-service, bedding, and the provisions not procurable on the road. But we failed to procure tents, which proved a serious drawback to the comfort and pleasure of our tour. At our request, the English consul-general commanded his cawas, Ashur, to accompany us, whose business it was to call upon the governor or military commander of each town, present our passports, and secure whatever military escort might be required. We were to furnish him with a saddle-horse, defray his incidental expenses, and make him the customary present.

Monday, March 23d, dawned cold and cloudy. At 6 A.M. all was ready. With sincere regrets we took leave of our generous and hospitable friends. Mrs. Newman and Mr. Collins occupied one pair of *khajawahs*, and presented a picture worthy a Nast. Fatoheh and Ashur were mounted; the baggage mules were loaded; the signal was given, and slowly we passed through the narrow streets of Bagdad, followed by a crowd curious to see us start. When we had passed the guard at the north-east gate, we halted, and a novel scene occurred. The hour had come for the distribution of presents to propitiate the Lord for a prosperous journey. Our "go-between" Oriental was there in smiling expectation; the cawas of the British consulate, who desired to accompany us, but was not permitted, was there, bland and attentive, assured that his desire would be rewarded; those from whom we had made our purchases were there, feeling sure that they deserved a parting present; and even those of whom we had asked a question as to the road or the prospect of the weather expected a backsheesh. Most of them received a token of our regard; and then came the parting scene between those who were going with us and the friends they left behind. The men embraced each other; they fell upon each other's neck: they kissed one another and wept aloud, sorrowing most of all that they should see each other no more.

It was seven o'clock when we left the old brick gateway of Bagdad for an overland journey of a thousand miles. The attempt was bold, and not without its perils. For at least twelve days, our only companions were to be the Arabs of our caravan, not one of whom we had ever seen or known before, and whose only attachment to us must spring from the hope of future reward. We were to sleep where we could find shelter, and eat what we could buy of the natives. Yet there is a sublime reality in the faith that binds man to man, and strangers are made friends by a common cause. The men whom we had employed gained a living by the transportation of travelers, and the selfishness of business would prompt them to be true to us. For personal safety, for kind attentions, for a prosperous journey, we felt we must trust in the goodness of Him who is high over all, and to the display of discretion, courage, and kindness, which never fail to control and attract others. It required a higher faith, a loftier moral nature, an intenser enthusiasm for a lady to essay the tour, especially so as Mrs. Newman was the first American lady who had attempted the journey. But she dared to do whatever became a woman, and was rewarded with the honor of being the pioneer tourist of her sex through the localities which were the earliest abodes of civilization, and which are consecrated by the most sacred associations.

For an hour and a half, the two gilded domes and four stately minarets of Kathimain were seen amidst the palm-groves west of the Tigris, while on our right the green fields of grain and pasture stretched far away to the east. Soldiers on horseback, merchants on camels, pilgrims on mules, peasants on foot, were on their way to the city, and our presence on the road was so novel as to prompt them to inquire whither we were going. Most of them bade us godspeed, while others passed on in silence. No one in our party felt inclined to converse. Each one was thoughtful of the morrow. We had severed the last link that connected us with civilization. We were strangers in a strange land. The leaden skies imparted seriousness to the mind, and the chilly air cooled the ardor of our emotions. Our mode of conveyance was altogether new. It requires time to become accustomed to the *khajawah*, and the longer you ride the less accustomed you become. The hours passed drearily. At noon we stopped near a small mud village, and lunched. A horse auction was being held near the place, and Jebarah, with an eye to business, wished to remain all night; but a sharp refusal was sufficient to impress him that he was subject to authority. To avoid the marshes and swollen streams along the Tigris, we were compelled to make a détour eastward; and during the afternoon we came to the river Shirnun, deep and

INTERIOR OF A KHAN.

rapid, with banks steep and high. And that night, after a ride of nine hours, we slept in the khan Bar Goobbah, two miles from the village of Yengejee. We had thus compressed two days into one. The first stage is put down in the itineraries as seven hours to Jedideh, and the second as five hours to Yengejee; but we had made the distance in less than ten hours. We were quartered for the night in a gloomy alcove of an old khan, but accepted it as part of the journey, and did not complain. The two soldiers who had accompanied us from Bagdad were here dismissed, with a present of ten piastres, and, on leaving the khan, stole Fatoheh's saddle-bags, which contained his clothes and our candles. It was a loss to him and an inconvenience to us. But Turkish soldiers are neither honest nor honorable. They are forced into the service. Their pay is nothing. They believe in blood and booty. They are quartered on the people, and appropriate to themselves whatever comes within their reach.

The morning skies were brighter, and the air warmer than on the previous day. At 6 A.M. we were *en route* for Delli Abbass, ten hours, or thirty miles, distant. About nine o'clock, we met six mounted soldiers, in charge of robbers to be taken to Bagdad for trial and punishment. The thieves had plundered a caravan, but had been caught with their booty. Each robber was fastened to a horseman by a long, strong cord, and, with pinioned hands, was compelled to walk to his doom.

Beyond, we met shepherds leading their flocks to pasture, and trains of donkeys loaded with the oranges and dates of Bagdad for the northern and inland towns. An hour later, we came to a small village with a large khan, which our muleteer called the "half-way house;" but it was like the Irishman's wall, which was two feet high and four feet wide, and when he turned it over it was two feet higher than before. We came the first half in four hours, but it required seven hours of hard riding to reach the end of the second half. The "half-way house" had excited our expectation of an early arrival at the end of our day's journey, but when we found the second half was twice as long as the first half, the hours wore wearily away. It was not till 5 P.M. that we passed beneath the old, smoked arched portal of the khan at Delli Abbass, and were quartered for the night in an arched vault with a wooden door and no window. A warm dinner of chicken-soup, roast mutton, boiled rice, sweet milk, nuts, and fruits, with Albert crackers and Arab bread, gave good cheer to the festive board, and caused us to forget for the while that we were to sleep with the beasts of the stall. Other caravans arrived later, and the braying of the unloaded ass, and the guttural clatter of the driver, made harsh music on the dull ear of night. But provender for the ass and tobacco for the Arab lulled the discordant sounds, and man and beast were soon silent in sleep. But "sleep that knits up the ravel'd sleeve of care" came not to us. So painful was the biting of the fleas that I left the doleful place, and sought relief in the chilly air of night. They, however, awaited my return, and covered me as soon as I had stretched myself on the stone floor. They are the pest of the East, and fill the land. The inhabitants are so accustomed to them that the insects do not bite them, or they are so inured to their attacks that the bites are not felt. But not so with travelers from the West, who suffer from their attacks the greatest pain and annoyance. When all hope of relief was gone, I devoted the sleepless hours to a soliloquy on the benevolence and malevolence of creation. On this occasion I had abundant proof of the latter; and as I had just come from the Garden of Eden, I wondered if Adam had been troubled with fleas in paradise. It may be fair to suppose that they had other food than human. As creation is from the beginning, without additions or deductions, it is reasonable to suppose their existence in the time of Adam, as the paws, jaws, and appetite of the lion, tiger, and hyena were the same then as they are now. It was, therefore, some relief to conclude that the fleas of Delli Abbass were not a recent creation for our torment, but could boast of a venerable ancestry, more ancient than Father Adam. And I was almost consoled to sleep by Urquhart's suggestion, "that these creatures act as a wholesome irritant to the skin, and that the last two mouthfuls of every meal are for the benefit of the fleas."

The rosy light of a new day was never more welcome. Near the khan flowed the river, whose banks we followed yesterday. It is called by Layard, Shirnun, and is probably the Tornadotum of Pliny, the Physcus of Xenophon, and the Gyndes of Herodotus. If the latter, it is the same river whose mouth Cyrus divided into three hundred and sixty channels, to avenge himself for the death of one of the sacred horses, which was carried away by the stream, in the attempt to cross it, when Cyrus was marching against Babylon. Around the khan and on the margin of the river were the homes of the villagers, whose complexion, features, language, and manners indicated that they were of the purest Bedouin blood, rather than that of the Fellah, or cultivating, class. Their flocks were large and in good condition, and from them we obtained supplies for the day before us.

We had started at 5 A.M., and for an hour we were in the marshes, wading through water knee-deep, and through a tall thick grass, which rendered locomotion difficult. But once out of the marshes, we were thrilled with delight by the glorious landscape around us. The vast pasture-fields were covered with flocks and herds, and the shepherds were chanting some pastoral lay. The long, low hills of Hamreen stretched far away to the north-east, while beyond were the Luristan Mountains, covered with snow for many miles, and their higher peaks touching the clouds. On a beautiful mound, carpeted with grass and perfumed with flowers, we rested for the morning meal, and sung with the birds, and laughed with joy awakened by beautiful nature.

Soon after leaving the khan where we had breakfasted, we entered the hills of Hamreen, composed of sand, gravel, and stone. They cross the road at right angles, and extend widely over the plain. They are shapeless, and without a " head." They describe a vast irregular circular area. Deep paths have been worn by the constant passage of animals, and are dangerous except to sure-footed beasts. They are infested with robbers, and during the day we passed the spot where, yesterday, a caravan of donkeys, loaded with dates, had been plundered; and we found the soldiers in pursuit of the thieves. We reached the summit in two hours, and before us lay a noble pasture plain dotted with the black tents of Bedouin shepherds. Our guides would not allow us to remain to enjoy the view, lest from behind some rugged hill might come forth the dreaded robbers. Our descent was rapid to the plains below, covered with white, pink, and yellow flowers, some of which resembled the hyacinth. I was only too glad to escape from my cramped position in the *khajawah*, to enjoy an hour's walk among the "flowers of the field." Later in the afternoon, we crossed a brick bridge spanning the river Narreen, which had cut a deep channel in the soft soil, and left on either side high, perpendicular banks. On our right was an old khan, surrounded by a few huts, and near them peasant-women were gathering brush-wood, who gazed with rapt wonder on our " elect lady." Onward we rode through fields of grain and grass, and at half-past 3 P.M., after ten and a half hours on the road, we entered the village of Kara-teppeh. There we found a new, clean khan, and near it a native café, in which were large wooden settees, which we hired for the night to sleep on. Immediately after our arrival, a blind man was led in, who requested a prescription for his eyes. He had heard of our coming, and had fondly hoped that we could restore his lost vision. The Arabs believe that the people of the West have a cure for every disease, and they pay Divine honors to the "medicine-man." We dismissed the poor fellow with a present, which was some compensation for his sad disappointment.

After a frugal repast, we strolled through the small village of a hundred huts, and were watched with evident curiosity by groups of women and children who had congregated to see the strangers. On the corners of the flat-roofed houses the storks had mated, and had built their nests. They are regarded with affection and superstition by the natives. Their return is always welcomed as a sign of continued good fortune; and, notwithstanding the great distances over which they pass, and the many lands in which they sojourn, yet they regularly return to their nest when the breeding season comes round. And when one of a pair dies, the survivor finds another mate, and the same home is kept up by successive generations of storks, much as among men the same ancestral mansion is inhabited by a series of members of the same family. The Arabs regard them with affection, as the storks devour reptiles, worms, grubs, and annoying insects. When they settle upon a tract of ground, the storks divide it among themselves in a very systematic manner, spread themselves over it with wonderful regularity, and each bird appears to take possession of a definite amount of ground, and seems to be under contract to keep it clear of all sorts of vermin. They build their nests on high rocks, in craggy trees, among old ruins, on

the top of a chimney, on the dome of a mosque, on the
corners of a human habitation, but generally on a firm
foundation, and the more elevated the better. Their
nests are very large and heavy, and are constructed of
reeds, sticks, and the smaller branches of trees, arranged
in a circle, with a depression in the centre, wherein the
eggs are laid. We passed near one nest in which the female
bird was brooding, and near it the male bird, standing
on one leg, was keeping guard, and resented our approach.
Opposite where we were was a mosque, and on
its dome two storks had built their nest of brush-wood.
During their absence for food, the mollah of the mosque
destroyed the nest. On their return, the birds seemed
surprised, but immediately regathered the scattered wood,
and commenced to rebuild their nest. The mollah thought
the place too holy for such a purpose, and again scattered
the fragments to the winds; but the birds thought the
spot none too good to lay their eggs and rear their brood.
Once more they commenced to construct their nest. Each
vied with the other, and with skill and taste they placed
the pieces, first this way, and then that; but, while absent
for more material, the strong wind had blown away
the pieces that had been laid. This was a new enemy
with which to contend, and for a while the birds appeared
in deep thought. In a moment, however, they seemed to
have decided how to prevent the destructive effects of
the wind. Both descended to the ground, and soon returned
with their building materials, which were carefully
laid on the highest part of the dome, and then one of
the birds remained, and placed its broad feet upon what
had been placed in order, while the other bird continued
to bring more material until the nest was completed.
Having observed these interesting characteristics, I was
prepared to believe what some naturalists say, "that the

storks are remarkable for their filial piety; that, in turn, they support their parents in old age; that they allow them to rest their necks on their bodies during migration; and that, when their parents are tired, the young ones carry them on their backs."

On our return to the khan, we had another instance of the avarice of the Arab. We had paid Jebarah seventy-five dollars in advance, and were to pay him the balance at the end of the journey. He had left at home what we had given him, where it was doubtless drawing good interest, and trusted to our good-nature to make him further advances to buy provender for his animals and food for himself. He now asked ten dollars of the forty-five due him when his work was done. He evidently was embarrassed by the stern manner with which we received his request, and began to realize that we regarded contracts as sacred and binding. But this incident was in keeping with his character. He had agreed to furnish us with three mules and two horses; but, when the morning to start came, he brought one horse and four mules. He had promised to provide two men to attend us, but came himself, and brought his son, a boy ten years old. He assured us of speed, but, when on the road, requested the muleteers to go slowly. To us he was bland as a saint, but to the men he was passionate as a savage. He was a Moslem of the strictest sect, and chose the most public and conspicuous places to offer his prayers, until two almost murderous quarrels with members of our caravan, when he seemed ashamed of his conduct, and ceased his prayers. Although Arab was he, yet Hadji Jebarah had some good qualities. He was polite, attentive, and obliging to his superiors, and his courage was greatest when the danger was most imminent.

A kind Providence had given us another delightful day. We were up at 4 A.M., and in less than an hour thereafter we were on our way to Kifri, twenty-one miles to the north. We wandered over the hills and through rich fields, blooming with beautiful flowers. On either hand were the black tents of the Bedouin shepherds, surrounded with their herds and flocks. We had overtaken a train of donkeys loaded with Bagdad dates, which the shepherds halted, and seemed ready to buy or steal, as opportunity favored. We stopped for breakfast on a hill-side, where the grass was luxuriant, and the water cool and sweet. But the quiet of the scene was disturbed by a war of words between Jebarah and Hadji Merridj. The latter had driven his mule too fast, and was requested to go more slowly. But Hadji Merridj thought that the mule could walk as fast as he could, and he therefore resented the rebuke. He was a spirited fellow, and could not brook an insult. Our caravan was delayed till the quarrel was over. It lasted many minutes, and impressed me with the fact that the Arabs can fight with their tongue as no other people on earth. Some peasants joined in the *mêlée*. One attempted to be a peace-maker; but in arranging the articles of agreement he quarreled louder than all the others put together. When the storm of human passion had ceased, I informed the parties that nothing of the kind must occur again; and they obeyed my instructions till the next quarrel, which was longer and louder than the first. But this war of words resulted to our advantage, for Hadji Merridj walked faster by two miles to the hour. I pitied both man and beast, but admired the walking abilities of the Arab. The two men who led the *khajawah* mules walked thirty miles a day for ten consecutive days, with only an hour's rest at noon, and were as vigorous and fresh at the end of the journey as at its commencement. Their food was rice, coarse bread, cucumbers, and sour milk, without meat or strong drink. They forded rivers; they waded through marshes; they traveled through mud knee-deep, without a chill to shake them or a fever to burn them.

TOWN OF KIFRI.

At 10 A.M. we crossed a dilapidated brick bridge over a large stream, and soon the hills and domes of Kifri were in sight. At noon we entered the gates of the city, and found, to our comfort, a two-storied coffee-house, of the upper story of which we took possession. It was the largest and best constructed town we had seen thus far on our journey. Pleasantly located at the base of picturesque hills, it is inclosed by a mud-wall, which is surmounted with a high parapet, pierced with loop-holes for musketry. A stream of clean water runs through the village, which is distributed by small canals through the central parts of the town, contributing to the cleanliness of the place and the comfort of the inhabitants. Within the walls were palm-groves and orchards of the sweet-lemon. The principal bazaar was in a brick arcade, wherein oranges, lemons, dates, apricots, pomegranates, and Manchester goods were for sale. On the banks of the stream were the coffee-houses, where idlers and travelers lounged, took their coffee, and smoked their pipes. Near our quarters was a small mosque, from whose minaret the muezzin called the faithful to prayers. The inhabitants numbered from three to five thousand, whose language, features, and manners indicated that they were of Turkish extraction; which fact is suggestive of the origin of the place, that originally it was a post-station for the accommodation of the couriers between Constantinople and Bagdad. And this is the probable origin of most of these villages between Bagdad and Mosul, which will sufficiently account for their being placed at equal distances from each other, while the rest of the country between them is desert and unpeopled. In process of time, a population was gathered around these halting-places, some of which are now flourishing villages. To the east of the town is a range of picturesque hills, streaked with red and white strata, and in which is found a clouded marble that might be utilized for building purposes. At the base of the hills was a large cemetery, wherein were many monuments of open domes.

While we were dining, a regiment of Turkish soldiers entered town, with banners flying and bugles blowing. The line of march was through the bazaar, across the stream to the coffee-house where we were quartered.

First came the small guns, mounted on horses; then came the smiths, with their tools on mules; then came the colonel, a fine-looking old man, dressed like a European except the fez, mounted on a splendid gray, and followed by the rank and file, with full band of music. It was a merry episode to us, but not so to the bazaar-men, who immediately closed their shops, or they would have been emptied of their contents by the soldiers, without asking and without paying. These troops had come to relieve another regiment which had been stationed here, and, according to the oppressive system of the Turks, were billeted on the people. They were seen in every house, and for the time being were the acknowledged masters of the homes where they were quartered. They strolled through the streets; they lounged about the coffee-houses; they made the night hideous with their drunken songs and shouts of revelry.

At midnight, the long-gathering storm broke in fury upon the town of Kifri, causing the stream to overflow its banks and flood the streets. All the next day the rain fell in torrents, and we were only too happy that necessity was laid upon us to rest from the fatigue of the journey. But at five o'clock the succeeding morning we were again in motion. It was a relief when once out of the narrow, crooked, filthy streets of Kifri, wherein the mud was two feet deep. Our path lay over a rich prairie, bounded on the east by hills of many colors. The bright skies of the early dawn were now black with the pent-up storm, which too soon burst upon our unsheltered heads. The wind had changed to the north-east, and hastened the storm, which had seemed to linger in mercy till we could reach some friendly tent. Wind, rain, and hail combined their energies to make that desert storm a discomfort never to be forgotten. But He who is greater than nature charged the winds to harm us not, and commanded the rains to cease, and they obeyed his voice. In less than an hour the storm-capped cloud had passed to the south-west, and the sun shone resplendently on plain and mountain.

At noon we reached the dreaded Dooz, of which our guides had foretold us, and whose alarming stories had excited our fears. Nor were their representations unfounded. The recent rains and melted snows had swollen the stream to the width of half a mile. It is a mountain stream that flows down a narrow ravine in the red and white hills of Dooz. In summer the passing ox might exhaust it; but now it was deep, broad, and rapid. It flowed in three channels, each of which we had to ford, and the current in each was not less than six miles an hour. As the passage was near the foot of the steep hills, the tumultuous waters rushed, leaped, foamed in their descent to the Tigris. We paused on the gravel shore for consultation. The passing seemed forbidding. Horse and rider might be swept away. One of our soldiers refused to cross, and, to prove his cowardice, left without his pay. But Ashur and the other soldier were willing and brave enough to test the possibility. Into the foaming torrent they plunged up to their horses' bridles. Now to the right, now to the left, they turned; now they advanced, now they returned; again they moved forward, to find sure footing and the least water. An hour had passed, and they were safe on the other shore. The villagers had noticed our arrival, and had hastened to the river. Familiar with the "paths of the sea," and certain of a reward if they conducted us across in safety, a dozen natives offered themselves as guides. They waded across in water up to their armpits, two of them leading the horses ridden by Ashur and the soldier. We were compelled to abandon our *khajawahs* and cross on horseback. Three of the strongest of the natives took Mrs. Newman in charge, and led the way. Then followed Mr. Collins on a mule, led by two Arabs. I was on horseback, and started with the baggage mules and *khajawahs*, but midway the rapid current we came in collision, and for a moment our peril was imminent. My horse, however, sustained the shock without injury; but, in the confusion that followed, I was left alone in that unknown stream, mounted on a young and fractious horse, to reach the other shore as best I might. So rapid was the current that the horse seemed to go sidewise, and, to all appearance, I was borne down the stream. A moment's reflection, however, convinced me that neither was true, for my horse, although moving very slowly, still touched bottom, and a sidewise motion, like a crab, was impossible for a horse. By this time, Mrs. Newman and Mr. Collins had landed safely, which relieved me of anxiety for them, but allowed me to think only of my perilous situation. I had yet the third branch of the stream to cross. Neither soldier, servant, nor native thought it necessary to come to my aid. Once or twice the horse stumbled over the huge stones in the bed of the river, and once the water was so deep that he began to float. Self-possession was indispensable. Fixing the eye on the distant shore, and holding a taught rein, I kept steadily on, and, after a desperate struggle up the opposite bank, I joined the others in a doxology of praise to Him whose voice the floods obey. Overcome with grateful emotions, our "elect lady" rewarded the Arabs who had guided her over, and who mingled with their thankful expressions the wish that the floods might continue the year round, and American ladies might be compelled to cross every day.

In half an hour we were in the small and filthy town of Dooz Khurmuttee, whose only beauty is a date-palm grove. The mud was not less than a foot deep, through which we proudly rode, watched by veiled maidens, by gray-bearded, solemn-looking men, and followed by rollicsome boys, as if a circus had come to town. On reaching the khan, Fatoheh pointed me to a dark and vile hole in which to lodge; but that was too much for human nature to endure, and, at an expense of forty piastres for the night, we rented the whole of a coffee-house. The place was an open arcade, with six piers and six flattened domes, and had the virtue of having been recently whitewashed. Therein we spent the afternoon, and passed the night with measurable comfort. Four watchmen stood guard all night, and two soldiers were sent by the officer in command to patrol the streets. These proved necessary precautions, as, soon after we had fallen asleep, a row occurred. A drunken Arab had entered a house near-by and abused the family. All rushed to the coffee-house to settle the dispute. As usual, there was a war of words, and a peaceful separation.

A frugal breakfast of eggs, milk, rice, and Arab bread, and we were on our way to Tavok, seven hours through a rich and grand valley, with hills on the east and mountains on the west. The day was the sunniest of all our journey. As we passed the black tents of the Bedouins, surrounded with glorious flocks, they recalled the patriarchs of old who dwelt in similar tents, and whose flocks and herds were led forth to pasture by Joseph and his brethren. On the same road, a family was journeying to the North. The wife and mother was mounted on a mule, and held in her arms a little child. So traveled Joseph and Mary with the infant Saviour.

The East is changeless, and the pictures of such scenes are true to life.

At 11 A.M. we saw a great company of men approaching, some on foot, some on horseback. We had heard much of robbers, and, to all appearance, we were now in their power. But a nearer view disclosed the fact that they were a hundred conscripts, all young men who had been taken from their homes by force to recruit the Turkish army. Their hands were secured in large wooden frames, which answered the purpose of handcuffs, and were conducted by mounted soldiers *en route* for Bagdad. They were treated as so many convicts, and illustrated how weak and mean must be a government compelled to reinforce its army in such a way. An hour later, we were joined by a dandy Turkish officer. He was young and handsome. His uniform was richly ornamented, and over it was thrown a white military cloak. He rode a beautiful white horse, and was armed with cimeter and silver-mounted pistols. He declined conversation with our men, and contented himself with stroking his silken mustache.

It was noon when we reached the Tavok River, which was much swollen, and divided into six streams, all of which we crossed safely by aid of the natives. On the banks of the river were large encampments of nomads, and near-by were their cultivated fields. Hundreds of travelers, who had forded the river, were drying themselves and their goods in the glorious sunlight on the green hills of Tavok. The village of Tavok can boast a mosque, a coffee-house, and a post-office. The old khan is comfortable for neither man nor beast. It required time, patience, and money to rent the coffee-house for a night. The idlers and gamblers were unwilling to vacate, and the proprietor hesitated between our offer and the favor of his old patrons. But thirty piastres were a prize too great to lose; and, in consenting to our wishes, he stipulated that he should be permitted to boil coffee and light pipes for the use of his customers.

Here we met another dandy Turkish officer, who displayed his silver watch in a most conspicuous manner, and was anxious that I should show him mine, which would have been a very indiscreet thing to do in such a company as that. The afternoon was enlivened by a singing dervish, who sung for money and for bread. He was a young man, robed in white, whose hair was black, and combed smoothly behind his ears. He sung in Persian, and had a good bass voice. He was a religious enthusiast, like the fakir in India, or the barefooted friar in Italy. The people venerated him as a holy person, and crowds gathered to hear him sing, and loaded him with bread. But our dandy soldier treated him with less respect. Throwing him a piece of coin, he requested him to leave. His request and money were received with equal contempt. The dervish threw back the coin with the plucky remark: "I won't have your money, and I will sing as long as I please." The villagers dared not offend the soldier by applauding the independence of the saint; but they increased the number of barley loaves to such an extent that the fakir had bread enough and to spare. The dandy officer retired, the song of the dervish ceased, the sun declined, the night came on apace. idler and gambler had gone to their homes, and four watchmen were employed to guard us while we slept.

The dawn was beautiful, and we were up to welcome the first rays of a cloudless sun. At 4 A.M. all were ready for the journey of another day; but reports of robberies and murders on the road came in so fast, that we determined to take a larger military escort. It was after five o'clock when the tardy soldiers came, and our joy was boundless to be once more on the sweet, clean prairies of God's own creation. For two hours our path lay over a rolling plain covered with grass and flowers. At 7 A.M. we passed a caravan of four hundred mules loaded with wheat for the Bagdad market. During the morning we crossed several dried water-courses of black sand, and large stones which the floods had washed down from the mountains. In the richer fields, men and women were at work, digging for truffles, a favorite vegetable with the natives. We were now approaching the most dangerous portion of the road. The caravans that had preceded us had halted for reinforcements, and we gladly joined them for mutual protection. Our united strength consisted of thirty men and women, and fifty donkeys, mules, and horses. We now entered the hills, and were soon in a deep, narrow ravine, where yesterday a caravan had been robbed and four men murdered. All was excitement. The Arabs dismounted and carefully examined their weapons of defense. Some had guns; some carried swords; others were armed with long sheathed knives. A woman led the van. Whether from the excitement of fear or the better attribute of heroism, she outran the men, and, with the agility of the gazelle, she was first to mount the highest hill from which to reconnoitre the field of danger. All was hurry, yet all were silent as the grave. The point of expected attack was approached and watched with breathless anxiety. It was a relief to get through the dreaded ravine; and then came an Arab chatter mingled with every demonstration of joy, the reaction of fear incident to anticipated danger.

An hour beyond the "Robber's Pass," we crossed a large stream, wherein pretty maidens were washing clothes, which they spread on the green hills beyond. It is a beautiful site for the large town of Tashemuttee, where the hills are so green and graceful, the meadows so vast and rich, the streams so clear and abundant. Within high walls, surmounted with higher watch-towers, were peach and apple orchards; and adjacent thereto were fields of wheat and corn. Beyond the town, we met a caravan of fifty camels, the first we had seen since we left Bagdad. The hours passed merrily. The day was delightful; the scenery was beautiful; a gleesome spirit animated our souls. Although the Arabs know little of music beyond simple melody expressed in monotone chants, yet "Yankee Doodle," "Hail Columbia," and the "Star-spangled Banner" never failed to set our muleteers dancing on the road, and often excited them to the most grotesque antics. Nor were they insensible to the holier, sweeter songs of Zion, which charmed their untutored minds. Jebarah's son was specially fond of that delightful hymn:

"I want to be an angel, and with the angels stand,"

and which I succeeded in teaching him ere we parted.

At 2 P.M. we had come twenty-one miles, and, after fording a deep and rapid stream, we entered the city of Kerkook, which contains thirty thousand inhabitants. An hour thereafter, we were comfortably quartered in the second story of a large, clean khan, wherein we remained until the next day. The well-supplied bazaars furnished us with poultry, cracked wheat, fresh eggs and milk, and the fruits and preserves peculiar to the East. Taking Hadji Flash for a guide, we strolled through the town, to observe and note whatever of interest might be presented to our view. The large bazaars were thronged with people, and gayly-dressed maidens were everywhere seen returning from the river with well-filled pitchers, which they gracefully poised upon head and shoulder.

There can be no doubt that Kerkook was once a military station of the Romans during the existence of their power in the East. At present, the city is divided into three parts, each of considerable size. On a high and extensive mound, artificially shaped into an inclined slope, is the fortified portion of the town, within whose walls are the dwellings of privileged Moslems, and three mosques whose minarets are seen from afar. The second portion is spread out on the plain at the foot of the citadel, and in it are the principal khans, coffee-houses, and bazaars, and a mixed population of Moslems, Nestorians, and Syrian Christians. Half a mile from the citadel, and beyond the river, is the third and smaller portion, wherein are walled gardens, with date and orange groves, with extensive graperies and olive orchards. Adjacent to this section is the city of the dead, containing a larger population than the city of the living. As we passed, we saw six women weeping at a new-made grave, the last resting-place of some dear departed one. This is a melancholy custom in the East, and it is not uncommon for the mourners to spend days at the tomb of buried affection in recalling the virtues of those who have gone never to return.

Ashur had applied to the Pasha of Kerkook for a military escort of two soldiers, but was informed that not more than ten soldiers remained in the barracks, and the request was, therefore, not granted. This was an unforeseen embarrassment. All agreed that it would not be safe to proceed without military protection, as the country was in a disturbed state, and infested with Kurdish robbers, whose recent depredations had alarmed the people. The governor, however, was gracious enough to send me word that the family of the Pasha of Mosul would proceed North at an early hour, and invited us to join that caravan. We were to rendezvous on the opposite bank of the river, and thence proceed with the grand cavalcade. After waiting an hour, an officer rode over to inform us that the caravan was about to start. First came twenty soldiers on foot; then came twenty mules loaded with tents, trunks, and household furniture; then came twenty horsemen armed with lances, swords, and rifles; and finally came the *tukhteravan* in which sat the pasha's two wives, followed by four *khajawahs* containing Circassian and Nubian female slaves. The son of the pasha, a young man of one-and-twenty, rode a white mule, by way of distinction. It was a large and well-fed beast, and, according to custom in the East, the tail and ears were dyed with henna a bright red, and the body was spotted with the same color, resembling a heraldic talbot. Only persons of eminence in religion or in the government are permitted to ride such an animal, which is a custom as old as the Judges of Israel.* Near him, and mounted on a small donkey, was a Nubian slave, purchased by the pasha at Medina for the sum of sixty dollars in gold. He was not yet eight years old, but exceedingly bright, and the pet of all the company. He will yet be chief eunuch of his master's harem.

The place of rendezvous was where two roads met. One led over the plains, and was the longer by several miles. The other crossed a range of white limestone hills, and, although shorter, was to be dreaded as running through the stronghold of the Kurdish robbers. A consultation was held as to which road should be taken. The council of war was evidently divided, as

---

* Judges v., 10.

some of the foot-soldiers had started over the plains as the safer of the two routes; and with them had departed a number of small caravans of merchants. But the braver of the soldiers preferred the shorter, though more dangerous, road, and displayed their superior courage by proudly galloping over the plain, some brandishing the glittering sword, others poising the long lance, and giving it that tremulous motion which betokens military skill, and others discharging rifle and revolver, indicative of their preparation to meet the foe. It was a momentary contest between courageous prudence and courageous imprudence. It was not strange that the latter prevailed. The command passed down through the long caravan, and in a few minutes we were in motion for the hills. We followed the telegraph-poles, which indicated that we had chosen the shorter route. In less than two hours we reached the naphtha springs, which are very extensive, and are worked by the natives with considerable success. The steam issued from the deep pits, and the boiling liquid was conveyed through small canals to a large reservoir prepared to receive it. The native workmen were besmeared with the black naphtha, and were hideous to behold.

We were now approaching the dreaded spot. "Keep together" was the order from the commander of the troop. Soldiers on foot advanced to the front, and stood in the mouth of each ravine, while the horsemen galloped in the wildest manner over the hills, and commanded the summit of each bold and rugged peak. Every eye was on the watch; all marched with bated breath; not a word was spoken. The report of a rifle sent a tremor through horse and rider, through *tukhteraran* and *khajawah;* but it proved to be only the signal that all was well, which caused veiled women to laugh, and armed men to shout for joy. We soon reached the summit of the highest ridge, where we smiled at our fears, and rejoiced over the noble panorama presented to our view. Rich meadows, flowing streams, vast valleys, beautiful hills — smooth, conical, and green, with the immense snowy range of Media far away — its loftier peaks touching the clouds — composed a landscape never to be forgotten.

The descent was rapid and joyous. All prepared for luncheon. Arabs to the east; Americans to the west. The wives of the pasha sat in a charmed circle, which none were permitted to approach but the master of the harem and the black eunuchs. They were guarded with jealous care. Their freedom was restrained. They were not allowed to wander over the fields and gather the wild flowers of spring. They conversed in an undertone. Neither the merry song nor the gleeful laugh came from that forbidden circle. They were the prisoners of a suspicious love.

After an hour's rest, the journey was resumed. Our path lay through a vast, beautiful valley, bounded by a circlet of hills. In the fields were men plowing with oxen, who made furrows deep, broad, and straight. Along the way-side were reservoirs ten feet in diameter and as many deep. A hundred feet apart, they extended for miles on either side of the road. In the rainy season, when the nearer streams are full, the water is conveyed to these wells, to be used for irrigation in the rainless months of summer.

The minarets of Altoon Kupri were now in view. The rushing waters of the Lesser Zab could be heard in the distance. The whole caravan moved forward with quickened pace. Ashur and Fatoheh had preceded us, and taken the two best rooms in the miserable khan:

but, while absent to escort us to our quarters, a dozen soldiers of the pasha's caravan had taken possession of one of the rooms and refused to vacate. There was no help for the Americans. Submission was a necessary virtue. But close proximity to such men was neither safe nor pleasant. So, crossing the court, filled with horses, mules, and soldiers, we ascended to the upper terrace, and occupied an open space between two rooms, wherein were stored hides of sheep and goats, whose odor was more abundant than fragrant.

Attended by Ashur, who marched in advance with drawn sword, to show his importance and convince the Arabs and the dogs of my dignity, I sauntered through the well-supplied bazaars, and passed large coffee-houses, wherein merchant and muleteer, soldier and pilgrim, had congregated to smoke and gossip. On our way, we passed the gardens of the governor, whose residence was spacious and inviting to one who, in happier days, had seen the grand hotels in the civilized West. The town is divided into two unequal parts by the Altoon Sour, or Golden Water. The inhabitants can not number less than twenty thousand, the major portion of whom live on the island formed by the two branches of the Golden Water. There was nothing either in the form or comeliness of the buildings to please the artist or delight the traveler. The chief attraction of the place is the classic river, which is here spanned by a remarkable bridge. This stream is, no doubt, the Zabatus Minor of Xenophon, and the Caprus of Ptolemy. It is known to the natives as the Lesser Zab, to distinguish it from the Greater Zab, which is north of Arbela, and which we are to cross to-morrow. Its source is in the mountains to the east, and its volume is increased by lesser streams, which intercept it in its course to the Tigris. Its waters are sweet and have a golden tinge, which suggested the Arab name of the stream. Always considerable, its volume is immensely increased by the melting of the Median snows. It is then a tremendous torrent, whose waters rush by with unwonted violence. At such times the water rises twenty feet above the summer level, submerging the adjacent plains. To obviate this extraordinary rise in the spring-time, the Turks have constructed a remarkable bridge. This bridge is fourteen feet wide, one hundred feet long, and fifty feet high. It consists of five circular arches, the central and largest of which is eighty feet in diameter. The materials are brick and stone, and the structure is grand and substantial. It was sublime to hear the thunder of the tumultuous waters as they rushed through those vast arches, and formed as many foaming streams on the opposite side, where they once more united in their course to the Tigris. While taking the measurements of the bridge, I was surrounded by a crowd of natives, who asked a thousand curious questions, and wondered how a line one hundred feet long could be reeled in a box so small. They were Turks and Arabs, dressed in gay-colored shalloons and muslins, some of which were fantastic from their great variety. As it was the evening hour, the bridge was thronged with camels, mules, and donkeys, and shepherds returning with their flocks. The steepness of the bridge added to the difficulty of the passage. As it is one hundred feet long and fifty feet high, the ascent was steep and difficult. Few of the beasts of burden could carry their load to the top of the curvature, and this compelled the drivers to unload before attempting to cross, which caused much noise and confusion.

The first rays of the morning were hailed with delight.

It was a relief to each and all of our five senses, when we issued out of the old khan. Crossing the northern bridge, we were soon among the beautiful hills, where we watched the morning light chase the shades of night away, and beheld the snowy peaks of Media invite the sun's earliest beams. Here and there were cultivated fields, with tents and herds and orchards. It was pleasant to follow the mountain stream, with its foaming rapids and sparkling cascades. At 10 A.M., we halted for breakfast on a flowery meadow near a murmuring brook, and where we would have gladly spent the live-long day. An hour's rest, and our caravan was again in motion. We were approaching a memorably historic site, whereon an empire was lost and won between the rising and the setting sun. In three hours thereafter, we saw on our right the ancient Arbela, the Arbeel of the modern Turks. How grandly its old citadel stood out against the clear sky! An hour later, and we were on the battle-field where a million and a half of combatants fought for the empire of Asia; where Alexander the Great, with fifty thousand horse and foot, put to flight a million of soldiers, commanded in person by Darius of Ecbatana. That great battle was fought in the month of October, in the year 330 before the Christian era. Alexander had come from Egypt, through Palestine and Syria. He had triumphed at Granicus and conquered at Issus. He had been received with regal honors at the gates of Jerusalem. Intent on the mastery of the world, he had traversed the Syrian desert, and crossed the Tigris not forty miles above ancient Nineveh. His victorious army of forty thousand foot and seven thousand horse he commanded in person, aided by Parmenio, the most distinguished of all his lieutenants. His march was southward, with the Tigris on his right and the Kurdistan mountains on his left. He had less than one hundred miles to march to meet the enemy.

Darius had come from his palace at Ecbatana to expel an invading foe. His mighty army, a million strong, was composed of Scythians, Bactrians, Armenians, Cappadocians, Babylonians, Persians, Mardian archers, Greek mercenaries, and Indians, mounted on their war elephants, which had come from parts beyond the Indus. Sole master of the territory, he had caused the inequalities in the surface of the earth to be leveled, for the free movement of his two hundred chariots armed with scythes. His stores and treasures were deposited in the citadel of Arbela. From his base, he marched to the north-west, crossed the Greater Zab, and at the small village of Gaugamela, on the banks of the Bumadus, awaited the coming of the enemy.

Nor was he long in waiting. Just nine days from the time Alexander had crossed the Tigris, the great battle was fought in the beautiful weather of an Assyrian October; and ere the sun of that day had declined, Darius had lost his empire. Three hundred thousand dead lay upon the field. The kings met in single-handed combat. The spear of Alexander transfixed the charioteer of Darius. In the confusion which ensued, Darius escaped. He fled toward Arbela, which he reached at midnight, but left it at dawn the next day for his palace and fortress at Ecbatana, in the mountains of Media. To rescue Parmenio, Alexander had ceased his pursuit of Darius. But at noon the next day, the conqueror entered Arbela, where he found treasure in gold estimated at five million dollars, where he offered sacrifices to the gods, and where he distributed rewards among those who had distinguished themselves on the field of battle; and thus perished in a day the fifth and last of the five Eastern monarchies. Some suppose that the "he-goat" was Alexander, and the "ram" was Darius, as prophetically portrayed by the prophet Daniel: "And as I was considering, behold, a he-goat came from the west on the face of the whole earth, and touched not the ground: and the goat had a notable horn between his eyes. And he came to the ram that had two horns, which I had seen standing before the river, and ran unto him in the fury of his power. And I saw him come close unto the ram, and he was moved with choler against him, and smote the ram, and brake his two horns: and there was no power in the ram to stand before him, but he cast him down to the ground, and stamped upon him: and there was none that could deliver the ram out of his hand. Therefore the he-goat waxed very great: and when he was strong, the great horn was broken; and for it came up four notable ones toward the four winds of heaven."*

It was with no ordinary interest that we entered a city around which cluster so many historic associations. It stands on the banks of a small stream in the midst of a noble plain. The principal feature of the place is the great castle, built on an eminence in the centre of the town. The vast mound is half a mile from east to west, and two hundred feet high. Its summit is surrounded with a wall whose height is not less than thirty feet. From the plain there is an inclined slope—a broad, paved causeway, which leads up to an immense arched entrance, ancient and gloomy. Passing through this vast, dark portal, we joined the throng of men, women, and children, and, having obtained permission, we ascended to the summit, whereon are the residence of the governor and the head-quarters of the commander of the troops.

---

* Daniel viii., 5-8.

His excellency was sitting on the terrace smoking his elegant nargileh, and conversing with his officials. He courteously granted our request for a military escort for the morrow's journey, and permitted us to ascend to a higher terrace to enjoy the commanding view. Around us, and within the old walls of the citadel, were mosques and minarets, small and great dwelling-houses, and the military barracks filled with Turkish soldiers. Beyond the walls and down on the plains was a scene of greater variety. There were streets shaded by awnings of leaves and branches supported by poles; stores and dwellings constructed of sun-dried bricks, and on whose roofs grass and flowers were growing; pretty gardens and sparkling fountains; long bazaars filled with well-dressed people; khans crowded with caravans just arrived; the river gliding gently by; and the city of the dead, monumented with white domes over the buried ashes of past generations. Beyond the city of the plain were green fields, and beyond the fields of wheat and corn were snow-capped mountains, rosy in the reflected beauty of the setting sun.

We were quartered that night in a room on the ground-floor of the khan, but too near a pond of fetid water for health and pleasure. Our men were in gleeful spirits. There was but another day's journey to Mosul. The moon was full and the air balmy. Arab merchants, Persian pilgrims, muleteers of all ages, gathered around the fires of our cook, and watched him prepare the evening meal for the Americans. They told stories, they cracked jokes, they chanted some humdrum melody. Recent murders and robberies were related with tragic effect. The keeper of the khan was a Solon among them. He was an intelligent old Arab, and from him I ascertained that from ten to twenty thousand people lived in Arbeel, who are Moslems, Jews, and Christians; but only Moslems are permitted to reside within the walls of the citadel.

As we hoped, by a forced march of sixteen hours, to reach Mosul at the close of the next day, we gave orders for an early start. At 4 A.M. we were again in motion. The full moon was still high in the heavens. The dawn came on apace. How beautiful to watch the sunlight reveal in slow succession the mountain peaks; observe how the clouds darkened the lower hills, while the morning light made manifest the higher snowy summits far away! In four hours we passed the half-way khan. On either side of the road, the meadows were adorned with flowers in richest profusion—red, white, and blue, violet, pearl-colored, scarlet, and pink. Here, one bloomed in solitary glory; yonder, thousands blended their beauty in harmony with the rich grass of the fields. During the morning we rode along plains well plowed and ready for the seed. At times the landscape was surpassingly lovely. At 10 A.M. we caught our first view of the River Zab, and could trace its tortuous course for many miles as it flowed among the hills and over the meadow lands. It is, no doubt, the Zabatus of Xenophon, the Lycus of Ptolemy, and the Zerbis of Pliny. Because it is deep and rapid, it is called by the Persians the "furious water." Its source is near the frontier of Persia, and it is the great confluent of the Tigris. Its banks are dotted with villages, groves, and cultivated fields. Its volume is increased by the melted snows on the mountains of Kurdistan, and then it is difficult and dangerous to cross. Over its classic waters Xenophon retreated with his "ten thousand," and at a subsequent period it was crossed and recrossed by Alexander and Darius on the day when their contending hosts fought for empire.

Our course was to the north-west, and our objective point was the raft ferry a little to the east of the small town of Abou Sheeta. The first sight of the river had cheered us, but the crossing was not near. Hope deferred begets impatience. The hours wore on wearily. We were doomed to disappointment. Mosul could not be reached by sundown. The distance from the Zab ferry to Mosul is twenty-seven miles. It was now high noon, and none could tell the exact distance to the ferry. We had been on the road eight hours. All felt the need of rest and refreshments. There was no help for us but to ride on. Our path lay across a rolling prairie of apparently interminable hills. We now passed a small Arab village, where the women were winnowing grain and the children were playing in the flowery fields. Beyond was a second village, where the telegraph wires were stretched across the Zab. This gave us heart. In less than an hour the huts of Abou Sheeta were seen on our left. In a few minutes we were at the ferry. And now came the crossing. Dispatch was indispensable. The pasha's caravan was not far behind us. It would require all the afternoon to ferry so large a company over. They would claim precedence, and enforce it by cimeter and rifle. We must improve our advantage of being in advance. Our Arabs understood this fact. Hence all was hurry and confusion. *Khajawahs*, saddles, and luggage were removed and placed in a boat, which seemed to have been cut through the centre, and the stern end left open for entrance. Into this native craft our "elect lady," a native woman, and sixteen men entered. Two horses and four mules were tied to the side of the boat, and left to do their best to swim the rapid stream. The Zab flowed at the rate of eight miles an hour, and the distance between the two landings was a full mile. The signal was given, and we were swept by the tremendous current the fourth of a mile down the river. The horses and mules struggled desperately, and we were in danger of being submerged. Three other mules were driven into the water without the aid of the boat to guide them; but after a trial they returned to the shore. They were again driven in, and stoned till they found resistance useless. This time they swam with the current; but, hearing their master's voice, they gradually turned toward the opposite shore, and landed a mile below the point of starting. It was expensive crossing the Zab ferry. The Arabs of the adjacent villages own the boat and do the work; but an officer of the Turkish Government was stationed there, to collect a heavy toll for each person in the boat and each animal that swam the stream; and had we swum the river, we would have had to pay for the privilege.

Safely over, we lunched on the green banks, where flowers bloomed to please the eye and delight us with their odor. The pleasure of the hour was disturbed by a war of words. We desired to go on as far as possible; but Jebarah interposed all sorts of objections, notwithstanding he had promised to do his best to reach Mosul that night. It was finally agreed that we should go to the next village, four hours distant. Our path lay up a narrow defile covered with loose white stones, which reflected the sun with terrific force. As we advanced, the heat increased to almost melting power. Man and beast suffered intensely. But God was merciful. A cloud appeared in the west, in the form of an angel with wings outspread, and spread one of its great wings over the face of the burning sun. It was the realization of the promise: "He shall cover thee with his feathers, and under his wings shalt thou trust."* We were in a wild, hilly region, where shepherds wandered with their flocks, and the herdsmen watched their droves of cattle and camels.

At 4 P.M. we reached the Bumadus, on whose banks Darius encamped on the night previous to the fatal battle of Gaugamela; and on our right, and stretching far away, were the plains whereon a million and a half of men had struggled for victory. The river is now called the Harsar, and is deep, broad, and clear. The crossing occupied nearly an hour, and the charge of the ferry-master was twenty piastres, only five piastres less than we had to pay to cross the Zab. Instead of a boat, we now had a raft of ancient and novel construction. Forty skins

RAFT ON THE TIGRIS.

of full-grown sheep and goats had been inflated by the lungs, through an aperture which had been carefully tied up with a string. The skins had been arranged in eight rows, and upon them had been placed a frame-work of the branches of the poplar and oleander, and made fast by twigs of the osier, and then covered with green leaves, which completed the construction. The raftsmen guide

---

* Psalm xci., 4.

these rude vessels by means of long poles and with perfect safety. The idea is as old as Nineveh, for I afterward saw the raft of inflated skins among the bass-relief sculptures on the walls of the ancient palaces. According to Xenophon, these *killeks*, or rafts, were used in the time of the younger Cyrus to navigate the Euphrates, and on such a conveyance a certain Rhodian proposed to transport the "ten thousand" over the Tigris. They were also used by Alexander the Great in crossing rivers while on his victorious march through Asia. Encouraged by such illustrious examples, we stepped on board the raft, and were soon gliding down the Harsar. As we approached the opposite shore, a dozen naked Arabs swam to meet us, and guide the raft from the rapid current to the sandy beach.

It was now five o'clock. We had been thirteen hours on the road. All were exhausted. On the neighboring hills were the black tents of Arab shepherds, and thither we prepared to go and spend the night. But the soldiers interposed, followed by another war of words. They insisted that their orders were to take us to the next village, and not to an encampment of shepherds, and they must obey. We insisted on stopping. They assured us that the Bedouins would rob and murder us; but our men drew their long knives, and swore by their prophet to defend us and themselves. The scene was tragical. A fight seemed inevitable. Night was approaching. We were without shelter and food. Our "elect lady" required the best of both, yet she was the most patient, gentle, brave of the company. Our men carried the day. We were again in motion. For two dreary hours, and in the dusk of the evening, we wandered over those strange hills in search of the shepherds' tents. At last their camp-fires were seen on the distant

SHEPHERD'S TENT.

hills. As we approached, dogs barked, children screamed, women ran, and men grasped their guns to drive back the intruders. The situation was not flattering. But gentle lips whispered, "And there were in the same country shepherds abiding in the field, keeping watch over their flock by night. And, lo, the angel of the Lord came upon them, and the glory of the Lord shone round about them; and they were sore afraid. And the angel said unto them, Fear not: for, behold, I bring you good tidings of great joy, which shall be to all people."*

---

* Luke ii., 8–10.

Fatoheh and Ashur rode in advance. Our wishes were made known. The Arabs consented. A tent of black cloth was vacated for our reception, wherein our beds were spread. Dinner was soon ready. Fresh eggs, sweet milk, cracked wheat, boiled in the rich milk of the camel, composed the bill of fare. And then we sat around our camp-fire, wondering what would be the events of the night in that strange place. Observing a group of twenty Arabs engaged in a low conversation, I approached, and, to my surprise and delight, I found them to be Chaldean Christians! They told me, "To-morrow will be Good-Friday, and next Sunday will be holy Easter." How groundless had been our fears! How beautiful are the surprises in human life! It was the solution of Samson's riddle: "Out of the eater came forth meat, and out of the strong came forth sweetness."* The full moon shone in unclouded beauty on the encampment. The shepherds arranged for a native dance. One of their number played on a flute of bamboo, while the others danced and sung and clapped their hands. The dance over, the chief shepherd took me by the arm in a most affectionate manner, and led me to see by moonlight the herds and flocks folded for the night. During the day all the sheep of the large encampment feed together on the hills and in the valleys, whither they are led by their shepherds; but when they are led home at night, they separate and gather in front of their owners' tents. Before one tent were ten; before another were twenty; around a third were fifty. Just within the open tent lay the shepherd, with his gun resting on his arm, and his faithful dog lying by his side. He is a soldier-shepherd to protect his flock from the thief and from wild beasts.

---

* Judges xiv., 14.

His sheep look to him for care and protection, as a child looks to the parent. He can distinguish one sheep from another, and to each he had given a name. Just as a child answers when called, so his sheep came at the sound of his voice: "My sheep know my voice;" and "he calleth his own sheep by name." To the north of the encampment were folded some splendid white camels, and by the side of each was a baby camel; and beyond was the sire, of immense size and of great value.

During our moonlight stroll, I noted the construction of the Arab tent, and the order of the encampment. Each tent was made of black goat-hair canvas, supported by poles down the centre and on either side, and held in their place by strong cords. The tents were arranged in parallel lines close together, with the sheikh's occupying the foremost place, facing the side from which the guest, as well as the enemy, is expected, that he may be the first to exercise hospitality, and the first to meet the foe. This position, however, is changed in winter, when the tent is closed completely on one side, according to the prevailing wind; so that when the wind changes, the whole camp suddenly, as it were, turns round, the last tent becoming the foremost. During the warm weather the whole canvas is raised on poles, to allow the air to circulate freely, a curtain being used in the morning and evening to ward off the rays of the sun. Rude as these Arab shepherds are in many things, yet they have their rules of politeness. It is thought indecorous to approach by the back of a tent, or step over the tent-ropes, or ride toward the woman's compartment, which is always on the right. And the owner has a right to claim as his guest any one who passes in front of his tent, and would consider it an insult to pass by without stopping to eat his bread.

Returning to our camp-fires, we sat down, and conversed about the habits and customs of the Bedouins who dwell in tents. They are creatures of necessity, and their nomadic life is compulsory, as the existence of their flocks and herds depends upon the pasturage they can find. With each change of the season, they change their locality according to the wants of their flocks. Ever subject to change, their wants must be few, and their household furniture must always be at the minimum, and such as can be easily transported. Their food is simple and their raiment coarse. When free from care, they are witty, cheerful, and of gentle temper. They are the most incessant talkers in the world. Their quickness of perception enables them to appreciate a good story, and they give themselves up to immoderate laughter. When excited they gesticulate in a violent manner, and vociferate in explosive tones. They are passionate, and quick to resent an insult. Their love of money passes all knowledge; it is an insatiable greediness; a ruling passion that knows no bounds. They are generous, but theirs is a generosity inspired by the hope of an equivalent in return. They are a nation within a nation. At the head of each tribe is a sheikh whose word is law, and who administers a rude justice among his people. The most common source of litigation is stolen property; the penalty is in money or in kind, and he who gains the suit has to pay the fee. They not unfrequently test a man's innocence by compelling him to lick a red-hot iron, and if his tongue is burned there is no doubt of his guilt. One of the most ancient laws among them is the law of blood, called the Thar, which prescribes the degrees of consanguinity within which it is lawful to revenge a homicide. According to this law, any one related to the murderer within the fifth degree is held responsible, and, although this seems like manifest injustice, yet it tends to the prevention of bloodshed among the wild tribes of the desert; and, were it not for the operation of this law, the warlike tribes would have exterminated one another centuries ago. When a murder is committed, an effort is made to prevail on the family of the victim to accept a compensation for the blood in money or in kind; but if the "blood-money" is refused, then any relative within the fifth degree of consanguinity may be legally killed.

ARAB MAN AND WOMAN.

This law has a remarkable effect upon the manners of the Arabs. They are cautious in disclosing to a stranger their name, or that of their father, or their dwelling-place, lest they may fall victims to the blood-revenge. They have another law which is as universal, and even more salutary. It defines the relations between the protector and the protected, and a breach of which is regarded as a lasting disgrace. If a man can touch the canvas of a tent, or throw his mace toward it, or touch with his teeth any article belonging to another, he has a right to protection; especially if he eats a man's salt or bread, he is under his protection. A woman can protect any number of persons, or even of tents, under the operation of this law.

Within the encampment were many girls of a marriageable age, which naturally suggested the usages relating to marriage. While among the Arabs of the towns daughters are literally sold to their husbands, yet a Bedouin of the desert will never ask money for his daughter. He may consult her wishes, but she is at liberty to accept or reject a suitor, provided he is not her cousin. But if the damsel accepts a present from her lover, whether a jewel or a donkey, she is bound to have him.

At two o'clock the next morning we were again on the road. The clouds separated, and the moon lighted up our way over the pasture-fields of Karagoosh. We soon regained the highway, and passed a ruined village. The light was sufficient to reveal the well-cultivated fields on either side, where the wheat was growing rich and in abundance. But there was a shade of loneliness in a start so early, and all naturally wished for the morning. Hour after hour wore slowly away. At length the day dawned; the stars faded; the moon grew pale; the sun rose. It was Good-Friday in ancient Assyria. We were amidst the ruins of buried empires. On either hand were great mounds wherein are the remains of former greatness. The domes and minarets of Mosul now appeared on the west bank of the Tigris. All felt the excitement of the moment. It was the eleventh day since we left Bagdad. We had come three hundred miles. Before us flowed the river whose banks we hoped soon to reach; but the floods compelled us to make a long

CITY OF MOSUL.

détour, and defer the consummation of our wishes. Patience was never more difficult to practice, and an even temper required an effort. We rode through deep ravines, crossed bridges that trembled with our weight, passed villages bereft of beauty, and encountered caravans of merchants bound for Bagdad. But the goal was not far. An hour later, and we were at the gates of ancient Nineveh. On our right was the palace of Sennacherib; on our left was the tomb of Jonah. A mile beyond was the landing where we waited for the boat. Swollen by the vernal rains and the melted snows on northern mountains, the Tigris rushed by with unwonted force. In the bed of the river are several islands, which were now nearly submerged. From the main-land on the east to the edge of the largest of the several channels of the river, and where the current is strongest and the stream deepest, there is a brick bridge supported by forty arches, and constructed some two hundred years ago. Owing to the rapidity of the current and the accumulated waters, the main channel is spanned by a bridge of boats, extending from the end of the brick bridge to the western bank of the Tigris. These boats are held together by iron chains, and covered with planks, on which earth is spread. When the river is high, the boats are removed, and a ferry is established. And such was the case when we reached the Tigris. It was a sore disappointment, as we had had enough of Turkish ferries for all practical purposes. But it was the harvest-time for the boatmen, who clamored for our patronage with loud vociferations and violent gestures. Had we been Arabs, we could have crossed for one-half less than was demanded, but we cheerfully paid double the amount for the privilege of being Americans. The boat was similar in construction and form to the one in which we had crossed the Greater Zab, but of larger dimensions. It was a moment of intense excitement when we entered the swift current, with an island on our right and a pier of the brick bridge on our left, with imminent danger of being dashed against the latter. At such a time minutes are magnified into hours. How wishfully we watched the opposite shore! Never was relief more sweet than when the rude boat thumped against the river-bank. Nor was the landing-place inviting—high, steep banks, down

LANDING AT MOSUL.

which flowed the blood of slaughtered sheep, and the colored waters from the tanners' yards which lined the bluffs. It required the aid of many Arabs to assist us up the slippery paths; and not a few men and boys proffered their aid, certain of a reward of a few piasters.

A letter of introduction secured us a temporary home in the house of Abboo Jizrawee, dragoman to the French consulate. Mr. Jizrawee was a large, fine-looking, richly dressed, genial Mosulian. He was jovial, volatile, talkative, of unbounded hospitality, and popular with his townsmen. His great fat face beamed with smiles, and his laughter was uproarious. His long connection with the consulate had made him familiar with the manners of foreigners, and he considered himself honored to be the host of three American travelers. His residence was large and comfortable, and the guest-chamber was the best of all his apartments. His wife was beautiful, and was unwearied in her attendance to our "elect lady."

INTERIOR OF A HOUSE AT MOSUL.

Our apartments were furnished in Oriental style. There were divans for bedsteads, rugs for carpets, elegant cimeters and richly ornamented rifles for decorations on the walls.

It was soon known in Mosul that Americans had arrived. A letter of introduction to Khowaja Meekha brought that worthy Christian to our abode. He was the elder in the American Presbyterian Mission Church, and universally esteemed for his intelligence and piety. His generosity prompted him to invite Mr. Collins to be his guest. He spoke English fluently, and was well posted as to the religious condition of the city.

But a greater pleasure awaited us. Mr. Hormuzd Rassam was in Mosul, and hastened to honor us with a call. A native of Mosul, he is an accomplished Oriental scholar. His preferences led him to marry an English lady, and he is now a British subject. He was associated with Layard and Rawlinson in Assyrian excavations, and is mentioned by them in terms of highest compliment. He has the honor of having discovered the palace of Asshur-bani-pal, which contained the stone library of that king, which is now in the British Museum. He had returned to Mosul to settle the estate of his deceased brother, who for many years was the English vice-consul in this city. With a generosity we can never forget, Mr. Rassam invited us to be his guests, in the elegant residence of his departed brother. Neither wealth nor painstaking had been spared to make this the abode of comfort. The structure was in the form of a square, with a court-yard in the centre, wherein was a beautiful garden. On the ground-floor, and opening into the court, were the dining-hall, reception-room, and a drawing-room of superb adornments. The oval ceiling of the latter was beautifully painted in blue, and ornamented with gilt vines, flowers, and stars. Three lofty arches also opened into the court, whose concave domes represented the star-lit heavens. In the second story, and surrounding the court, were marble-paved balconies, and adjoining them were elegant sleeping-apartments. As a retreat from the intense heat of an Assyrian summer, an under-ground residence had been constructed of Mosul marble, and consisted of broad arches supported by sculptured piers. Within this palatial abode we remained for a week, enjoying a hospitality as elegant as it was abundant. Never did host anticipate the pleasure of his guests with greater success. Each day some new dish peculiar to the East was served up to tempt our never-indolent appetites; and chief among these favorite dishes was *kaïmmak*—the cream of the buffalo's milk, eaten with the white, hard Syrian honey.

Mosul occupies a portion of the suburbs of ancient Nineveh, but its primeval history is unknown. Xenophon mentions a castle as standing here, and now known as the ruins of Yarumjah, and designates the site of Nineveh as Mes-pylæ, the middle gate or pass, which this point of the river has ever been; but he does not allude to the existence of a town. Although the city is scarcely noticed in history during the time of the caliphs, yet when the Turks came into power, Mosul became the seat of a race of independent princes, and to their times belong the old Saracenic structures which still remain.* During the reign of Selim I. it became part of the Turkish empire. In 1554, Suleiman the Great made a treaty of peace with the King of Persia, by which the city became a boundary of his dominions. Since then it has been ruled by a class of pashas who have been despotic and rapacious. Its present population of fifty thousand is composed of Chaldeans, Syrians, Arabs, Turks, Kurds, and Jews. Its walls are less than three miles in circuit, within which are large gardens and many ruins. The buildings are of stone, with arched roofs, and with court-yards faced with slabs of sculptured alabaster. Its streets are narrow, crooked, and never clean. Few cities have suffered greater vicissitudes. In 1825, a famine prevailed for three years, followed by the plague, which lasted nine months, and

---

* Ainsworth.

during the prevalence of which eighteen thousand persons died; and in the year 1832, the whole city was flooded for months, causing extraordinary suffering. In earlier years, the commerce of Mosul was extensive and lucrative; but under the oppressive rule of the Turks, it has dwindled to nothing. The bazaars are well supplied with grapes, melons, pomegranates, apricots, cucumbers, and truffles for home consumption, and with gall-nuts from the valonia-oaks in Kurdistan, which are exported. The once famous Mosul cloths, or muslins, have given place to a blue cotton cloth of an inferior quality. But Mosul excels in the manufacture of red, yellow, and green leather for the showy boots and shoes worn by the natives.

Were a stranger to infer the religious condition of a town from the number of places of worship therein, he would naturally conclude the Mosulians to be a devout people. According to universal custom among the Turks, the census is based on the number of families, and not on the number of individuals, and they are classified by their religious faith rather than by their nationality. Of the three thousand three hundred and fifty families in Mosul, two hundred are Jews, one thousand one hundred are Christians, and two thousand and fifty are Mohammedans. The Moslems have twenty large mosques, and two hundred and fifty places for prayer. Near the old ruined mosque of Noor-el-Deen is a grand minaret, ninety feet high, whose projecting and receding courses of bricks represent a fancy work of arabesque; and, whether by intention or accident, it *leans*, like the Tower of Pisa.

The Christians are not so numerous as their Mohammedan neighbors, but superior to them in thrift and intelligence. Their sectarianism is patent to all, and supported by a zeal worthy a better cause. They are known as Nestorians, Jacobites, Papists, and Presbyterians. Their numerous churches are largely attended. The French Roman Catholic church is an imposing structure. It is constructed of Mosul marble, crowned with two domes, which are supported by marble columns. The interior is adorned with pictures, and on the high altar is a life-size statue of Mary. I was present at the eight-o'clock mass on Easter-Sunday. Two French monks officiated on the occasion. Seven French nuns, in charge of a large company of native orphans, sat on the right of the chancel. The congregation was large. The men sat in front, on the carpeted floor, and the women sat in the rear. On the preceding Good-Friday, the monks dramatized the scene of the Crucifixion; and on the Easter anniversary they presented to the gaze of the devout the empty tomb perfumed with flowers, and brilliantly illuminated. From Rome I went to Chaldea, and witnessed the worship of the Nestorians, who are by birth Chaldeans. Their ceremonies are not unlike those of the Papists, but toward each other they cherish the most cordial antagonism. The bitterness of their enmity springs from their similarity. They are too near alike to live in peace. It was my privilege to meet Joseph Ado, Patriarch of Babylon, and Primate of the Chaldean Christian community, whose official residence was formerly in Mosul; but the Romish monks intrigued to get him away, on the principle that two of a trade could not agree. His appearance is most venerable, and he is held in high repute by the people. He is now the Chaldean bishop of Malabar, which is more nominal than real. He had returned to his old residence as more congenial to his tastes, and spends his time in praying, reading, and smoking.

It was more in accord with my sentiments and feelings to attend the eleven-o'clock services in the small church wherein worship the members of the American Presbyterian Mission. Notwithstanding the storm, forty men and ten women were present, to whom the native pastor preached with commendable zeal. The members of this little community are among the most intelligent and enterprising citizens of Mosul. They are a light shining

JOSEPH ADO.

in a dark place. Their greatest need is the presence of a foreign missionary to instruct, encourage, and defend. But this boon is denied them, from an impression that an American missionary can not survive in Mosul; and the impression has been strengthened by the remarkable mortality which has attended those who have made the attempt. In 1833, Rev. Messrs. Hinsdale and Mitchell, with their wives, were appointed to this mission; but

Rev. Mr. Mitchell died on the way, and his wife died within ten days thereafter; and Mr. Hinsdale died after a residence of one year. Their place was supplied by the coming of the Rev. Mr. Lowry, whose wife died within a year from the date of his arrival. Then followed the death of Dr. Grant; and at a subsequent period, the death of Rev. Messrs. Marsh and Williams and their wives; and, still later, the death of Rev. Messrs. Lobdell and Haskell. But old Elder Khowaja Meekha thinks that these good servants of the Lord would have died had they lived in Jerusalem or Mardeen or Beirut, and is strong in the opinion that the little community should not be neglected because so many missionaries found Mosul to be the gate of heaven to their ascending souls.

The Monday and Tuesday succeeding Easter-Sunday are holidays with the Christians of Mosul, and are devoted to exchanging calls, not unlike our calls on Newyear's-day. They are festive days, and in each house a feast of fat things awaits the callers. Mr. Rassam had provided for his many guests with that good taste and elegance so characteristic of himself. It was a favorable opportunity for us to observe the social customs prevalent in this far-off Assyrian city, and especially the rich costumes of the Chaldean ladies. The weather was charming, and the ladies appeared in all the gorgeousness peculiar to the East. The display was reserved entirely for the house. They appeared at the portal of the court wrapped in a huge checkered blue sheet, and with the face hidden beneath a square horse-hair veil; but these were removed as they entered the court, and then was displayed the splendor of their attire. The high head-dress was resplendent with gold and pearls; the necklaces were elaborately wrought; the frontlets, anklets, and bracelets sparkled with the richest gems; the bust and arms were covered with the finest lace inwrought with gold, and their ample robes of silk were embroidered with gold and silver thread in many a curious device. The youthful wife of Mr. Rassam's eldest brother was adorned like the daughter of a king. But these outward adornments were the least of their many charms. Nature had left the impress of beauty on each lovely face, and bequeathed to each a grace of carriage worthy of an Esther. Nor had the mind and heart been neglected. Their conversation evinced an appreciation of the beautiful and the true; their graceful deportment was proof of the careful culture of the refined amenities of social life; and the joyousness of their smile bespoke a soul conversant with the higher and better sentiments of our humanity.

CHAPTER V.

Among the Ruins of Ancient Nineveh.—Historical and Scriptural Allusions.—Nimrod, the Mighty Hunter.—Asshur and his Colony.—Extent and Duration of the Assyrian Empire.—Extent and Glory of Nineveh.—Its Walls, Gates, and Palaces.—Identity of its Ruins.—Jonah's Visit to Nineveh.—His Mission and his Tomb.—Sail down the Euphrates.—Beautiful Scenery.—Selamiyah.—Donkey-ride.—Birthplace of Saladin.—Great Image of Nebuchadnezzar.—Exploring the Ruins.—Tower of Nimroud.—Ancient Temples.—Wonderful Sculptures.—Palace of Asshurizir-pal.—Splendid Remains.—Palaces of Shalmaneser II., and of Tiglath-pileser II.—The Marble Obelisk.—Palace of Esarhaddon.—God Nebo.—Horrid Night with the Arabs.—Return to Mosul.—Grand Palace of Sennacherib, and its Magnificent Sculpture.—Annals and Will of Sennacherib.—Palace of Sardanapalus, and its Splendid Bass-reliefs.—Assyrian Wars.—Fall of Nineveh.—The Last Battle.—Prophecy Fulfilled.

SEVEN days among the ruins of ancient Nineveh gave me the rare opportunity to trace its walls, to stand within its monumental gates, to wander through its excavated palaces and examine their sculptured halls, to recall the mighty past, to read prophecy in the light of modern discoveries, and compare Herodotus with Isaiah, Ctesias with Nahum, and Diodorus with Jonah. The three sources of information as to the origin, extent, and fall of the Assyrian empire are, the Bible, the Greek historians, and the cuneiform inscriptions. These authorities synchronize in the main, and supplement each other. The earliest record of the empire of Assyria, in authentic history, is by Moses, in the tenth chapter of Genesis. The allusion thereto is brief, but definite: "Out of that land went forth Asshur, and builded Nineveh, and the city Rehoboth, and Calah, and Resen between Nineveh and Calah: the same is a great city."* It is apparent, from this concise statement, that Asshur was a colonist, and the founder of Nineveh. "Out of that land went forth Asshur," is an expression that clearly indicates the existence of an antecedent kingdom. That kingdom was founded by Nimrod in the land of Shinar, the lower section of the great valley between the Tigris and the Euphrates, and near the confluence of those two historic rivers. The sacred historian is no less concise than definite in his allusion to that fact: "And Cush begat Nimrod: he began to be a mighty one in the earth. And the beginning of his kingdom was Babel, and Erech, and Accad, and Calneh, in the land of Shinar."† That was the first kingdom established subsequent to the Flood, and probably about two thousand four hundred years before the Christian era. The Tower of Babel is the only remaining monument of the oldest empire known to mankind, and of the identity of that tower there is but little doubt. From a point so advantageous in location, the "mighty hunter" rapidly spread his dominion inland and northward; and other cities than Babylon were founded by him, who is among the foremost men of the Old World, and whose memory will last while time endures. Even now his name is mentioned with reverence by the people of Chaldea, and wherever a mound of ashes or an extraordinary ruin is to be seen in Babylonia or the adjoining regions, the local traditions attach to it the name of Nimrod.‡

From the dominions of the "mighty hunter," Asshur went forth and laid the foundations of a rival empire, whose remains are now exciting the attention of the civilized world. Whether his emigration was voluntary or

---

* Genesis x., 11, 12.   † Genesis x., 8, 10.   ‡ Rawlinson.

compulsory, or in obedience to a royal decree of Nimrod, are facts not known to history; but that the Assyrians and Babylonians were of a common origin, and that the former were colonists from the land of the latter, is evident from the similarity of religion, of language, and of architecture. And whether this colonization took place two thousand two hundred years before our era, or one thousand four hundred years, is a point on which the Assyrian archæologists do not agree. At present the weight of the evidence favors the earlier of the two dates; and, accordingly, the empire of Assyria continued during fifteen centuries, or from B.C. 2182 to B.C. 606. The grandeur of such a duration has scarcely a parallel in history. Rome, whether kingdom, commonwealth, or empire, lasted but twelve centuries. The Chaldean monarchy endured but a thousand years, from Nimrod to Tiglathi-Nin. The first Persian empire continued less than two and a half centuries. The kingdom of Babylon, founded by the father of Nebuchadnezzar, did not survive a century. The continuity of Egypt was interrupted by foreign domination; and the same is true of China. It is thought that there are sufficient grounds for the conjecture that there were two distinct Assyrian dynasties—the first commencing with Asshur, and ending with Sardanapalus; and the second, including the kings mentioned in the Scriptures, and ending with Saracus, in whose reign Nineveh was finally destroyed by the combined armies of Persia and Babylon.*

But of the extent and magnificence of the empire of the Assyrians there is greater certainty. While the true heart of Assyria was on the banks of the Tigris, and within the limits of the four great cities, marked by the

---

* Layard.

mounds at Kuyunjik, Nimroud, Khorsabad, and Karamles; yet from this imperial centre the empire extended eastward to the Kurdistan Mountains, southward to the Greater Zab, westward to the Euphrates, and northward to Mount Masius. The probable area was not less than seventy-five thousand square miles, the length of which area from north to south was less than three hundred and fifty miles, and the breadth from east to west not more than three hundred miles. But this was only, as it were, the base from which her kings went forth to subdue other realms, and extended their dominion from the Persian Gulf to the Caspian Sea, and from the western provinces of Persia to the shores of the Mediterranean. There was a time when the Assyrian kings held in vassalage, and received tribute from, Susiana, Chaldea, Babylonia, Media, Mesopotamia, Armenia, Cappadocia, Cilicia, Syria, Phœnicia, Palestine, Idumea, Arabia, nearly all of Egypt, a portion of Ethiopia, and the rich island of Cyprus. The records of these conquests are sculptured in alabaster on the walls of the royal palaces in Nineveh, and thereon, in bass-relief, may be seen the king in his triumphal chariot, the conquering army returning laden with the spoils of victory, the long line of captives, and the bearers of the tribute from the conquered nations.

It was with no ordinary zest that I wandered through the ruined palaces of an empire whose dominion was so vast, and whose power had been felt in regions so remote. The identity of these ruins, as marking the remains of Nineveh, is no longer called in question; but the extent of the imperial city is still a matter of dispute. The historian Rawlinson is disposed to limit the city to the mounds opposite Mosul, and to regard the adjacent mounds as marking so many distinct royal cities;

but Mr. Layard regards them as parts of one grand metropolis, "called by different names, but included within the area of that great city known to the Jews and to the Greeks as Nineveh." In the days of its glory, when it was "an exceeding great city," Nineveh described an oblong square, eighteen miles long and twelve miles broad. The circuit of the vast quadrangle was sixty miles, and the inclosed area two hundred and sixteen square miles, about ten times that of London. The four corners of the square were marked by the magnificent palaces of Kuyunjik, Nimroud, Khorsabad, and Karamles, whose abiding ruins bespeak their pristine grandeur. Nimroud is supposed to represent the original site of the city, and from that point the city was gradually extended as the population increased and the demands of the empire multiplied. It was an ancient custom that when a king founded a new dynasty, or was ambitious to perpetuate his name, he signalized the former, and sought the latter, by the erection of a new and grander palace. So with the Assyrian kings. To the first palace the son of its founder added a second, and therein recorded his name. Subsequent monarchs followed the same rule; which accounts for the number and magnificence of the palaces whose remains have been exhumed at the four corners of the Assyrian capital. Although Nineveh is said to have contained an area ten times that of London, yet it is not probable that the whole space inclosed was occupied with dwellings. To the many palaces were attached parks, wherein game was kept for the diversion of the king. Within the larger inclosure were extensive gardens and much arable land. This was true of Babylon, within whose precincts was space sufficient for the cultivation of corn enough to supply the whole population in case of siege. Nineveh was a walled city of gardens, parks, orchards, and farms. The smaller and larger dwellings of the people were arranged in villages, which formed so many garden districts. The dimensions of an Eastern city do not bear the same proportion to its population as those of an American or European city. Nineveh might have been larger than London, Paris, or New York now is, yet the population might have been much less. The rural character of the Assyrian capital is more than intimated by the concluding words of the book of Jonah, that within the city were " much cattle."

Around the city were walls of extraordinary dimensions, and at certain distances were immense gates, flanked by towers, and adorned with human-headed bulls and lions. According to Herodotus and Diodorus Siculus, the walls were a hundred feet high, and sufficiently broad for three chariots to be driven abreast thereon. There were fifteen hundred towers, each two hundred feet in height, and in them troops were stationed for the defense of the capital. The walls were probably constructed of bricks of clay dried in the sun; or they may have been earthen ramparts cased with stone slabs at the base, and with bricks from the stone casings to the top. Although the relative positions of the mounds of Kuyunjik, Nimroud, Karamles, and Khorsabad form very nearly a perfect parallelogram, yet the walls which once inclosed the same can not now be traced in their entirety. There are, however, consecutive mounds whose present breadth of base proves their former magnitude. They can be traced for many miles in extent; they have an average height of fifty feet, and are now sufficiently broad on the top for the free movement of three chariots abreast.

We have the testimony of two prophets touching the strength and size of Nineveh. Nahum alludes to its "strongholds" and "barred gates," which doubtless refers to its fortified palaces, and its immense gate-ways, flanked by towers capable of holding many troops, and deemed impregnable.* But the more extended account is recorded in the book of Jonah. In his mild rebuke to the offended prophet, the Lord inquires: "Should not I spare Nineveh, that great city, wherein are more than sixscore thousand persons that can not discern between their right hand and their left hand, and also much cattle!"† If the hundred and twenty thousand persons herein described were children, then the total population was not less than six hundred thousand, which would have constituted Nineveh "an exceeding great city." But if the phrase is to be understood as descriptive of moral ignorance, then a city containing a population of one hundred and twenty thousand adults who could not "discern between their right hand and their left hand," would be no less worthy of the title "great," as it is reasonable to suppose that the children were not included in the number; and it is equally reasonable to conclude that there were many thousands of adults who could discern between good and evil. It is, therefore, fair to infer that such a population could not be accommodated within the ascertained limits of any one of the four great sections of the ancient city.

In another place it is said, "Now Nineveh was an exceeding great city of three days' journey,"‡ which is an intended description of a city of unusual size. The passage may imply that it required three days to traverse the city from end to end, or to traverse its circumference, or to visit its four principal centres. Of the commencement of his Divine mission it is said: "And

---

* Nahum iii., 13, 14. † Jonah iv., 11. ‡ Jonah iii., 3.

Jonah began to enter into the city a day's journey, and he cried, and said, Yet forty days, and Nineveh shall be overthrown."* Coming on his solemn errand, it is probable that the prophet entered the city at Kuyunjik, through whose lengthened streets he went a "day's journey," impressively proclaiming the coming doom. Having delivered his solemn warning in Kuyunjik, the prophet passed southward eighteen miles, to Nimroud; thence to the north-east twelve miles, to Karamles; thence to the north eighteen miles, to Khorsabad; and thence to the west twelve miles, to Kuyunjik, which completed the circuit of the city of sixty miles; and, as twenty miles is a day's journey in the East, we have here "the three days' journey" of the prophet, which is a remarkable coincidence with the well-ascertained measurements of the city.

And there is another interpretation of this passage, as simple as it is rational. Having entered Nineveh at Kuyunjik, the prophet may have gone in silence "a day's journey" to Nimroud, and from that point commenced the circuit of the city, proclaiming as he went the terrible message of Heaven. Whether he accomplished his mission in three days or three weeks is a fact not stated in the text; nor would the time he occupied affect the statement that "Nineveh was a great city of three days' journey." But, as his solemn business required dispatch—the "forty days" to date from the last utterances which fell upon the ear of an astonished people from his inspired lips—it is highly probable that he uttered his last note of warning on the evening of the third day.

In whose reign these words of awful import were

---

* Jonah iii., 4.

uttered by the prophet, we have no certain knowledge. His visit to the Ninevites may have been in the year 840 B.C., during the flourishing reign of Shalmaneser II., or a hundred years later, when Sardanapalus was on the throne, living in inglorious ease and vicious indulgences, careless of his crown, and indifferent to the welfare of his people and his obligations to his God. In either case, it was at a time when the magnificence of Nineveh excited the admiration of the world; when her massive walls and lofty towers inspired a sense of security; when her royal palaces were adorned with those extraordinary sculptures and inscriptions which have since been exhumed; when her temples were resplendent with all that art could create and wealth procure; when her vast gardens were laden with the fruits, and bloomed with the flowers of the East; when her merchants were princes, and her citizens proud of their wealth; when her inclosed parks were filled with game for the diversion of the king and his nobles; when the voice of revelry resounded through her streets, and each returning night was spent in scenes of merriment; when captives from all nations were the slaves of their conquerors, and the spoils of victory had rendered a great people vain and luxurious. It was doubtless at such a time when the pale, haggard, travel-stained seer of Judea appeared in their midst, like a visitant from another world. Twenty-seven centuries have since passed away. Nineveh is now a mass of ruins; the memory of her mighty kings is perpetuated by no recognized mausoleum; but the name of the Hebrew prophet has outlived the lapse of time and the fall of empires. Opposite Mosul is the traditional Tomb of Jonah. On one of the mounds of Kuyunjik is a mosque, and within the mosque is the tomb of the prophet. The square sarcophagus is covered with a green cloth, embroidered with sentences from the Koran, and around it are the emblems of affection and respect. From that mound have been exhumed colossal human-headed bulls, figures of the Assyrian Hercules slaying a lion, and inscriptions containing the name and titles of the great Esar-haddon. And thus upon one of the buried palaces of Assyria is the supposed tomb of the immortal seer of Judea.

From a review of these important historic facts, we turned to explore the remains of the ancient city. Sending our horses across the Tigris, in charge of Bene-Jebarah, with instructions to meet us at Nimroud, we chartered a native boat, and were borne southward by the rapid current. Our crew consisted of six men and a boy, and the cost was two hundred and twelve piasters. We were attended by Khowaja Meekha and his son, who were our interpreters, and an Arab who had excavated under Messrs. Layard and Rassam. Our departure had been delayed by the inevitable discussion and boisterous talking of the boatmen. What talkers the Arabs are! They are bound to discuss a subject down to the least point before they decide a question, and each man present, whether boatman, soldier, or tanner, must "speak his little piece." To our relief, the last man had spoken the last word, and we swung out into the swift current, and were soon drifting at the rate of eight miles an hour. Just south of Mosul, and on the right bank of the Tigris, are the Turkish barracks, where the soldiers were preparing for the morning drill. Far out in the centre of the current was a man floating on an inflated goat-skin, using his lower limbs for a rudder. He was a farmer going to his farm, which was some miles below, on the eastern shore. He held the inflated skin under his arms, and across his breast. He conversed and laughed with our boatmen, with as much composure and sense of safety as one sailing on the *Great Eastern*. It is customary for both men and women to carry about them a goat-skin, and, when they wish to cross a stream or descend a river, they inflate the skin, and sail away. And this is a very ancient custom, as I have seen the same portrayed in the bass-reliefs on the walls at Kuyunjik.

Far away among the western hills, we observed a caravan of camels *en route* for Mosul. An hour later, we landed at Tel-Sabbat (the Hill of the Sabbath), and proceeded to visit the Sulphur Springs. At the base of the beautiful, conical hill, fifty feet high, and covered with grass and flowers, is a small village, and near the shore are the Hot Springs. The water is black as ink, and of a high temperature. Over the springs is a stone building, crowned with a series of small domes. The water is contained in a circular room twenty feet in diameter, whose roof is a dome. There was a strong smell of sulphur as we entered the inclosure. The water is regarded as efficacious to cure cutaneous diseases. Six lepers were there testing its efficacy, and who implored our charity. Having resumed our voyage, the boat was driven against an island by the force of the current. Our boatmen leaped into the water, and, after a hard and long struggle, succeeded in getting it afloat again.

As we descended the river, the scenery increased in interest. On our left was Assyria; on our right was Mesopotamia. The landscape was variegated by green hills, rich valleys, winding streams, small hamlets, and cultivated fields. At noon we landed at the small village of Selamiyah, supposed to mark the site of "Resin" of Scripture, and once important as a commercial centre. It is now a miserable Arab town, but surrounded with mounds which indicate the antiquity of the site. As our horses had not arrived, we called on the Sheikh of Selamiyah, and offered a good price for mules to carry us to Nimroud, three miles distant; but his demand being exorbitant, we started on foot. On the way we were overtaken by a peasant with four donkeys, who gladly accepted five piastres for a ride to the ruins. Within an hour thereafter, I stood upon the pyramid which Xenophon saw, and which he describes. The view was extensive, and the prospect pleasing. The vast and fertile plains of Assyria stretched away for miles, rich in meadow lands and fields of grain, dotted with villages and diversified with ancient mounds. The Tigris flowed rapidly within a mile to the west, and the snow-capped mountains of Media appeared in the distant east. West of the river, and forty miles to the south, were the mounds of Kalah Sherghat, supposed to mark the most ancient of all the Assyrian cities, and founded by Asshur himself. On the opposite side of the river, and ten miles beyond, was Tekrit, the birthplace of the great Saladin, the son of a Kurdish chief, and the conqueror of the Crusaders at the battle of Kurûn Hattin, and which is the supposed site where "Nebuchadnezzar the king made an image of gold, whose height was three-score cubits, and the breadth thereof six cubits: he set it up in the plain of Dura, in the province of Babylon," and commanded that "whoso falleth not down and worshipeth shall the same hour be cast into the midst of a burning fiery furnace."*

From the summit of the pyramid, I could best survey the remains of Nimroud, considered the most ancient of the four great sections of Nineveh, and founded by Shal-

---

* Daniel iii., 1, 6.

ENTRANCE TO A TEMPLE.

maneser I., about one thousand three hundred years before our era. The ruins now cover an area equal to one thousand acres, and in their general outline describe an irregular quadrangle, whose sides face the four cardinal points. On the north and east could be traced the old rampart, once flanked with towers, and pierced with gates. The royal quarter of the city, occupied by the

TUNNEL IN THE TOWER OF NIMROUD.

palaces of the kings, was on the west, bounded by the Tigris, which, no doubt, once flowed close to the city walls. On a raised platform, forty feet high, and covering an area of sixty acres, constructed of sun-dried bricks, and incased with solid stone masonry, were erected the palaces of successive monarchs, and two temples dedicated to the gods of Assyria. At its north-west angle is the Tower of Nimroud, one hundred and fifty feet high, and the fourth of a mile in circumference. Descending from its summit, we entered its deep, long trenches, made for purposes of exploration. Its foundations are constructed of large, square blocks of stone, laid upon each other without mortar. At the north-west corner is a circular projection or bastion; and in the interior of the tower is a gallery, six feet broad, twelve feet high, and one hundred feet long, which some suppose leads to the tomb of the king, but that has not yet been discovered. Adjoining this tower are the remains of two temples, whose portals were guarded by colossal lions, and whose walls were ornamented with sacred figures and sculptured inscriptions. The sculptured lions measured sixteen and a half feet high and fifteen feet long, and were flanked by winged figures, and between them was an inscribed pavement slab of alabaster. At a second entrance was a group designed to represent the expulsion of the evil spirit by the good deity. The representation of the bad spirit is hideous in the extreme. The monster's head is as frightful as it is fanciful. The ears are long and pointed; the jaws are distended, and armed with huge teeth. The body is covered with feathers; the forefeet are those of a lion; the hind legs terminate with the talons of an eagle; it has spreading wings, and the tail of a bird. It is pursued by a winged man dressed in fur, and bearing in each hand a three-forked thunder-bolt, which he is represented as hurling against the monster, who had turned toward him with an expression of the utmost fury. Near the temple stood a solid block of limestone, representing the king in high-relief. It is, perhaps, the best specimen of Assyrian art yet discovered. The monarch is clad in sacrificial robes,

ENTRANCE TO A TEMPLE.

STATUE OF A KING.

and in his right hand is the sacred mace. From his neck depend the four sacred signs—the sun, the crescent, the trident, and the cross. To his girdle are attached three daggers, and above his head are the winged globe. the sun, the crescent, the trident, and the horned cap. At his feet is a triangular altar, not unlike the tripod of the Greeks, and whereon were placed the offerings to the deified king, who had been decreed divine honors.

From the site of the temples we passed to examine the remains of the once magnificent palace of King Asshur-izir-pal, who reigned in the ninth century before our era. His is regarded as the most prosperous period in Assyrian history, and the one in which art was carried to its highest degree of perfection among the Assyrians. He was no less renowned as a warrior than famous as a hunter. Ten of his great campaigns are recorded in cuneiform inscriptions. His ninth was against Syria, during which he compelled Tyre and Sidon, Byblus and Aradus, to pay him tribute. On his return from the shores of the Mediterranean, he crossed the Lebanons, and brought therefrom beams of cedar wherewith to adorn his palace. Next to Nimrod, he is the most noted hunter in history. He loved the chase, and is said to have killed three hundred and sixty large lions. Near his palace he had a menagerie park, wherein he kept lions, leopards, elephants, and other animals, for his royal sport.

His grand palace was three hundred and sixty feet long and three hundred feet broad, and consisted of eight large halls and smaller chambers, arranged around a central court, one hundred and thirty feet in length and one hundred feet in breadth. The largest hall was one hundred and fifty feet long and thirty-three feet wide. Built upon a high platform, it had two splendid façades. The gate-ways thereto were flanked with sphinxes or winged lions, sculptured to represent the human form down to the waist. The grand portal to the king's audience-chamber was ornamented with winged human-headed bulls, of yellow limestone. The pavement of the palace was of slabs of alabaster, whereon were inscribed the titles, the genealogy, the achievements of the king. The ceiling was frescoed, representing flowers and animals, and inlaid with ivory and plates of gold. On the walls were the sculptured records of the empire, so that he who entered might read; and thereon were traced in bass-relief, and with great spirit and freedom, battle scenes, triumphal processions, exploits of the chase, ceremonies of religion, and grand

ENTRANCE TO THE GREAT HALL OF THE NORTH-WEST PALACE.

state occasions, when monarchs received embassadors from foreign lands. Within the palace stood the statue of King Asshur-izir-pal, which is now in the British Museum.

Through this forsaken palace I wandered from room to room and from hall to hall, where, thirty centuries ago, kings had been banqueted with all the luxuries an empire could afford, and where the crowned and sceptred had received the homage of conquered provinces. How inadequate is language to express the emotions thereby awakened in the soul, and to voice the thoughts which come trooping through the mind! The past returned with the reality of the present, and the imagination reproduced the royal structure in its completeness and splendor. "Art is long," said a great poet, whose words were here verified in a remarkable manner. The king is dead, and the master-builder is unknown; but the creations of the latter, which were the pride of the former, abide, and excite the admiration of the modern traveler. Many of the grander specimens of Assyrian art have been removed to adorn the capitals of Europe, but enough remains to interest and instruct. Some of the bass-reliefs are as perfect to-day as when they received their finishing touch centuries ago, while others have suffered from exposure to the elements and the vandalism of the thoughtless Arab. In some of the rooms the alabaster slabs which face the walls remain in their original position, and measure from six to ten feet square. In each corner is a triangular block, deftly cut, and in ornamentation is the "chief corner-stone." On the walls in one room are sculptured in relief, and in a beautiful manner, elaborate tracery, fruitful vines, and the honeysuckle—the "sacred tree" of the Assyrians; and on the same are inscriptions in the cuneiform character. Beyond, we came to a room whose walls are covered with historic records. It is a library in stone, whose volumes are ever open to him who enters therein. On the sides of an adjoining apartment are representations of winged bulls, with knotted girdles and inscribed records. On those of another room, perhaps a votive hall, is the image of a man with wings, whose beard and hair are massive, and in whose hand is an offering to the gods. At the entrance of a hall, and on either side, is a human-headed lion, with five legs, two seen from the

EXCAVATIONS.

front view and four seen from the side view, the object being to supply thereby what was then an imperfection in art. From the hall we passed through a series of apartments on whose walls are described soldiers with round shields and drawn daggers, beasts and birds, beautiful flowers, and garlands elegantly wrought, horses and chariots, with archers therein drawing the bow at a venture, and a priest whose hands are raised in prayer.

Turning from these marvelous works of ancient art, which seemed to echo back the mighty past, we traversed the intervening mounds and ravines, to examine the central palace, wherein had lived in regal splendor two Assyrian kings, whose military expeditions into Syria and Palestine are recorded in the Bible. The earliest of the two was Shalmaneser II., the son of Asshur-izir-pal, who ascended the throne about 860 B.C., and whose reign continued for thirty-five years. His power was felt from Media to the Mediterranean, from the Persian Gulf to the mountains of Armenia. Three of his twenty-seven campaigns were against Syria, when Ben-hadad and Hazael were upon the throne of Damascus, and during the successive reigns of Ahab and Jehu, the kings of Israel. Against their confederated strength, he marched with an army, "in multitudes that were not to be counted," and returned to his capital crowned with victory.

To commemorate his reign, he built for himself a magnificent residence less than five hundred feet from the splendid palace of his father; and, although subsequently despoiled of its rarer specimens of art, to adorn the palace of Esar-haddon, yet enough remains to illustrate its proportions and beauty. Among its ruins were discovered two gigantic winged bulls, covered with inscriptions, and an obelisk of black marble, now in the British Museum. On the four sides of the obelisk are twenty compartments of bass-reliefs; and in the space above, between and below the figures, is cuneiform writing of two hundred and ten lines, sharply cut and well preserved. It is seven feet high, and twenty-two inches wide on the broad face. The material and the workmanship are superior. It is a record in marble of the military annals of Shalmaneser II., for thirty-one years, commencing about 860 B.C. The bass-reliefs represent the king on two several occasions, attended with his chief officers of state, receiving the tribute of conquered nations, whose envoys prostrate themselves before the great king, and at his feet lay their offerings of gold, silver, copper in bars and cubes, goblets, shawls, and the tusks of elephants. In addition to such offerings as could be carried in the hand, there are also presented animals, such as the two-humped camels from Bactria, together with monkeys and baboons, lions and antelopes, the elephant and the rhinoceros, emblematic of different countries. Among the nations thereon portrayed are the Jews, whose peculiar features are unmistakable. And among the tributary kings whose names are inscribed on the obelisk is the name of "Jehu, the son of Omri," and Hazael, whom Elijah anointed king of Syria; which furnish an interesting instance of corroborative evidence of the fidelity of the Bible historians.

And other historic facts cluster around these ruins; for on the spot where the marble obelisk was found a subsequent king had his royal abode. It was Tiglathpileser II., the supposed Pul of the Scriptures, who repaired and adorned the palace of Shalmaneser II., and on its walls had caused to be sculptured in relief, but in colossal proportions, winged figures struggling with mystic animals; and, to delight his high martial spirit, he had also scenes of war portrayed, such as sieges, with mounds

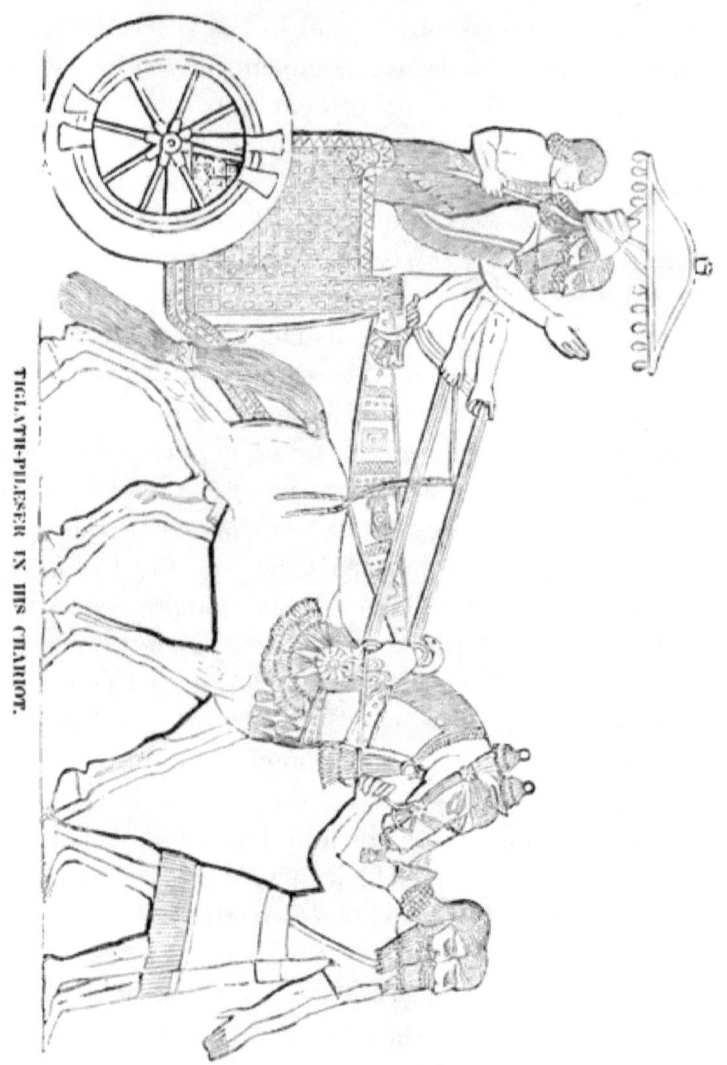

TIGLATH-PILESER IN HIS CHARIOT.

and battering-rams, archers masked by loop-holed screens, and captives impaled alive.

Having ascended the throne in 745 B.C., Tiglath-pileser II. sought to restore the kingdom to its ancient glory and ascendency. His wars were many, long, and bloody. By his energy and unwearied activity he subdued a revolt in Southern Mesopotamia, and thereupon assumed the title of "King of Babylon." From the south, he led his victorious legions to the west, and, after a struggle which lasted eight years, he conquered Rezin, King of Damascus; Menahem, King of Samaria; Hiram, King of Tyre; and Queen Khabila, whose dominions were on the borders of Egypt. And having subdued these, he defeated Azariah, King of Judah; but the victory was dearly bought, and the Assyrian king retired to his own dominions. Resolved upon the unconditional surrender of all those provinces which had revolted, he returned, after the lapse of ten years, and commenced an attack on Samaria, when Pekah was the king. This campaign is thus recorded in 2 Kings: "In the days of Pekah king of Israel came Tiglath-pileser king of Assyria, and took Ijon, and Abel-beth-maachah, and Janoah, and Kedesh, and Hazor, and Gilead, and Galilee, all the land of Naphtali, and carried them captive to Assyria."* And this inspired account is corroborated by the inscriptions found in the palace of this Assyrian monarch.

A year later, Tiglath-pileser was again in Syria. He had been summoned by Ahaz, King of Jerusalem. A powerful confederation had been formed by Pekah, of Samaria, and Rezin, of Damascus, who sought to compel Ahaz to join the alliance against Assyria. To accomplish their object, they had "come up to Jerusalem to war, and besieged Ahaz, but could not overcome him." In his extremity, "Ahaz sent messengers to Tiglath-pileser king of Assyria, saying, I am thy servant and thy son: come up, and save me out of the hand of the king of Syria, and out of the hand of the king of Israel, which rise up against me. And Ahaz took the silver and gold that

---

* 2 Kings xv., 29.

was found in the house of the Lord, and in the treasures of the king's house, and sent it for a present to the king of Assyria. And the king of Assyria hearkened unto him: for the king of Assyria went up against Damascus, and took it, and carried the people of it captive to Kir, and slew Rezin."* All these Bible facts are recorded in the Assyrian inscriptions which have been exhumed in our own day. There is a notice of the defeat and death of Rezin in a mutilated cuneiform inscription, now in the British Museum, and also the reception of the tribute from Ahaz, king of Judah.

Crossing what seemed to be a deep ravine, we soon stood within the palace of Esar-haddon, who succeeded his father, Sennacherib, some time in the year 680 B.C. He is justly renowned for his military success and the monuments he caused to be erected. Phœnicia, Cilicia, Egypt, Idumea, Chaldea, and Palestine surrendered to his conquering sword, and were compelled to pay the tribute exacted by his father. He was at once and at the same time "King of Assyria and King of Babylon;" and to these titles he proudly added, "King of the kings of Egypt, and Conqueror of Ethiopia." It was during his reign that Manasseh, King of Judah, revolted, and refused to pay the annual tribute: "Wherefore the Lord brought upon them the captains of the host of the king of Assyria, which took Manasseh among the thorns, and bound him with fetters, and carried him to Babylon."† From a cylinder inscription in duplicate, and now in the British Museum, it appears that this Assyrian monarch caused to be erected four palaces and thirty temples. Of his great palaces, one was at Kuyunjik, one at Nimroud, and one at Babylon, which he occupied as taste

---

* 2 Kings xvi., 5-9.   † 2 Chronicles xxxiii., 11.

might incline or state policy demand. The one at Nimroud was spacious and grand, and was probably modeled after the Temple of Solomon in Jerusalem. Its great hall was two hundred and twenty feet long by one hundred feet in breadth. On its northern front was a noble terrace, which commanded an extensive view. At one end of this hall were winged bulls, and at the opposite end, which had a triple portal, were placed three pairs of colossal sphinxes, which overlooked the Tigris winding through the plain. Judging from the excavated portions, the interior of the palace had been designed on a scale more magnificent than that of any other Assyrian palace yet discovered. Its chief room measured one hundred and sixty-five feet long by sixty-two feet wide, and must have contained an area of not less than ten thousand square feet. The ornamentations of the interior were on a scale of corresponding grandeur; and it is thought that the curious mythical and grotesque figures portrayed on the walls suggested to the prophet Ezekiel his vision of the four living creatures. But the grand palace of Esar-haddon was never completed; or, if finished, it was destroyed by fire. Both may be true. When the ruin was excavated, piles of sculptured slabs were discovered ready for use; and the quantity of charcoal found within the mound indicated the action of the fire.

Leaving the blackened remains of this once gorgeous palace, we crossed a field of young spring wheat, and, following our Arab guide, descended a deep, circular excavation, wherein stood the statue of the god Nebo. He was in the East what Mercury was in the West, and his special function was to preside over knowledge and learning; and hence he was called by the Assyrians "the god who knows, and who hears from afar." The great statue is twelve feet high, and of harmonious proportions; it is richly ornamented with elegant robes and garlands of flowers. The hands are folded in repose, and the face is calm, and expressive of wisdom. From the waist down to the knees is a lengthened inscription in the cuneiform characters. But the surroundings of the deserted god were melancholy in the extreme. The accumulated earth of ages had been removed, and Nebo stood in a deep, dark hole, without a follower to do him reverence. Poor fellow, he had seen better days!

From this deserted shrine, we crossed the intervening mounds and ravines, on our return to Selamiyah; but, when opposite the "Castle of Nimroud," we were overtaken by a storm which lasted four consecutive hours. The lightning was vivid; the thunder was deep-toned; the rain was gradual and incessant. We took shelter in one of the subterranean trenches around the foundations of the castle, where we remained during two hours. In addition to our own party, a large company of Arabs

THE GOD NEBO.

were there, who had been attracted thither by the hope of gain. Among the number was the sheikh of the tribe who had aided Layard in his excavations. He invited us to an entertainment in his encampment, distant half an hour's ride; but when he saw we hesitated to accept, he relieved our embarrassment by informing us that we could formally accept his invitation, and, instead of going, we could make him a present. This was Arab etiquette. The proffered entertainment placed us under an obligation to reciprocate; and the formal acceptance of the invitation demanded that we should go, or make him a present. Feeling sure that he was more anxious for our money than for our company, we gave him five piastres, which were as the oil of gladness to his countenance. But the love of money was not peculiar to the sheikh. Six of his tribe now advanced, and claimed a revenue as the guardians of Nimroud, and insisted that all who look upon the ruins must pay for the privilege thereof. This impudence could hardly be excelled in a better civilized land. We disputed their right to tax us; and they, waiving their right, appealed to our benevolence, which we expressed to the extent of one piastre for each man.

It was now 4 P.M., and there was no prospect that the storm would soon abate. Mine was the only horse at the mound, which I gladly offered to Mr. Collins for the return journey to Selamiyah, some three miles distant to the north-west. Old Mr. Meekha was mounted on a mule hired for the occasion. The rest of the party started on foot over the hills, through plowed fields and across meadows whereon the water was a foot deep. Our discomfort was increased by snow and hail that fell with the rain, and made the ground slippery. At length the western sky grew bright, and a rainbow appeared in the east—a bow of promise to some, but not to us. A rain-cloud followed us to the last, pouring upon us its drenching floods. All this would have been endurable had we had in prospect a change of clothing and a comfortable house. We were to lodge that night with the Sheikh of Selamiyah, the entrance to whose wretched hovel was almost inaccessible by the depth of the mud around it. On the earthen floor of the hut was a fire that filled the place with smoke. Sixteen Arabs—men, women, and children, and, in addition thereto, dogs, cats, goats, and donkeys—were to be our companions for the night. Our frugal repast consisted of a few cakes that we had brought from Mosul, and some eggs and milk purchased from the sheikh's homely wife. Each person measured his length upon the floor for a night's rest; and, as the feet of all were placed toward the little fire, our bodies were as so many spokes in a wheel resting on its hub. But there were too many animals in that hovel for an American to sleep without the annoyance of warlike dreams; and, after hours of fruitless resistance, I said, with David, "Make me to know mine end, and the measure of my days, what it is; that I may know how frail I am."

At two o'clock in the morning, I roused my companions to start for Mosul. In a moment every Arab in the hut was awake, and ready for a present. Hassin and his wife, Meriam, were the proper occupants of the place, and the others were neighbors, who had come to spend the night with their distinguished guests. A large, muscular Arab, who boasted the proud name of "Sultan," who was a walking armory of old swords and pistols, who had volunteered to accompany us to Nimroud, and for whose voluntary services I had offered five piastres, refused the proffered sum, and left the house in a rage; but this was only a feint, for, on finding he could get no more, he returned, and took what had been offered.

By the light of the moon, we started on horseback for Mosul. The distance was not more than fifteen miles, which we should have gone in four hours; but it soon transpired that our horses had not been fed, and we struggled on at the rate of two miles an hour. Yet the mind found relief in the recollections of history. We were passing over the same ground trodden by the feet of Jonah, when he startled the people with the cry, "Forty days, and Nineveh shall be overthrown." These hills heard that voice, which a repentant people reverently heeded. For many miles we could trace the walls of the ancient city, once the causeway for the war-chariots of Nineveh; and here and there were mounds marking the site of the garden-houses of the populace, and around which the soil is now as rich and fertile as in the days of yore. Slowly the day dawned; the sun rose above the dense fog; and, after a ride of seven hours, we reached the great mounds of Kuyunjik.

Around us were the ruins of the grand palaces of Sennacherib and of Sardanapalus, whose names are recorded in the sacred annals, and whose deeds fill so large a space in the history of the Eastern world. We were on a fertile plain, dotted with the gardens and cottages of the poor, and traversed by the great caravan road leading to Kurdistan on the north-east, and to Aleppo and the sea on the north-west. Two immense mounds of ruins are less than a mile from the Tigris, and directly opposite Mosul. Between them flows the river Khausser, which issues from the hills of Makloub and empties into the Tigris. In the dry season it is small and sluggish, but at other times it is an impetuous torrent, and has worn for itself a deep and broad bed. It is now spanned by a modern brick bridge, beneath which the swollen stream rushed with unwonted force. It is an

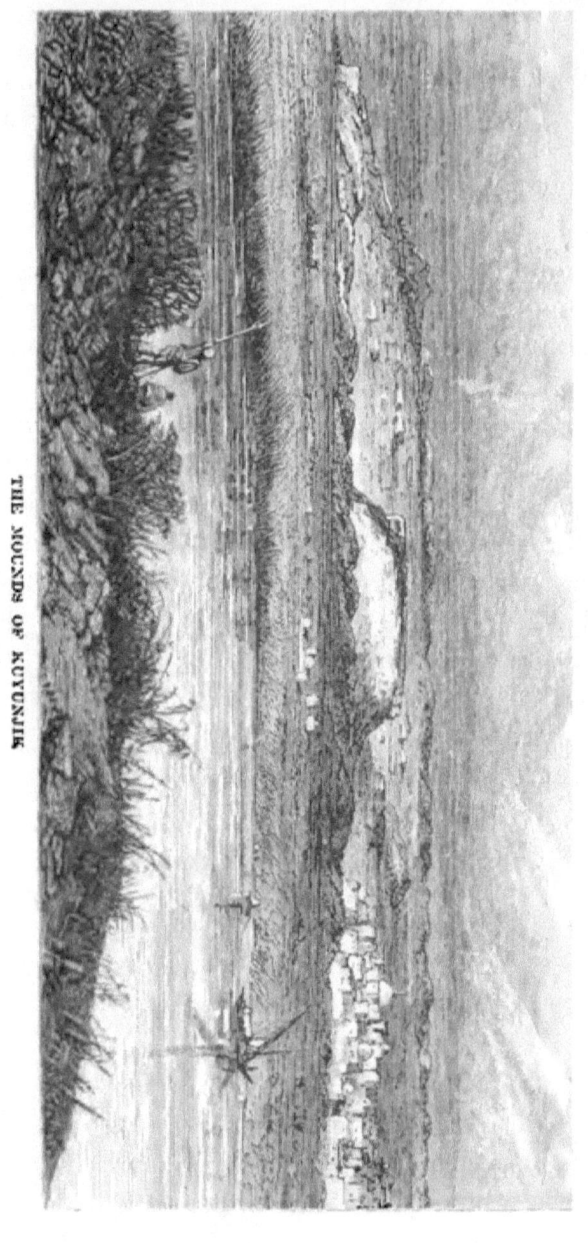

THE MOUNDS OF KUYUNJIK

ancient river, and occupies the channel through which it flowed when Sennacherib was king of all Assyria. But it is evident, both from historic records and the rich alluvium deposited on the plain, that the Tigris has gradually retreated to its present bed. Once it flowed along the city wall on the west, and was a section, with the Khausser and two artificial canals, of the deep moat that encompassed this portion of Nineveh. To the east of the great mounds are the remains of the ancient wall, and in it is a deep cut for the modern caravan road, and through which the telegraph extends to Mosul, and thence to Constantinople. It is estimated that the circuit of the walls was eight miles, and the area inclosed was about two thousand acres. Of the grand gate-ways only one remains to reflect its original grandeur. It is the north-west gate of the city, through which Sennacherib and his hosts had often gone forth to battle, and returned crowned with victory, laden with spoil, and leading in triumph captives from the Holy Land. When complete, it must have been exceedingly imposing. The noble entrance was fifteen feet wide, paved with limestone slabs, that still bear the marks of chariot-wheels. The roof was arched, and surmounted with a lofty tower one hundred feet high. It was a triple gate-way, and within were two chambers, each seventy feet in length and twenty-three feet in breadth, wherein troops were stationed. The triple portal was flanked by majestic human-headed bulls, each fourteen feet long, a pair of which remain, exciting the wonder and admiration of the modern traveler. The mound in which they have been buried for more than twenty-five centuries is fifty feet high, through which the explorers have tunneled to the chambers and to the outer entrance, where the gigantic sculptures now are seen. How impressive the sight of these half-human, half-animal, mysterious creatures, the creation of the genius of the past, and the embodiment of a faith of which so little is now known! The workmanship is extraordinary, and not altogether unworthy of Greece. The sentiment impressed on the marble is grand: the human head represents intelligence; the body of the bull illustrates strength; the

A WINGED BULL.

wings of the eagle symbolize ubiquity; and thus we have here three attributes of Deity—omniscience, omnipotence, and omnipresence. The lofty head-dress, the richly ornamented rosettes, the wide-spreading wings which rise above their backs, and the curled hair which profusely adorns their bodies, indicate a taste and finish not elsewhere seen. Behind them are colossal winged figures of the same height, each bearing the traditional pine-cone and basket. Their human faces are in full, and the relief is high and bold. On all these figures, and on the great slabs near them, are the cuneiform inscriptions cleanly cut, and still distinct. Was it not of these grand portals Nahum said, "The gates of thy land shall be set wide open unto thine enemies?"* And what the enemies spared, time is gradually destroying. The motley marble of Mosul, out of which they are sculptured, is yielding to the elements, after a burial of so many centuries. The face of the great image on the right remains quite perfect, and is remarkable for its fullness of expression; but the body is broken through the centre, and will soon fall to pieces. Its companion figure is much more injured; except the massive beard, the head is gone; and there are large cracks in its marble sides. It has been suggested that this splendid gateway was in process of completion when Sennacherib was murdered by his sons, which may account in part for the apparent fact that the great work was left by the sculptor incomplete.

Of the two principal mounds within the ancient inclosure, that which is known as Nebbi-Yunus is the smaller and less explored. Loftier and steeper than its companion, it is a triangular area of forty acres. If an artificial mound, it is estimated that it required the labor of ten thousand men during five years to complete it. It has a deep depression in the middle, on one side of which is a Moslem cemetery, and on the other side is a small village of Kurds and Turcomans, to whom the hill belongs. The most conspicuous object on the mound is the mosque,

---

* Nahum iii., 13.

beneath which is the traditional tomb of the prophet Jonah. Although the fanaticism of the Moslems is a bar to thorough explorations, yet sufficient antiquities have been discovered to confirm the opinion that the mound is the site of more than one Assyrian palace yet to be exhumed when the power of the Turk is broken, and the people are ruled by an intelligent and liberal government. Among the relics found there were inscribed

TOMB OF THE PROPHET JONAH, AND THE RIVER KHAUSSER.

tablets, a pair of colossal human-headed bulls, two figures of the Assyrian Hercules slaying the lion, and the walls of an antique chamber. These, however, are but the promise of richer results, which the impatient explorer is now anticipating with confidence and delight.

Half a mile to the north-west is the larger of the two mounds of Kuyunjik. The river Khausser flows near its south-eastern base. It is nearly a mile and a half in circumference, and is ninety-five feet high at its south-east corner. The area is equal to a hundred acres, and ap-

PALACE OF SENNACHERIB RESTORED.

pears to be a mass of transported earth. If artificial, it occupied twenty thousand men six years to complete the platform. Its flat summit is annually plowed, which is the fulfillment of prophecy. The rains of the centuries have cut deep ravines down its sides, which are now channels for the torrents in the rainy season. On the northern end is a ruined village; near it is the white tomb of some Moslem saint; and between the village and the tomb is the broad, steep road that leads to the summit.

Ascending the beaten path in company with Mr. Hormuzd Rassam, the distinguished explorer, we were soon within the excavated palace of the renowned Sennacherib. The great structure had been uncovered by Mr. Layard, so that we could now traverse its spacious courts, its lengthened halls, its many rooms, and examine with admiration its beautiful bass-reliefs, and contemplate its grand façades. It stood on an artificial platform ninety feet high, which was covered with a pavement of bricks. The public and private apartments were connected by a noble corridor two hundred and eighteen feet long and twenty-five feet wide, from which passage-ways led into the public courts, and from the latter other passage-ways led into the king's seraglio. From the two chief entrances extended immense halls, whose length was not less than one hundred and eighty feet, and whose width measured forty feet. From these halls were the entrances into the twenty large rooms and into the fifty smaller ones, all of which were elegantly adorned with sculptures in relief. When complete, with all its terraces, façades, courts, halls, and rooms, the grand palace covered an area equal to eight acres of ground. Lofty flights of marble steps led up to the three façades—one on the north-east, one on the south-east, and the third on the south-west;

BASS-RELIEFS.

and each of these magnificent entrances was ornamented by five pairs of human-headed bulls and lions and other colossal figures. It is supposed that the western face of the palace overlooked the Tigris, which once washed the

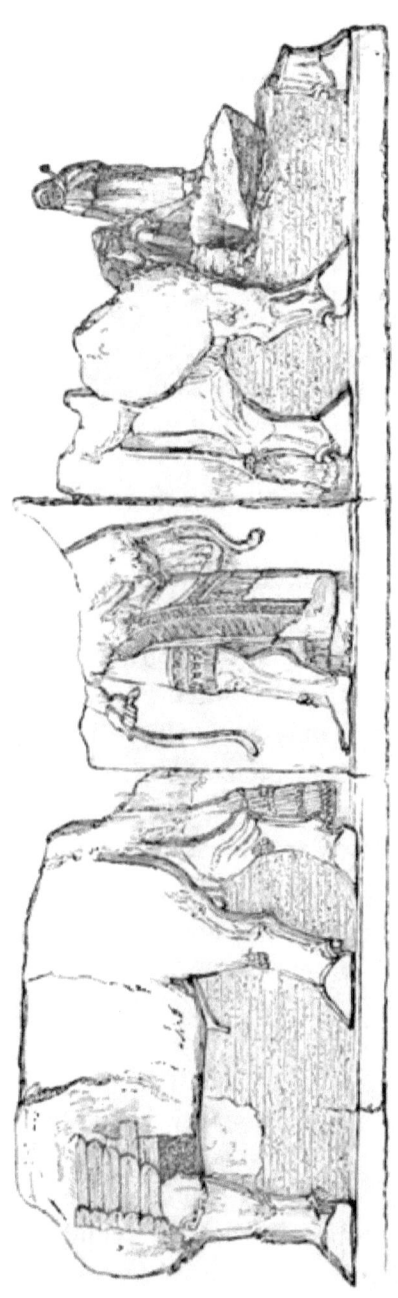
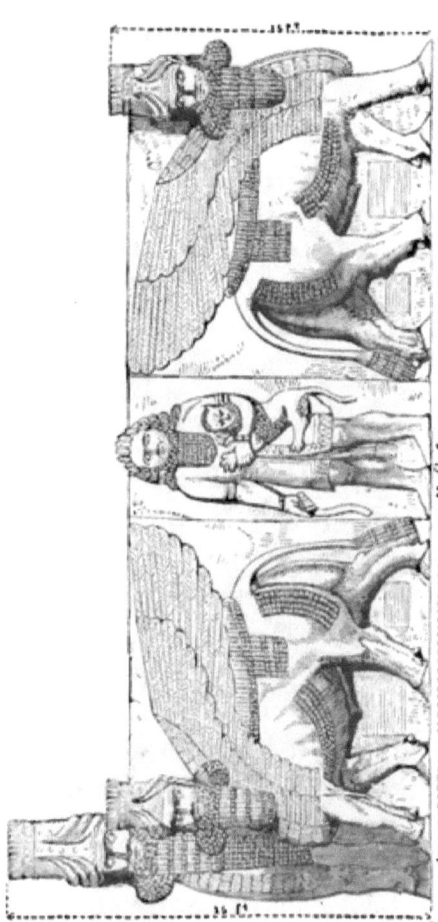
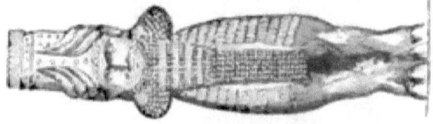

base of the great platform, and which was reached by an inclined way, or steps, leading down to the water's edge. But the principal approach to the royal abode was on the eastern side, where the great bulls were found bearing the inscribed annals of Sennacherib.

From this eastern entrance we passed through the halls and larger rooms of the deserted palace, and experienced an enthusiasm which language is inadequate to express. Many of the bass-reliefs remain in their original positions, and evince a degree of perfection in sculpture not excelled in later times. There is more of the picturesque in these than in those at Nimroud, and a greater fullness of detail. The sculptor sought to transfer to the marble the landscape where occurred the historic events he aimed to portray. The high mountain, the extended plain, the flowing river, the spreading palm, the rugged rocks, the embattled city, the contending armies, are traced with marvelous reality. On the walls of one hall is sculptured a lofty mountain covered with trees, and at its base a broad and flowing river, filled with fish, whose motion in the water is almost perceptible. On the walls of other apartments through which we passed are portrayed battle-scenes; triumphal processions; captives taken in war; superb horses led by grooms; the Tigris, wherein fish are swimming; a garden, wherein are fruitful trees and blooming flowers; a palm with six branches; and gigantic human-headed lions, whose sides are covered with the arrow-headed characters.

When in its glory, this palace was an art-gallery, on whose walls were sculptured in relief the national and domestic life of the Ninevites; their religious ceremonies; their hunting-scenes; their mechanical arts; the natural history of their country; their methods of warfare; the chief incidents in their famous battles; the treatment of captives taken in war; their military equipments; their domestic and public architecture; their modes of navigation; their ornaments in glass, ivory, metals, and pottery; their household furniture; their musical instruments, such as the harp and the lyre; the variety of their food and style of cooking; their implements of agriculture; their festal scenes; the ornaments worn by the ladies; the private life of the king, and the royal honors paid him at court and on his return from victorious war. So numerous were the bass-reliefs in this magnificent palace, that, were they arranged in order, their aggregated length would not be less than two miles; and to these should be added the colossal winged lions, bulls, and sphinxes which adorned the twenty-seven portals that have been discovered. By a careful study of these sculptures, it was easy to learn what were the birds, the beasts, the fishes, the plants and flowers, the minerals and metals, the topography and landscape scenery of Assyria; the size and features of the people; the style of the costumes worn; and the peculiar features of the government of the Ninevites.

On the northern wall of the great hall of the palace were a series of reliefs, which convey to the mind the skill of the artist and the state of mechanical science which then obtained. They represent the process of transporting the great human-headed lions from the quarry whence the marble was taken to the place for which it was designed. There is the low, flat-bottomed boat floating on the river which conveyed the huge mass to a point opposite the city; there are the strong cables by which it is held in its place, and to which are attached smaller ropes held by a large body of men, who are tracking the boat to its destination; there are the

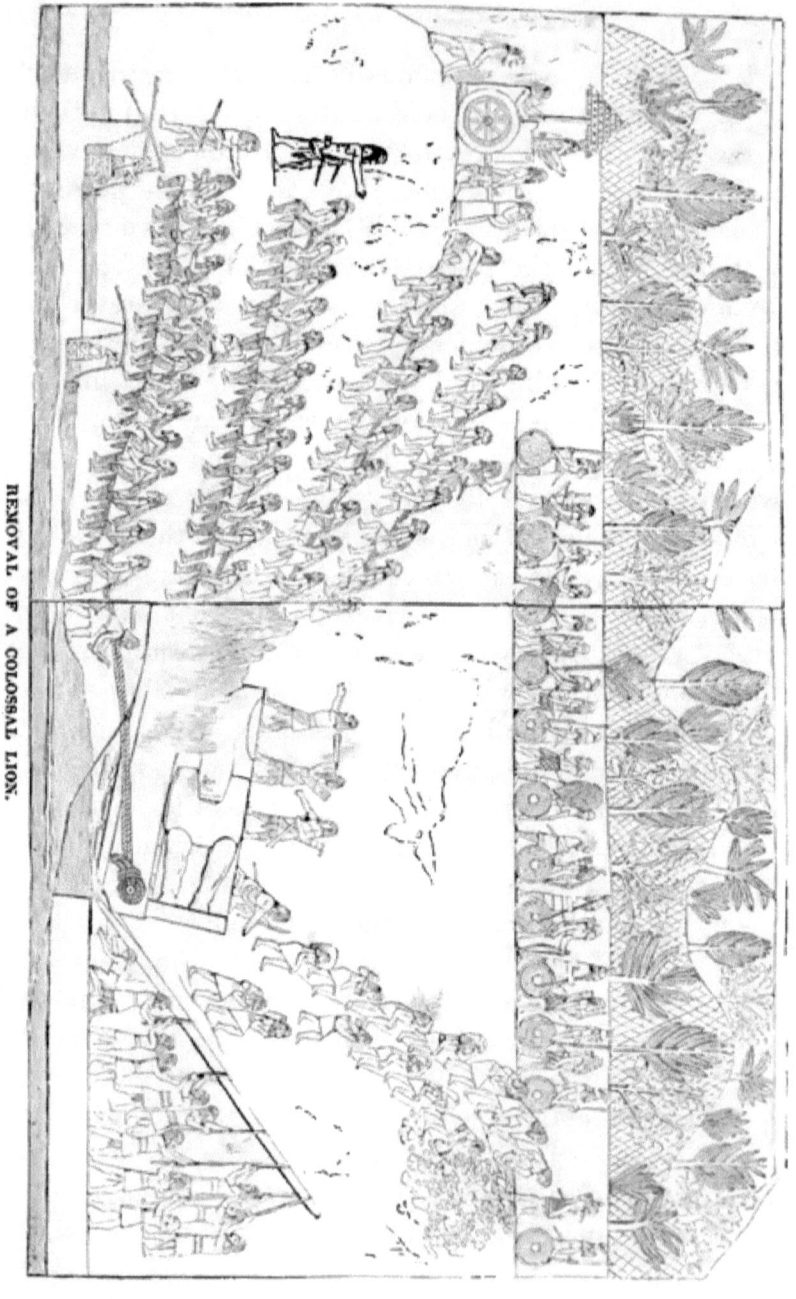

REMOVAL OF A COLOSSAL LION.

task-masters, armed with swords, who are placed over the captives; and seated astride the stone is the overseer, whose outstretched hands indicate that he is issuing his commands; there is the sledge on the river-bank on which the sculptured block is placed, to be hauled to its place in the palace. The sledge is impelled by levers, and dragged by men, over whose shoulders the ropes are passed. Beneath the sledge are placed rollers, to facilitate the motion; and there is depicted the whole process by which the great image is elevated to its pedestal, by means of props, the wedge, the lever, and the pulley, with which the Assyrians were acquainted.

In another hall was portrayed, with equal spirit and greater detail, the siege of Lachish by Sennacherib and his mighty army. The scene is in the land of the fig and the vine. The besieged city is defended by double walls, with embattled towers and strong outworks. The warriors are drawn up before the beleaguered town: some are archers, some spearmen, some slingers. From the castellated towers, the besieged are hurling javelins, stones, fire-brands, and discharging arrows on their enemies. Undaunted, the Assyrians seek to scale the walls by means of ladders; and, to intimidate their enemies, they are impaling those who have fallen into their hands. At length the city capitulates, and in long processions the captives are marched out, and brought before the king, who is seated on a gorgeous throne.

It was while the occupant of this stupendous and gorgeous palace that Sennacherib was murdered by his sons, Sharezer and Adrammelech. The great king was worshiping in the temple of his patron deity, when the parricides dispatched their father, impatient to wear his crown. And thus perished in an evil hour the most celebrated of all the Assyrian kings. Proud and haughty, self-confident and fearless, he displayed a strength of will and a fertility of genius beyond all his predecessors. Ascending the throne in B.C. 705, his prosperous reign lasted through a quarter of a century. By his military prowess, he excited a sense of dread in the minds of his most formidable enemies; he enlarged the limits of his dominions, and created for himself an imperishable name. Egypt and Ethiopia, Susiana and Babylon, Syria and Palestine, felt the power of his arms. He is best known to the general reader by his expedition against Hezekiah, King of Judah. Crossing the Tigris and the Euphrates with an immense army, he descended from the Lebanons to the Mediterranean, and seized Phœnicia. By the dread his arms inspired, all the petty monarchs of the coast hastened to pay the tributes which they had dared to withhold. Tyre and Sidon, Sarepta and Joppa, Ashdod and Ascalon, Hazor and Beth-dagon, were taken by the conqueror. But the King of Ekron had presumed to defy the coming of the Assyrians. He had for his allies the Egyptians and Ethiopians, whose combined forces were posted at the city of Eltekeh, mentioned by Joshua as a city of the Levites.* The battle was long and bloody, and resulted

SENNACHERIB ON HIS THRONE.

---

* Joshua xix., 44.

PLACING A HUMAN-HEADED BULL IN POSITION.

in an overwhelming defeat of the confederated kings. The spoils of the victors were vast and rich. Thousands of captives were sold as slaves. The princes captured were slain, and their bodies exposed on stakes around the whole circuit of the walls of the city; and the imperial city of Ekron opened its gates to the victor.

Flushed with success, determined and revengeful, intent on the punishment of all who had opposed his authority, Sennacherib prepared to measure arms with King Hezekiah. It appears from history that the citizens of Ekron had deposed King Padi, who had been loyal to Assyria, and had sent him in chains to Hezekiah for safe-keeping. Having accepted the charge of the deposed king, Hezekiah had thereby become party to the rebellion of the Ekronites against their Assyrian master. To punish the King of Judah for this complicity, and to compel him to surrender the person of Padi, was the double object of Sennacherib in invading Judea.

From the gates of Ekron the King of Assyria marched to attack Jerusalem. On his way he captured many smaller cities, and took not less than two hundred thousand captives. Having reached the Holy City, he besieged it with a determination which alarmed Hezekiah and all his men of war. Fearing a disastrous issue of a persistent resistance, Hezekiah concluded to surrender conditionally, and his proposal was at once accepted by Sennacherib. He consented to surrender Padi, and to pay an enormous tribute in gold and silver and the chief treasures of his palace.

The terms of the capitulation are recorded in the Bible and in the Assyrian annals, which records agree in a most remarkable manner. In the Second Book of Kings it is said: "Now in the fourteenth year of king

Hezekiah did Sennacherib king of Assyria come up against all the fenced cities of Judah, and took them. And Hezekiah king of Judah sent to the king of Assyria to Lachish, saying, I have offended; return from me: that which thou puttest on me will I bear. And the king of Assyria appointed unto Hezekiah king of Judah three hundred talents of silver and thirty talents of gold. And Hezekiah gave him all the silver that was found in the house of the Lord, and in the treasures of the king's house. At that time did Hezekiah cut off the gold from the doors of the temple of the Lord, and from the pillars which Hezekiah king of Judah had overlaid, and gave it to the king of Assyria."*

INSCRIBED TABLETS.

Among the ruins of the palace of Sennacherib were found the inscribed annals of his reign. They cover a period in all of sixty-six years, and consist of three

---

* 2 Kings xviii., 13-16.

separate records. The first consists of inscriptions on the winged bulls which ornamented one of the grand façades, and extend over a period of six years; the second is inscribed on a large barrel-shaped terra-cotta cylinder, embracing two years; and the third is engraved on a hexagonal cylinder of the same material, and includes eight years in all. These several records have been deciphered by those thoroughly versed in the translation of the cuneiform characters, and their translations are accepted as correct.

INSCRIPTIONS ON THE WINGED BULLS.

The account of his campaign against Hezekiah is supposed to have been written by Sennacherib himself, and is as follows: "Because Hezekiah, king of Judah, would not submit to my yoke, I came up against him, and by force of arms and by the might of my power I took forty-six of his strong fenced cities; and of the smaller towns which were scattered about I took and plundered a countless number. And from these places I captured and carried off as spoil two hundred thousand one hundred and fifty people, old and young, male and female, together with horses and mares, asses and camels, oxen and sheep, a countless multitude. And Hezekiah himself I shut in Jerusalem, his capital city, like a bird in a cage, building towers round the city to hem him in, and raising banks of earth against the gates, so as to prevent escape..... Then upon this Hezekiah there fell the fear of my arms, and he sent out to me the chiefs and the elders of Jerusalem with thirty talents of gold and eight hundred talents of silver, and divers treasures, a rich and immense booty..... All these things were brought to me at Nineveh, the seat of my government, Hezekiah having sent them by way of tribute, and as a token of his submission to my power."*

The agreement between these two independent accounts is one of the most remarkable coincidences of historic testimony on record, and mutually prove the general accuracy of the translations of the Biblical and Assyrian records. The principal discrepancy relates to the amount of treasure demanded and given. Both statements correspond as to the amount of gold, but there is a difference of five hundred talents in the amount of silver, which may be accounted for on one of two suppositions: Sennacherib gives the sum demanded; the Bible gives the sum paid; or, the Bible account includes the actual amount of money to have been three hundred talents of silver, while the Assyrian records comprise all the precious metal received.

In less than two years after his return in triumph, Sennacherib was again in Palestine. His frontier on the south-west was threatened by Egypt, which claimed dominion to Lachish on the extreme verge of the Holy

---

* Translation by Sir Henry Rawlinson.

Land. He therefore besieged Lachish "with all his power," and determined to crush, if possible, an enemy which had disputed his right to hold in vassalage the kingdoms that bordered on the Mediterranean. The example of Egypt had revived the hopes of Hezekiah, who had thrown off his allegiance to Sennacherib, and had entered into an alliance with the Egyptians. Sennacherib had, therefore, a twofold object to accomplish in his second expedition to Palestine. To have his authority respected, he must reduce Hezekiah to a state of helpless submission, and must crush with a blow the daring Sethos, a powerful prince who ruled in Lower Egypt. While engaged in the siege of Lachish, he dispatched Rab-shakeh, his chief cup-bearer, and Rabsaris, his chief eunuch, to summon Hezekiah to an unconditional surrender. These two high officers of his court were supported by a strong body of troops, under the command of Tartan. Their coming alarmed the king, and sent consternation to the hearts of the people of the Holy City. Standing "by the conduit of the upper pool, which is in the highway of the fuller's field," Rab-shakeh addressed the king's messengers in most uncourtly terms, and then sought to excite the popular fears and hopes by a direct appeal to the people. "But the people held their peace, and answered him not a word." Unable to take the city by the force under Tartan, and disappointed in the effect of his eloquent blasphemy, Rab-shakeh and his colleagues returned to report their ill-success to their royal master. Sennacherib, however, resolved to make another effort to overcome the obstinacy of Hezekiah, and accordingly sent him an autograph letter, in which he warned him not to trust in God, who could not save him. "And Hezekiah received the letter of the hand of the messengers, and read it: and Hezekiah went up into the house of the

Lord, and spread it before the Lord," and prayed: "Lord, bow down thine ear, and hear: open, Lord, thine eyes, and see: and hear the words of Sennacherib, which hath sent him to reproach the living God." The king's prayer prevailed. Isaiah was commissioned to allay the fears of the good Hezekiah, and to assure him: "I will defend this city, to save it, for mine own sake, and for my servant David's sake," and " I will put my hook into the nose of Sennacherib and my bridle into his lips, and I will turn him back by the way he came." "He shall not come into this city, nor shoot an arrow there, nor come before it with shield, nor cast a bank against it. By the way that he came, by the same shall he return, and shall not come into this city, saith the Lord."*

These prophetic words received a fulfillment beyond their seeming scope. From Lachish and Libnah, Sennacherib advanced to Pelusium, where Sethos was encamped with his Egyptian host. The time was probably coincident with the prayer of Hezekiah in the house of the Lord. The day had declined, and the shadows of night were falling on the embattled hosts. The morrow was to be the day of battle. To the coming of that morn the Egyptians looked forward with anxious fears; the Assyrians, with confidence as to the issues of the combat. But no morrow was to come to the hosts sleeping peacefully in the tents of Assyria. "And it came to pass that night, that the angel of the Lord went out, and smote in the camp of the Assyrians a hundred fourscore and five thousand: and when they arose early in the morning, behold, they were all dead corpses."†

From that unfought battle Sennacherib returned to Nineveh shorn of his glory, and leaving, as the ghastly

---

* 2 Kings xix.   † 2 Kings xix., 35.

JEWISH CAPTIVES.

monument of his defeat, one hundred and eighty-five thousand Assyrian corpses, to be swept by the simoom and devoured by the vulture and hyena. It is not strange that he has left no record of that terrible reverse to his military success. His annals thereon are silent as the voiceless dead he had abandoned unburied. He would not perpetuate the memory of his own overthrow. Jerusalem and Pelusium were cities to be forgotten. Hezekiah and Sethos were names to be consigned to oblivion. In all time to come, the West was to be avoided as the land of ill-fortune. He was content to hand down to coming generations that he had compelled Hezekiah to pay him tribute, and to have sculptured on the walls of his palace the forms of the Jewish captives taken in a previous campaign. His subsequent years were spent in wars against Babylon, Susiana, and Cilicia; and his obituary is thus written by the inspired penman: "And it came to pass, as Sennacherib was worshiping in the house of Nisroch his god, that Adrammelech and Sharezer his sons smote him with the sword."*

---

* 2 Kings xix., 37.

Among the ruins of his palace was found his will, which is considered the earliest copy of a will extant. The translation is as follows: "Sennacherib, king of multitudes, King of Assyria, has given chains of gold, stores of ivory, a cup of gold, crowns and chains besides, all the riches, of which there are heaps, crystal and another precious stone and bird's stone: one and a half manchs, two and a half cibi, according to their weight: to Esarhaddon my son, who was afterward named Asshur-ebil-mucin-pal, according to my wish; the treasure of the Temple of Amuk and Nebo-irik-erba, the harpists of Nebo."*

From the palace of Sennacherib, we passed a few hundred yards to the north-west, and entered the long, deep trenches which had been made to uncover the once magnificent palace of Asshur-bani-pal, the grandson of Sennacherib, and the Sardanapalus of the Greeks and Romans. The honor of discovering the site of this celebrated structure belongs to Mr. Hormuzd Rassam, who was our mentor on this interesting occasion. The royal structure resembled in general outline a gigantic cross, and it is supposed that in the western arm thereof were the private apartments of the monarch. Here was a grand hall, one hundred and forty-five feet long and thirty feet wide, which opened into a large court paved with slabs, on which were traced designs of exquisite beauty. From this court there were openings into smaller rooms, and on the south and south-west of these was a second spacious court. In the eastern arm of the cross was a grand hall, one hundred and eight feet in length and twenty-four feet in breadth, in the centre of which was a door-way that opened into a square ante-

---

* "Records of the Past," vol. i., p. 136.

chamber, and into another apartment eighty feet long. The central portion of the building was reached by a long, ascending gallery adorned with sculptures, and at the entrance of which was a gate-way of extraordinary beauty. No other Assyrian palace was comparable to this in the elaborate character and elegant finish of its ornamentation. The flowery pavement of the courts, the rosetted ceilings of the arched door-ways, the minute and delicate reliefs on alabaster slabs that lined the walls of hall and court and chamber, imparted to the whole an elegance nowhere else apparent in Nineveh.

And the sculptures in relief expressed the tastes of the king. He loved flowers and trees and birds; he was fond of the chase; he delighted in aquatic sports, and had them portrayed on the marble. As a hunter, he excelled all his royal predecessors. He hunted the stag, the gazelle, the wild ass, and the lion. He is represented as hunting in the parks attached to his palace, wherein lions were kept in cages, and turned loose for him to kill. Now he hunts from his chariot; anon, on horseback; again, on foot. Now he is attended by armed warriors and protected by a shield, and dead and dying lions lie scattered around him, transfixed with his arrows. In moments of greater daring, he is on foot in single-handed combat with the lion, who is speared by the kingly hunter. The return from the hunt is celebrated by music, and by the king pouring a libation on the body of a dead lion. Although living in a country where the seclusion of woman is a proverb, yet he so far disregarded the conventional customs of society as to have his queen represented as being present at some royal banquet. Nor did he fail to perpetuate the sadder, grander details of war. The assault and the defense, the flight and the pursuit, the gathering of the spoils,

TORTURING THE CAPTIVES.

the capture and cruel treatment of the prisoners, are delineated with a master's hand.

Coming to the throne in the year 668 B.C., he was ambitious to enlarge his dominions and subdue all his enemies. He pursued the fugitive Tirhakah from Memphis to Thebes, and compelled Urdamane to fly in the same direction. Having marched in triumph along the Syrian coast, he crossed the Taurus range, and penetrated Asia Minor to a point never before visited by an Assyrian monarch. Elam, Chaldea, and Arabia felt the power of his arms, and yielded to a warrior whom it was madness to oppose. But his familiarity with blood in war and in the chase made him cruel and vindictive. He practiced tortures, mutilations, and executions on the prisoners he took in battle, and perpetuated his modes of extreme punishment in the bass-reliefs on his palace walls. Thereon may be seen the helpless captive thrust through with a spear, and his tongue torn from his mouth; a conquered king beheaded on the field of battle; a prisoner led to execution with the head of a friend suspended about his neck; a captive flayed alive; and the victors returning home, each one holding by its hair the head of some less fortunate combatant. No marvel the prophet called Nineveh "a bloody city."

It is a venerable saying, and confirmed by all history, that "with what measure ye mete, it shall be measured to you again." The sword of conquest was to pass into other hands. The day of retribution had come. Asshur-bani-pal was to witness the decline of a monarchy which he had crowned with glory. The end of his great empire was at hand, not from inherent weakness or premature decay, but from a combination of circumstances, which he was powerless to resist. Coming from the frozen regions of the North, the brave, the cruel, the countless Scythians overran the richest portions of Assyria, besieged and plundered many of the oldest cities, rich in the accumulated stores of ages, and wantonly burned the noblest palace of the empire. They found it a garden; they left it a wilderness. In their barbarous cruelty, they flayed their enemies alive; they drank their blood; they stripped the scalp from the skull, to be a trophy on their horse's bridle, and of the skull they made a drinking-cup. Against such a foe, Asshur-bani-pal could not successfully contend. But he was permitted to see the departure of an invader he had failed to conquer. Although aged, he might have restored his empire to somewhat of its former greatness; but, after a reign of forty-two years, he died, and was succeeded by his son Saracus, destined to be the last king of ancient and renowned Assyria.

The enemies of the father were the enemies of the son. The Medes were prepared to renew their effort for the conquest of the Assyrian empire. Their leader was the skillful and daring Cyaxares, who had for his allies the Susianians, so often defeated by the kings of Assyria. To provide against the impending danger, Saracus resolved to command in person the defenses of his capital, and to dispatch his general, Nabopolassar, to Babylon, to defend the provinces of the South. But the young king had not provided against a foe in the person of his chosen general. Taking advantage of the difficulties that surrounded his monarch, Nabopolassar joined the allies, and received as a reward for his treachery the daughter of the Median king, to be the wife of his eldest son, the celebrated Nebuchadnezzar. The forces of the allies, under the joint command of Cyaxares and Nabopolassar, marched against Nineveh, and besieged the imperial city. Never was a beleaguered town more bravely defended. If we may credit Diodorus, the allied army numbered more than four hundred thousand. The siege lasted during three years. In the third year, the floods accomplished what the enemy had failed to effect. Superstition hastened a result which embattled hosts could not attain. The king gave heed to an oracle which had told him to fear nothing till the river became his enemy. The swollen and overflowing Tigris had destroyed two miles of the city wall. The oracle was revered as divine. Bereft of faith, conscious that all the means of resistance were exhausted, and inspired by despair, Saracus resolved to burn his palace, and perish in the flames thereof. Amidst the smoke and flame of the royal abode, the allied forces entered the city on the side which the floods had breached, and, having plundered it of its wealth, left it a desolation.

Two Hebrew prophets had foretold the fall of the empire, the destruction of the capital, and the present desolate appearance of the site thereof. In a strain of invective, astonishing for its richness, variety, and energy, the seer of Elkosh had denounced the Assyrians, and described the capture and destruction of Nineveh. His prophecy is "The Burden of Nineveh;" wherein he says, "I will make thy grave, for thou art vile;" and, "Woe to the bloody city! it is all full of lies and robbery." Its hunting-parks and royal menageries, wherein the kings indulged in the pleasures of the chase, are referred to in designation of the place: "Where is the dwelling of the lions, and the feeding-place of the young lions, where the lion, even the old lion, walked, and the lion's whelp, and none made them afraid?" As if he himself were there, he repeats the orders to prepare to resist the approaching foe: "Draw thee waters for the siege, fortify thy strongholds; go into clay, and tread the mortar, make strong the brickkiln." So vivid is his description of the struggle that ensued, that one can almost see and hear what then transpired: "The shield of his mighty men is made red, the valiant men are in scarlet: the chariots shall be with flaming torches in the day of his preparation, and the fir-trees shall be terribly shaken. The chariots shall rage in the streets, they shall justle one against another in the broad ways: they shall seem like torches, they shall run like the lightnings. He shall recount his worthies: they shall stumble in their walk; they shall make haste to the wall thereof, and the defense shall be prepared." Bridging over, as it were, the intervening century, the prophet is an eye-witness to the taking of the city, and chronicles aforehand what subsequently occurred. Did the floods destroy the river wall of the city? "The gates of the rivers shall be opened, and the palace shall be dissolved." "The gates of thy land shall be set wide open unto thine enemies." Did Saracus burn his palace? "There shall the fire devour thee." "The fire shall devour thy bars." "The palace shall be dissolved." Was there a panic in the captured city? "Stand, stand, shall they cry; but none shall look back." Were the victors enriched by the booty taken? "Take ye the spoil of silver, take the spoil of gold: for there is none end of the store and glory out of all the pleasant furniture." And the prophetic vision is projected far beyond the time of the siege, and the traveler of to-day is the witness to the fulfillment thereof in the desolation he beholds. "Nineveh is laid waste." "Thy people is scattered upon the mountains, and no man gathereth them." Where once the proud city stood, a marsh is created by the overflow of the Tigris and the Khausser. "But Nineveh of old is like a pool of water."* Where formerly were the garden-homes of the Ninevites, between Kuyunjik and Nimroud, are now pasture-fields whereon the Arab shepherd feeds his sheep and goats. "And flocks shall lie down in the midst of her." And at the great centres, where were the magnificent palaces of the kings, where the "rejoicing city dwelt carelessly, and said in her heart, I am, and there is none beside me," *there* "is she become a desolation, a place for beasts to lie down in! every one that passeth by her shall hiss, and wag his hand."†

---

* Book of Nahum. † Zephaniah ii., 14, 15.

CHAPTER VI.

Discovery of the Royal Library of Asshur-bani-pal.—Rawlinson on the Nature and Style of Assyrian Writing.—Eminent Cuneiform Scholars.—Layard's History of the Process of Deciphering the Cuneiform Characters.—Triumphant Success.—Specimens of the Translated Tablets.—Promissory Note.—Bill for the Sale of Slaves.—Deed of Conveyance.—Religious Views of the Assyrians.—Forms of Prayer.—Death of a Righteous Man.—Harmony between the Bible and the Assyrian Records.—Daniel in the Lion's Den, and his Companions in the Fiery Furnace.—Modes of Punishment.—Chaldean Account of the Creation and of the Deluge by Berosus.—Original Account of the Flood by the Assyrians, Discovered by Mr. Smith, and his more recent Translation of the Same.—Copy of the Record.—Its Agreement and Disagreement with the Bible.—Probable Future Discoveries, and their Bearing on Biblical Interpretation.—What the United States should do in the Work of Exploration.

TWENTY-FIVE hundred years after the destruction of the palace of Asshur-bani-pal, there was exhumed from the ruins thereof his "Royal Library." Consisting of more than twenty thousand inscribed terra-cotta tablets and fragments of tablets, it contains the records of the past, and evinces the literary taste of a king who excelled all his kingly predecessors in his love of learning, and in the advancement of the same. In the adjoining palace of his grandfather, Sennacherib, there had also been discovered a chamber, whose floor was covered with similar tablets to the height of a foot, and which room is supposed to have been the depository for such earthen documents. Some are broken, but many are entire; and the inscriptions thereon are as distinct to-day as when the impression was made upon the plastic clay. Some are slightly convex, and an inch in length; others are flat, and measure nine inches in length and six inches in breadth. They contain comparative vocabularies, lists of deities and their epithets, chronological tables of kings, records of astronomical observations, grammars, histories, scientific works of various kinds, and royal decrees. Others contain the names of the months, a list of weights and measures, the Assyrian calendar, a code of laws, a table of square roots, private business contracts, prayers for protection against the Evil Spirit, omens, hymns, the religious belief of the Assyrians, the movements of the planet Venus, the eclipses of the moon, the vernal equinox, royal-birth portents, the names of tributary cities, the annals of Sennacherib's invasion of Judea, and the Assyrian account of the Deluge.

Many of the fragments have been put together by patient and laborious scholars, and, having arranged the broken parts, they have successfully translated the inscriptions thereon. From these deciphered records, we are permitted to form a general idea of the manners and customs, of the arts and literature, of the religion and history, of a people of whose remarkable civilization we have hitherto known but little. And, inferring the future from the past, we may confidently look for additional information as the work of cuneiform translation is successfully advanced.

"We may now proceed to consider the style and nature of the Assyrian writing. Derived evidently from the Chaldean, it is far less archaic in type, presenting no pictorial representations of objects, and but a few characters where the pictorial representation can be traced. It is in no case wholly rectilinear; and indeed preserves the straight line only in a very few characters, as in ⌐▼ for 'house,' ▭▼ for 'gate,' ▣ for 'temple, altar,' and ▷ for 'fish,' all which are in the latter inscriptions superseded by simpler forms. The wedge may thus be said to be almost the sole element of the writing—the wedge, however, under a great variety of forms—sometimes greatly elongated, as thus ▶︎, sometimes contracted to a triangle ▶, sometimes broadened out ▶, sometimes doubled in such a way as to form an arrowhead ◁, and placed in every direction—horizontal, perpendicular, and diagonal.

"The number of characters is very great. Sir H. Rawlinson, in the year 1851, published a list of two hundred and forty-six, or, including variants, three hundred and sixty-six characters, as occurring in the inscriptions known to him. M. Oppert, in 1858, gave three hundred and eighteen forms as those 'most in use.' Of course it is at once evident that this alphabet can not represent elementary sounds. The Assyrian characters do, in fact, correspond, not to letters, according to our notion of letters, but to syllables. These syllables are either mere vowel sounds, such as we represent by our vowels and diphthongs, or such sounds accompanied by one or two consonants. The vowels are not very numerous. The Assyrians recognize three only as fundamental—*a*, *i*, and *u*. Besides these they have the diphthongs *ai*, nearly equivalent to *e;* and *au*, nearly equivalent to *o*. The vowels *i* and *u* have also the powers, respectively, of *y* and *v*.

"The consonant sounds recognized in the language are sixteen in number. They are the labial, guttural, and dental *tenues*, *p, k, t;* the labial, guttural, and dental *mediæ, b, g, d;* the guttural and dental aspirates, *kh* (= Heb. ח) and *th* (= Greek θ); the liquids *l, m, n, r;* and the sibilants *s, sh* (= Heb. שׁ), *ts* (= Heb. צ), and *z*. The system here is nearly that of the Hebrew, from which it differs only by the absence of the simple aspirate ה, of the guttural ע, and of the aspirated פ (*ph*). It has no sound which the Hebrew has not.

"From these sounds, combined with the simple vowels, comes the Assyrian syllabarium, to which, and not to the consonants themselves, the characters were assigned. In the first place, each consonant being capable of two combinations with each simple vowel, could give birth naturally to six simple syllables, each of which would be in the Assyrian system represented by a character. Six characters, for instance, entirely different from one another, represented *pa, pi, pu, ap, ip, up;* six others, *ka, ki, ku, ak, ik, uk;* six others, again, *ta, ti, tu, at, it, ut.* If this rule were carried out in every case, the sixteen consonant sounds would, it is evident, produce ninety-six characters. The actual number, however, found in this way is only seventy-five, since there are seven of the consonants which only combine with the vowels in one way. Thus we have *ba, bi, bu,* but not *ab, ib, ub; ga, gi, gu,* but not *ag, ig, ug;* and so on. The sounds regarded as capable of only one combination are the *mediæ, b, g, d;* the aspirates *kh, th;* the sibilants *ts* and *z.*

"Such is the first and simplest syllabarium: but the Assyrian system does not stop here. It proceeds to combine with each simple vowel sounds two consonants, one preceding the vowel, and the other following it. If this plan were followed out to the utmost possible extent, the result would be an addition to the syllabarium of seven hundred and sixty-eight sounds, each having its proper character, which would raise the number of characters to between eight and nine hundred! Fortunately for the student, phonetic laws and other causes have intervened to check this extreme luxuriance; and the combinations of this kind which are known to exist, instead of amounting to the full limit of seven hundred and sixty-eight, are under one hundred and fifty. The known Assyrian alphabet is, however, in this way raised from eighty, or, including variants, one hundred, to between two hundred and forty and two hundred and fifty characters.

"Further, there is another kind of character, quite different from these, which Orientalists have called 'determinatives.' Certain classes of words have a sign prefixed or suffixed to them, most commonly the former, by which their general character is indicated. The names of gods, of men, of cities, of tribes, of wild animals, of domestic animals, of metals, of months, of the points of the compass, and of dignities, are thus accompanied. The sign prefixed or suffixed may have originally represented a word; but when used in the way here spoken of, it is believed that it was not sounded, but served simply to indicate to the reader the sort of word which was placed before him. Thus, a single perpendicular wedge, ⌐, indicates that the next word will be the name of a man; such a wedge, preceded by two horizontal ones, ⊤, tells us to expect the appellative of a god; while other more complicated combinations are used in the remaining instances. There are about ten or twelve characters of this description.

"Finally, there a certain number of characters which have been called 'ideographs,' or 'monograms.' Most of the gods, and various cities and countries, are represented by a group of wedges, which is thought not to have a real phonetic force, but to be a conventional sign for an idea, much as the Arabic numerals, 1, 2, 3, etc., are non-phonetic signs representing the ideas, one, two, three, etc. The known characters of this description are between twenty and thirty.

"The known Assyrian characters are thus brought up

nearly to three hundred! There still remain a considerable number which are either wholly unknown, or of which the meaning is known, while the phonetic value can not at present be determined. M. Oppert's Catalogue contains fourteen of the former and fifty-nine of the latter class.

"It has been already observed that the monumental evidence accords with the traditional belief in regard to the character of the Assyrian language, which is unmistakably Semitic. Not only does the vocabulary present constant analogies to other Semitic dialects, but the phonetic laws and the grammatical forms are equally of this type. At the same time, the language has peculiarities of its own, which separate it from its kindred tongues, and constitute it a distinct form of Semitic speech, not a mere variety of any known form. It is neither Hebrew, nor Arabic, nor Phœnician, nor Chaldee, nor Syriac, but a sister-tongue to these, having some analogies with all of them, and others, more or fewer, with each. On the whole, its closest relationship seems to be with the Hebrew, and its greatest divergence from the Aramaic or Syriac, with which it was yet, locally, in immediate connection."*

But the decipherment of the cuneiform inscriptions on the tablets, the cylinders, the obelisks, the bulls, and walls discovered at Nineveh, required much patient and persistent labor. There were, however, eminent scholars equal to the task; and all honor to Grotefend, Dr. Hinks, M. Oppert, Mr. Norris, Fox Talbot, Sir Henry Rawlinson, G. Smith, and Mr. Layard, who have not only overcome the chief difficulties which beset the subject, but have had the satisfaction to know that their

---

* Rawlinson's "Ancient Monarchies," vol. i., pp. 268-272.

translations have been accepted as reliable. At first all was conjecture; then the process of investigation was purely tentative; but conjecture was superseded by certainty, and the tentative by the demonstrative. Step by step these patient toilers advanced, till results assured them of success. To verify what had been done, translations of the same inscription, but made by different persons, were carefully compared, one with the other, and then compared with the well-ascertained facts of contemporaneous history. By this thorough and honorable method were the translations of the Annals of Sennacherib tested, and which were found substantially correct when compared with the Bible account of his wars against the Jews. And it is no mean compliment to the translators that the French Academy, justly considered the first literary and scientific body in the world, has recognized the progress made, the correctness of the principles upon which the decipherment of the cuneiform inscriptions are based, and the importance of the results already obtained, by recommending one of the foremost of the translators, Dr. Oppert, as entitled to receive the great prize of twenty thousand francs, conferred periodically upon the author who has rendered the greatest service to literature or science. It is to Mr. Layard that we are indebted for the following lucid account of the process and progress in the difficult task of deciphering the Assyrian inscriptions:

"Although our knowledge is far from complete, yet the sculptures and inscriptions have enabled us to put together a part of the skeleton of Assyrian history, and to illustrate to a certain extent the manners, arts, sciences, and literature of the Assyrian people. So much unreasonable incredulity still exists as to the extent to which this has been effected through the interpretation of the cuneiform inscriptions, and the evidence upon which that interpretation rests has been so summarily rejected by English writers of great and deserved authority, that a short account of the history of cuneiform decipherment may be interesting to some of my readers, and may tend to remove those erroneous impressions which exist on the subject.

"The investigation of the arrow-headed character is by no means a new study. It was first seriously attempted in the year 1802 by Grotefend, a learned German scholar. At that time the only materials accessible for this purpose, with the exception of the well-known inscribed bricks from the ruins of Babylon, were the inscriptions carved on rocks, and on the remains of edifices at Persepolis and Hamadan (Ecbatana), and near other ancient sites in Persia. Copies of these inscriptions, more or less accurate, had been brought to Europe by various travelers from the time of Tavernier and Chardin. Fortunately, although short, they afforded the most important materials for breaking ground and taking the first step in the interpretation of the cuneiform character. They are trilingual, that is to say, that the same inscription is repeated three times in a different language and in a different character; but, unfortunately, unlike the trilingual inscription on the celebrated Rosetta stone, which furnishes a key for the decipherment of the Egyptian hieroglyphics, neither the languages nor the characters were previously known to us. The trilingual inscriptions of Persia are generally divided into three parallel columns, or arranged in three distinct tablets, each containing the same inscriptions expressed in a different language, and in a different modification of the cuneiform character—the letters and signs in each column being formed by the same elementary wedges arranged in different combinations or groups. That the inscriptions are the same is evident from the fact of the recurrence of the same groups of letters or words in each column or tablet, at the same regular intervals. I give a copy herewith of one of these trilingual tablets from Persepolis, in order that my readers may understand their nature, and the process by which they are deciphered.

"It will be perceived that the combination of wedges forming a letter or sign differs in each column. The most simple combination, and that which usually takes the place of honor in the first column of these tablets, is only found on monuments of the Persian period; and the language of the in-

SPECIMEN OF A CUNEIFORM INSCRIPTION.

scriptions is allied to the ancient Sanscrit. This is called the Persian cuneiform character. The characters in the second or centre column are commonly called the Median, or, more correctly, the Touranian or Scythic, because they are believed to express a Touranian or Tartar language, one of the then families of languages spoken by the subjects of the ancient Persian kings. The inscriptions of the third column are in a character and language nearly identical with those of the monuments of Nineveh and Babylon. They have been, consequently, termed the Assyrian and the Babylonian, or sometimes the Assyro-Babylonian.

"It will be further observed that in the first, or Persian, column a single oblique arrow-head or wedge constantly recurs. It first occurred to the German scholars, Tychsen and Münter, that this sign might mark the division of words. This conjecture was confirmed by the recurrence of the same group of letters forming a word, sometimes with terminal variations which might indicate case-endings, marked off, as it were, by these single oblique wedges. Instances of this will be perceived in the first and second lines of the inscription which I have given. A comparison of a number of inscriptions led to the further discovery that, while the greater number of words or groups of signs in each were generally the same, certain groups had disappeared, and other groups, which had before appeared in another part of the inscription, had taken their place. These, again, were succeeded by a new group. This circumstance led Grotefend to conjecture that these signs so changing position represented proper names of persons in the relation of father and son, and that when a new king had ascended the throne his name appeared in the place of his predecessor. The name of the grandfather would then disappear altogether, and be replaced by that of the father. For instance, if in one inscription Darius was called the son of Hystaspes, in a second, carved after his death, Xerxes would be called son of Darius, the name of Darius taking the place of that of Hystaspes, which would no longer be found in the inscription.

"This ingenious conjecture led to the discovery of the clue to the decipherment of the inscriptions, and Grotefend assumed that these groups of letters or signs were the names of these very Persian kings. Supposing such to be the case, and admitting that the ancient Persian forms of these names varied considerably from those handed down to us by the Greeks, yet he felt convinced that the value of certain letters in them must be the same. By various tentative processes he satisfied himself that he had hit upon the right names, and that he had determined the proper value of some, if not all, the letters composing them. This enabled him to verify the conjecture, based upon historical evidence, that the language of the inscription was in Indo-Germanic dialect, spoken in Persia at the time of the Macedonian conquest, and allied to the Zend or Sanscrit, and consequently, in a certain degree, to the modern Persian.

"Proceeding always in the same tentative way, Grotefend next attempted a translation of some of the inscriptions, and the results of his investigations and an analysis of his method of interpretation were given in an appendix to Heeren's work on the principal nations of antiquity, which was published in 1815.

"Lassen, Rask, Burnouf, and other eminent Sanscrit and Oriental scholars, applied themselves to the examination of Grotefend's system and his interpretations, bringing to bear upon the inquiry a profounder knowledge of the ancient Indo-Germanic tongues than he claimed to possess, though scarcely more skill and ingenuity as decipherers. Through their labors, what had been at first the result of happy conjecture was reduced to a certainty. It was proved that Grotefend had been mistaken in the value he had assigned to several letters, but that he had been right in his method of interpretation, and in his conjectures of the names of the kings contained in the inscriptions which he had examined.

"The short trilingual inscription which I have given contains the name of Xerxes, and may be translated thus:

KHSHIYÁRSHÁ . KHSHÁYATHIYA . WAZAR-
   Xerxes   the king   great
-KA . KHSHÁYATHIYA . KHSHAYATHIYÁ-
     The king   of kings;
-NÁM . DÁRYAVHAUSH . KHSHÁYATH-
    Of Darius   the king.
-IYAHYÁ . PUTRA . HAKHÁMANISHIYA.
     the son   the Achæmenid.

"Hitherto the materials for the investigation of the cuneiform character had been comparatively limited. The inscriptions copied by travelers in Persia were short, rarely consisting of more than ten or twelve lines, and they were for the most of nearly the same import. A trilingual inscription of great length was known to exist on the rock of Behistun, near Kermanshah, on the western frontiers of Persia; but it was in a position inaccessible to the ordinary traveler, and too high to admit of its being copied from below. Sir Henry Rawlinson was the first to obtain an imperfect transcript of it by the aid of a powerful telescope in the year 1835; but it was not until 1844 that, assisted by Captain Jones, and other gentlemen attached to the mission at Bagdad, he was able to reach the tablets, and to make copies and paper casts of the inscriptions. Like those of Persepolis and Hamadan, they consist of the same record, repeated three times in the three languages spoken by the three great races under the dominion of the Persian kings, and written in different modifications of the cuneiform character. The Persian column contains no less than four hundred and six lines. The application of this great inscription of the key furnished by the short records previously deciphered by Grotefend and other investigators, completely corroborated the soundness of their system of interpretation. The Behistun tablets were found to contain a narrative of the principal events of the reign of Darius, the son of Hystaspes, which, in many respects, coincide with those recorded by the Greek historians. The effigy of the king himself is sculptured on the rock. Behind him stand his attendants, and in front are nine captive kings or chiefs, one of whom lies prostrate at his feet. Above each figure are short trilingual inscriptions, recording the name of the person represented.

"By the aid of the Behistun inscription, which has furnished the most ample and reliable materials we yet possess for the investigation of the cuneiform characters, Sir Henry Rawlinson has been able to add largely to the results obtained by Grotefend, Lassen, Burnouf, and others, from the scanty records in their possession. He published the text of the Persian column, with a complete translation of it, in the 'Journal' of the Royal Asiatic Society for 1846. This translation has been subjected to the most rigorous examination and criticism by Sanscrit scholars; and those who have taken the trouble to acquaint themselves with the subject, and are competent to form an opinion upon it, do not hesitate to admit that the interpretation of the Persian cuneiform is placed beyond a doubt.

"The Persian column of the trilingual inscription having thus been deciphered, a key was afforded to the interpretation of the two other inscriptions, supposing always that their contents were the same, and that the language was one which either still existed or was allied to one still spoken or written. That the contents of the three inscriptions were the same was evident from the corresponding recurrence of certain groups in each column. But Assyro-Babylonian inscriptions offered far greater difficulties than the Persian. The letters or signs used in the Persian were limited in number, not exceeding thirty-six; and, as we have seen, each word was separated, and marked by an oblique wedge. In the Assyrian inscription there was no division between the words; the letters and signs seemed not only to be unlimited in number, but to be used in the most arbitrary manner. As, however, the inscriptions contained names of persons, countries, cities, etc., many of which could be identified with those preserved in classical or Biblical literature, the value of many letters could be determined with sufficient confidence; and thus a clue was afforded to a few words of constant recurrence, and proof afforded that the language of the Assyro-Babylonian inscriptions, as might have been expected, was a Semitic dialect, allied to the Chaldee, Hebrew, Arab, and other cognate languages, either still existing or of which written remains have been preserved.

"While European scholars were thus occupied in deciphering the trilingual tablets, the discoveries of Nimroud, Khorsabad, and Kouyunjik, and among other Assyrian ruins, furnished a vast number of inscriptions, which will afford materials for years to come for the study of the cuneiform character. During the excavations in Assyria, I was too much occupied to be able to devote much time to the decipherment of the inscriptions; but, while copying them, I was able to compare them, and to classify to a certain extent the various signs and letters which they contain. One fact soon became evident to me—that the Assyrians, unlike the Persians, rarely, if ever, divided a word at the end of a line, preferring to finish it by cutting letters on the sculpture itself, or on the side or even back of a slab. As the 'Standard inscription' of the north-west palace of Nimroud, containing the names, titles, and part of the annals of the founder of the edifice, was repeated upon almost every slab discovered in the ruins, and in every variety of space, sometimes only one or two letters forming a line, I was able, by a careful comparison of the endings, to determine and mark off almost every word in the inscription. I soon, also, found, by the relative position of certain groups, the signs or letters marking the names of the kings, their titles, and the names of their fathers, and, in many instances, of their grandfathers.

"On my return to England from my first expedition, I edited, for the trustees of the British Museum, a volume containing transcripts of inscriptions from Nimroud, Kouyunjik, Kalah-Sherghat, and other Assyrian ruins. Their publication, and that of the cuneiform inscriptions discovered by M. Botta at Khorsabad, afforded fresh materials for investigation, and several eminent scholars took up the subject; among whom were the late Dr. Hincks, Mr. Norris, Mr. Fox Talbot, and M. Oppert. Sir Henry Rawlinson, in 1850, announced that he had succeeded in reading the inscription on the black obelisk discovered in the centre palace of Nimroud; and shortly after, communicated his version of its contents at a meeting of the members of the Royal Institution. On my return to England in 1851, after my second expedition, I spent some time with Dr. Hincks, in Ireland, in examining the cuneiform inscriptions which I had brought from Assyria and

Armenia, and I am indebted to him for the translation of these inscriptions which I published in the work of which this book is an abridgment. Dr. Hincks had already deciphered the names of Sargon, Sennacherib, and Esar-haddon, and had thus proved that which I had been led to conjecture, from a comparison of the monuments and from other evidence, that the palaces at Kouyunjik and Khorsabad, and in the south-west corner of the mound of Nimroud, owed their foundation to those kings. He also determined the Assyrian numerals from the Wan inscriptions. He had previously (in June, 1846) discovered the names of Nebuchadnezzar and Babylon on the well-known Babylonian bricks from the ruins of Hilla. On August 23d, 1851, Sir Henry Rawlinson announced in the *Athenæum* that he had found in the inscriptions from Kouyunjik notices of the reign of Sennacherib, which placed beyond the reach of dispute his historic identity; and he gave a recapitulation of the principal events recorded on the monuments, including the war with Hezekiah and the siege and capture of Lachish.

"Constant additions were made to our knowledge of the contents of the cuneiform inscriptions in communications from Dr. Hincks, Sir Henry Rawlinson, Mr. Fox Talbot, and Mr. Norris, to the 'Journals' of the Royal Asiatic Society, to the 'Transactions' of the Royal Irish Academy, to the *Athenæum*, and to other literary and scientific periodicals. But scholars in this country, whose learning was limited to the classics, were little inclined to accept these interpretations, and were rather disposed to reject them altogether as ingenious fictions. In the year 1857, Sir Henry Rawlinson had superintended for the Trustees of the British Museum the publication of a transcript of the inscription upon the clay cylinders discovered at Kalah-Sherghat. A copy of this inscription had been sent to Mr. Fox Talbot before its publication, and before Sir Henry Rawlinson had placed before the public any account of its contents. In March, Mr. Fox Talbot forwarded a sealed packet to the late Professor Wilson, then President of the Royal Asiatic Society, inclosing his translation of the inscription, with a request that it might not be opened until Sir Henry Rawlinson, with whom he had had no communication on the subject, had published the translation of the same inscription which he had announced, adding his opinion, that 'all candid inquirers must acknowledge that if any special agreement should appear between such independent versions, it must indicate that they have truth for their basis.'

"The Council of the Royal Asiatic Society considered that this was a favorable occasion for testing the general accuracy of the interpretation of the cuneiform writing, and they requested not only Sir Henry Rawlinson, but Dr. Hincks and M. Oppert also, to furnish them with the translations of the same inscription, under sealed covers, and without any previous communication with each other. A committee of gentlemen of the highest literary attainments, and of entirely independent opinions upon such matters, including Dr. Milman (the Dean of St. Paul's), Dr. Whewell, Sir Gardner Wilkinson, Mr. Grote, the Rev. Mr. Cureton, and Professor Wilson, were named to open the packets, and to examine and report upon the translations. Mr. Cureton, Dr. Whewell, and Professor Wilson were absent when the packets were opened; but the other three members of the committee, after having carefully examined and compared their contents, reported their opinions to the Council of the Asiatic Society. Dr. Milman and Mr. Grote certified that 'the coincidences between the translations, both as to the general sense and verbal rendering, were very remarkable. In most parts there was a strong correspondence in the meaning assigned, and occasionally a curious identity of expression as to particular words. Where the versions differed very materially, each translator had, in many cases, marked the passage as one of the doubtful or unascertained signification. In the interpretation of numbers there was throughout a singular correspondence.' Sir Gardner Wilkinson, in a separate report, expressed himself somewhat more strongly in favor of the decipherers, and declared that 'the resemblance (very often exactly the same, word for word) was so great as to render it unreasonable to suppose that the interpretation could be arbitrary, or based on uncertain grounds.' Professor Wilson declares in his report to the society that, 'upon the whole, the result of this experiment—than which a fairer test could scarcely be desired—may be considered as establishing almost definitively the correctness of the valuation of the characters of these inscriptions.'"

By the translations made by these eminent cuneiform scholars, we are permitted to know more definitely much of the daily life of the Assyrians. From them we obtain a clearer and fuller idea of the activity of trade and business in Western Asia in the seventh and eighth centuries before our own era. By them we are informed of the religious belief of a people who existed prior to Moses and the prophets; and they confirm, in a very remarkable degree, the historic portions of the Bible.

From these deciphered tablets we learn that the Assyrians bought and sold houses and slaves and other kinds of property; that they drew the deeds of sale, the leases, and promissory notes with a care and detail not unworthy a modern lawyer; that they loaned money and goods at three and four per cent.; and that security for the loan was often taken in houses or other property. To these transactions the names and seals of competent witnesses were affixed; and when they were too poor to possess a seal, they made in the soft clay their nail-mark, which was considered sufficient. All this appreciation and interchanging of property led to testamentary devolution, and to the accumulation of these legal documents.

Among the many business contracts exhumed and translated are the following, which relate to the loan of money, the sale of seven slaves, and the transfer of a piece of property:

PROMISSORY NOTE.

"Four manehs of silver according to the standard of Carchemish, which Neriglissar, in the presence of Nebo-sum-iddin, son of Nebo-rahim-baladhi, the Keeper of the Crown, from the City of Dur-Sargon, lends out at five shekels of silver per month interest. The 26th day of the month Iyyar, during the eponym of Gabbaru. The witnesses (were): Nebo-pal-iddin, Nebo-atsib, the holder of the two sceptres, Akhi-ramu, of the same office, Assur-danin-sarri, of the same office, Disi the astronomer, Samas-igur……. Sinmati-kali the executioner, (and) Merodach……the astronomer."

BILL OF SALE FOR SLAVES.

"The seal of Ebed-Istar, the master of the men. The giving-up of Hoshea, his two wives Mih'sa (and) Badia, 'Sigaba, Bel-kharran-cunucci, (and) his two daughters, in all seven persons, slaves, whom Ebed-Istar has sold; and 'Simadi for three manehs of silver has taken. The whole sum hast thou given. The exchange (and) the contract are finished: (there is) no withdrawal. The witnesses (are) Bel-nuri the priest, Amyatchu, 'Sangi, Kat-i-sa, (and) 'Sidur. [The name of the sixth witness is not filled in.] The month Tisri; the eponym of Dananu."

DEED OF SALE.

"The nail-mark of Sarru-ludari, the nail-mark of Atar-'suri, (and) the nail-mark of the woman Amat-'Suhala, the wife of Bel-duru, the……. the owner of the house (which) is given up. [Then follow four nail-marks.] The whole house, with its wood-work and its doors, situated in the city of Nineveh, adjoining the houses of Mannu-ci-akhi (and) Ilu-ciya, (and) the property of 'Sukaki he has sold, and Tsillu-Assur the astronomer, an Egyptian, for one maneh of silver (according to) the royal (standard), in the presence of Surru-ludari, Atar-'suru, and Amat-'subala, the wife of its owner, has received it. The full sum thou hast given. This house has been taken possession of. The exchange (and) the contract are concluded. (There is) no withdrawal. Whosoever (shall act) feloniously among any of these men who have sworn to the contract and the agreement, which (is) before (our) prince Assur, ten manehs of silver shall he pay. The witnesses (are): Su'san-kukhadnanis, Murmaza the......, Ra'snah the pilot, Nebo-dur-sanin the partitioner of the enemy, Murmaza the pilot, Sinnis-nacarat, (and) Zedekiah. The 16th day of the month Sivan, the eponym of Zazā of the city of Aspad, before Samas-itsbat-nacara, Latturu, (and) Nebo-sum-yut-sur."

Another class of these exhumed tablets open to us the religious thought of the ancient Assyrians, and illustrate the antiquity of some doctrines which are held to-day by the Christian Church. The Assyrians were polytheists, and chief in their Pantheon was their "great god," Asshur, the son of Shem, the progenitor of their race, and who, in process of time, they deified. Out of a man they made a god. He is represented in the bass-reliefs by a "man in a winged circle, holding a bow and shooting an arrow." All this was highly emblematical. The circle typified eternity; the expanded wings were expressive of omnipresence; the human form symbolized intelligence. But while Asshur was deity supreme, yet he was only one of the "lords many and gods many" in the Assyrian Pantheon. The first triad of divinities consisted of Anu, Bel, and Hea, whose pompous titles are inscribed on tablet, temple, and monument. Unwilling that only half of the human race should be represented in the list of the gods, the Ninevites had a shrine to Beltis, whom they styled "The Mother of the Gods," "The Queen of the Lands," "The Goddess of Battle;" and they also erected altars to Ishta, whom they called "their lady," and whose descent into Hades is elaborately described in cuneiform inscriptions. She was their Venus, and her symbol was the naked female form so common on the exhumed cylinders. In the list of the gods of the sterner sex was Vul, an Eastern Jupiter, "the lord of the whirlwind and the tempest, and the wielder of the thunder-bolt," whose emblem was a triple bolt gleaming with lightning. Their god of war was Nin, represented by the human-headed bull, the impersonation of strength and power. Equally honored with him was Nergal, "The Strong Begetter," "The Ancestor of Kings," "The God of the Chase," who was represented by the human-headed lion. In their appreciation of learning, they paid homage to Nebo, "The God who possesses Intelligence," "He who Hears from afar," "The Inventor of Writing and Literature."

There can be no doubt as to the belief of the Assyrians in the existence of evil spirits, of the necessity of sacrifice for sin, of penitence for pardon, of a future judgment, and of the immortality of the soul. Here is a translation of a penitential prayer:

> O my Lord! my sins are many, my trespasses are great; and the wrath of the gods has plagued me with disease, and with sickness and sorrow.
> I fainted; but no one stretched forth his hand!
> I groaned; but no one drew nigh!
> I cried aloud; but no one heard!
> O Lord! do not abandon thy servant!
> In the waters of the great storm, seize his hand!
> The sins which he has committed, turn thou to righteousness.*

Here is a short prayer for the soul of a dying man:

> Like a bird may it fly to a lofty place,
> To the holy hands of its god may it ascend.†

Similar to the above is the following address to the Sun:

> The man who is departing in glory, may his soul shine radiant as brass.
> To that man, may the Sun give life!
> And Marduk, eldest Son of Heaven,
> Grant him an abode of happiness.‡

---

* "Records of the Past," vol. iii., p. 136.   † Ibid., p. 134.
‡ Ibid., vol. iii., p. 134.

On another tablet was inscribed this prayer for the king:

Length of days — long lasting years — a strong sword — a long life — extended years of glory — pre-eminence among kings — grant ye to the King my Lord, who has given such gifts to his gods!

The bounds vast and wide of his Empire and of his Rule, may he enlarge and may he complete! Holding over all kings supremacy and royalty and empire, may he attain to gray hairs and old age!

And after the gift of these present days, in the feasts of the land of the silver sky — the refulgent courts — the abode of blessedness: and in the Light of the *Happy Fields*, may he dwell a life eternal — holy — in the presence of the gods who inhabit Assyria!*

On another tablet is the account of the death of a righteous man, of which the following is a translation by Mr. H. F. Talbot, F.R.S.:

Bind the sick man to Heaven, for from the Earth he is being torn away!
Of the brave man, who was so strong, his strength has departed.
Of the righteous servant, the force does not return.
In his bodily frame he lies dangerously ill.
But Ishtar, who in her dwelling is grieved concerning him, descends from her mountain, unvisited of men.
To the door of the sick man she comes.
The sick man listens!
Who is there? Who comes?
It is Ishtar, daughter of the Moon-god Sin:
It is the god (......), son of Bel:
It is Marduk, son of the god (......).
They approach the body of the sick man.

The next line is nearly destroyed.

They bring a *khisibta*† from the heavenly treasury.
They bring a *sisbu* from their lofty store-house; into the precious *khisibta* they pour bright liquor.
That righteous man, may he now rise on high!
May he shine like that *khisibta*!
May he be bright as that *sisbu*!
Like pure silver may his garment be shining white!
Like brass may he be radiant!
To the Sun, greatest of the gods, may he ascend!
And may the Sun, greatest of the gods, receive his soul into his holy hands!‡

---

* "Transactions of Society of Biblical Archæology," vol. i., part i., p. 107.
† Probably a drinking-cup.   ‡ "Records of the Past," vol. iii., p. 135.

But the greatest value of these exhumed tablets is the remarkable agreement between them and the historic portions of the Bible. They synchronize as to dates and proper names in a most extraordinary degree. They are national records of contemporaneous history, written from different stand-points and for different objects, but confirmatory each of the other. And although our faith in the integrity of the sacred historians is quite independent of any such confirmation, yet such proof from the "dead past," disentombed after a burial of so many centuries, will go far to strengthen the faith of the weak and to dissipate the doubts of others.

These Assyrian records contain the names of countries, of cities, and of kings, with which we have been familiar from childhood. On cylinder, on tablet, on monument may be read, "Babel, and Erech, and Accad, and Calneh," the cities built by "Nimrod," "Nineveh, Resin, and Calah," the cities founded by "Asshur;" "Ur of the Chaldees," the birthplace of Abraham and the cradle of the human race; "Babylon," where the Jewish captives sighed, and Daniel foretold the coming future; "Syria and Damascus," the country and the capital of "Benhadad and Hazael;" "Ashdod" of the Philistines, and "Tyre and Sidon of the Phœnicians;" "Samaria" of "Omri, Ahab, Jehu, Pekah, Hoshea, and Resin;" and "Jerusalem," the imperial city of "Azariah, Hezekiah, and Manasseh." In addition to these familiar names, others equally familiar occur in the Assyrian inscriptions; such as, "Menahem, Merodach-baladan, Pharaoh, Sargon, Sennacherib, Esar-haddon, Dagon, Nebo, Judea, Lachish, Gaza, Askelon, Lebanon, Egypt, Tigris, Euphrates, Haran, and Mesopotamia." And more than the names of countries, cities, and kings are recorded. The events which took place are portrayed in bass-reliefs, such as the capture of

Lachish, the coming of the tribute-bearers from King Hezekiah, and the sad march of the Hebrew captives from their native land.

While Biblical chronology is not unfrequently pronounced defective, and therefore unreliable, yet it is a noteworthy fact that the Assyrians had a chronology quite identical thereunto, and the coincidence of dates through a given period of years is one of the great facts demonstrated by the Assyrian archæologists. On this important point, Mr. George Smith remarks as follows:

"The close agreement between the contemporary Assyrian records and the Biblical chronology, from the reign of Ahaz downward, enables all the dates to be fixed with a fair amount of certainty; only one of the numbers in the Bible requiring rectification, the date of the expedition of Sennacherib against Hezekiah king of Judah (2 Kings xviii., 13), where I should read "twenty-fourth year" instead of "fourteenth year." And I can not quit this subject without pointing out the curious parallel in the order of the subjects between the first thirty-seven chapters of Isaiah, on one side, and the Assyrian history of Tiglath-pileser, Shalmaneser, Sargon, and Sennacherib, on the other. To exhibit this I place them in opposite columns:

ISAIAH.	ASSYRIAN ANNALS.
Ch. i. to vi.—During the time of Uzziah king of Judah.	B.C. 738.—Tiglath-pileser mentions Azariah (Uzziah) king of Judah.
Ch. vii. to x.—Relate to the expedition of Tiglath-pileser king of Assyria against Syria and Israel, in the reign of Ahaz.	B.C. 734–732.—Expedition of Tiglath-pileser against Damascus, Israel, and Philistia, tribute of Yauhazi (Ahaz) king of Judah.
Ch. xiii. and first half of xiv.—Against Babylon.	B.C. 731.—Tiglath-pileser conquers Babylon, and annexes it to Assyria.
Ch. xiv., vs. 28 to 32.—In the year of death of Ahaz, rod of smiter broken.	B.C. 727. Death of Tiglath-pileser.
Ch. xv. and xvi.—Against Moab.	B.C. 725.—Reign of Shalmaneser; details unknown.

ISAIAH.	ASSYRIAN ANNALS.
Ch. xvii.—Against Damascus, Aroer, and Israel.	B.C. 720.—Expedition of Sargon king of Assyria against Qarqar (Aroer), Damascus, and Samaria.
	B.C. 715.—Egypt makes alliance with Assyria.
Ch. xviii. and xix.—Against Egypt.	B.C. 712.—Egypt stirs up revolt in Palestine against Assyria.
Ch. xx.—In the year of capture of Ashdod, prophecy against Egypt.	B.C. 711.—Sargon takes Ashdod: king of Egypt abandons his allies.
Ch. xxi., v. 1 to 10.—Against Babylon.	B.C. 710.—Sargon conquers Babylon.
Ch. xxiii.—Against Tyre.	B.C. 702-1.—Phœnicia attacked by Sennacherib king of Assyria; the king flies from Tyre to Cyprus.
Ch. xxiv. to xxix.—Sennacherib's invasion.	B.C. 702-1.—Sennacherib marches through Palestine.
Ch. xxx. and xxxi.—Against relying on Egypt.	B.C. 702-1.—Sennacherib defeats the Egyptian army at Eltekeh.
Ch. xxxii. to xxxvii., v. 36.	B.C. 702-1.—Sennacherib attacks Judah.
Ch. xxxvii., v. 37 and 38.—Murder of Sennacherib and accession of Esarhaddon.	B.C. 681.—Murder of Sennacherib, and accession of Esar-haddon.

Other and equally interesting corroborative evidence has been brought to light by the painstaking and distinguished cuneiform scholars. They have shown that the modes of punishment related in the Book of Daniel were not uncommon among the Babylonians and Assyrians. It has been discovered that, in the days of Asshur-bani-pal, men who had fallen under his displeasure were cast into a fiery furnace, and others into a den of lions. It is a matter of record that Saul-mugina rebelled against his brother, Asshur-bani-pal, King of Assyria; and sought to make himself king of the province of Babylonia. But the rebellious brother and his associates were defeated after a severe battle, and, having been captured, were condemned to death. Implacable and revengeful, the King of Assyria did not spare his own brother, but commanded that he should be burned alive, as appears from the following words: "Saul-mugina my brother rebellious, who made war with me, into a furnace fiery burning, they threw him, and destroyed his life." And of those engaged with him in the rebellion it is said: "The rest of the people, among the bulls and lions, as Sennacherib my grandfather used to throw men among them, so I again, following in his footsteps, threw those men in the midst of them."*

Nor were the ancient Babylonians and Assyrians destitute of traditions and records relative to the Creation, to the Deluge, and to other great events of which Moses has left us an inspired account. There is an apparent difference as to many details in the two statements, but as to the general and principal facts there is a remarkable agreement. For the Chaldean account of the Creation and of the Deluge we are indebted to Berosus, a Chaldean priest, who lived in the third century before the Christian era, and who translated the records of Babylonia into the Greek language. His writings indicate that he was well acquainted with the history of his country, and competent to translate the inscriptions. It is supposed that his history of the Creation was derived from an old Chaldean tradition, which in its purer form was the basis of the Mosaic account. But whether Moses wrote his history of the Creation from a Divine vision of the successive acts of the Creator, or from a tradition which came from Adam to Noah, from Noah to Abraham, from Abraham to Moses, and inspired therein, are points on which the Bible is silent. While the whole spirit and tone of the Mosaic account is incomparably superior to that by Berosus, yet the general outline

---

* "Transactions of the Society of Biblical Archaeology," vol. ii., part 2, p. 361.

of the narrative in each is nearly the same. In both we have the earth at first "without form and void," and "darkness upon the face of the deep." In both the first step taken toward Creation is the separation of the mixed mass, and the formation of the heavens and the earth as the consequence of such separation. In both we have light mentioned before the creation of the sun and moon; in both we have the existence of animals before man; and in both we have a Divine element infused into man at his birth, and his formation "from the dust of the ground."* But the purity and historic importance of the Chaldean cosmogony, as given by Berosus, are marred by mythological additions and extravagance of language, which contrast most severely with the exalted simplicity and historic dignity of the Hebrew cosmogony as recorded by Moses.

There are two accounts of the Deluge. One is Chaldean, and translated by Berosus; the other is Assyrian, recently discovered at Nineveh by Mr. George Smith, of the British Museum, and by him translated from the cuneiform characters. The former is briefer, more pertinent, less mythological, and includes a statement relative to the confusion of tongues and the dispersion of mankind. The latter is less simple and exact, but is an original document, the work of some Assyrian annalist. Both, however, are concurrent as to the main facts of the story, and harmonize therein, not only one with the other, but with the Mosaic account.

The agreement between Moses and Berosus is no less curious than interesting. There is the warning to a single man; there is the command to construct a ship; there is the direction to take into the ark a chosen few of

---

* Rawlinson's "Ancient Monarchies," vol. i., p. 144.

mankind, and also the winged fowl and the four-footed beasts; there is the coming of the storm that submerged the earth; there is the sending-forth of birds which returned the first and second time, but not the third; there is the egress of Noah from the ark, and his building an altar for sacrifice immediately afterward; there is the resting of the ark upon a mountain in Armenia; and the subsequent building of the Tower of Babel. As the translation by Berosus is the Chaldean version of the Flood, I give it entire:

"God appeared to Xisuthrus (Noah) in a dream, and warned him that on the fifteenth day of the month Daesius, mankind would be destroyed by a deluge. He bade him bury in Sippara, the City of the Sun, the extant writings, first and last; and build a ship and enter therein with his family and his close friends; and furnish it with meat and drink; and place on board winged fowl, and four-footed beasts of the earth; and when all was ready, set sail. Xisuthrus asked 'Whither he was to sail?' and was told, 'To the gods, with a prayer that it might fare well with mankind.' Then Xisuthrus was not disobedient to the vision, but built a ship five furlongs (3125 feet) in length, and two furlongs (1250 feet) in breadth; and collected all that had been commanded him, and put his wife and children and close friends on board. The flood came; and as soon as it ceased, Xisuthrus let loose some birds, which, finding neither food nor a place where they could rest, came back to the ark. After some days he again sent out the birds, which again returned to the ark, but with feet covered with mud. Sent out a third time, the birds returned no more, and Xisuthrus knew that land had re-appeared; so he removed some of the covering of the ark, and looked, and behold! the vessel had grounded on a mountain. Then Xisuthrus went forth with his wife and his daughter, and his pilot, and fell down and worshiped the earth, and built an altar, and offered sacrifice to the gods; after which he disappeared from sight, together with those who had accompanied him. They who had remained in the ark and not gone forth with Xisuthrus, now left it and searched for him, and shouted out his name; but Xisuthrus was not seen any more. Only his voice answered them out of the air, saying, 'Worship God; for because I worshiped God, am I gone to dwell with the gods; and they who were with me have shared the same honor!' And he bade them return to Babylon, and recover the writings buried at Sippara, and make them known among men; and he told them that the land in which they then were was Armenia. So they, when they had heard all, sacrificed to the gods, and went their way on foot to Babylon, and, having reached it, recovered the buried writings from Sippara, and built many cities and temples, and restored Babylon. Some portion of the ark still continues in Armenia, in the Gordiæan (Kurdish) Mountains; and persons scrape off the bitumen from it to bring away, and this they use as a remedy to avert misfortunes.

"The earth was still of one language, when the primitive men, who were proud of their strength and stature, and despised the gods as their inferiors,

THE DELUGE TABLETS.

erected a tower of vast height, in order that they might mount to heaven. And the tower was now near to heaven when the gods (or God) caused the winds to blow and overturn the structure upon the men, and made them speak with divers tongues; wherefore the city was called Babylon."*

* Rawlinson's "Ancient Monarchies," vol. i., pp. 145-147.

Of greater importance, because we have the *original*, is the Assyrian account of the Deluge. We are indebted to Mr. George Smith, of the British Museum, not only for the discovery of the tablets on which the account is inscribed in the cuneiform characters, but also for the translation of the record. He was fortunate enough to find, amidst the ruins at Kuyunjik, twelve tablets, which purport to contain a record of the adventures of a hero called Izdubar, supposed by him to have been the Nimrod of the Bible. Associated with Izdubar was a seer, whose name was Heabani. The two heroes were no less distinguished as hunters than as conquerors. In one of their hunting expeditions, the seer Heabani was killed by a wild animal; and after this misfortune to his companion, Izdubar himself was smitten with some terrible disease, and went to the sea-shore in search of health. The place whither he went was a city on the shores of the Persian Gulf, near the mouth of the Euphrates, and called in the inscriptions Surippak—"the City of the Ark." In his distress and trial, he sought advice of Hasisadra, the Xisuthrus of the Chaldean account, and the Noah of the Bible. Of this eminent saint, who had escaped the Flood, Izdubar inquired how he could become immortal, and, after a homily on "life and death," Hasisadra related to Izdubar the story of the Flood.

Of all the tablets discovered by Mr. Smith, the "Eleventh" is the most perfect and important, as it contains the legend of the Flood, and is supposed to have been composed two thousand years before the Christian era. This tablet, together with its companion tablets, may now be seen in the Assyrian Department of the British Museum, where they are preserved as memorials of the past, and as monuments to the enterprise and success of modern discovery.

CHAMBER WHERE THE TABLETS WERE FOUND.

The harmony and the difference between the Assyrian and Mosaic accounts of the Flood are worthy of most careful attention. The two records agree that the Flood was a Divine punishment for the wickedness of the antediluvian world; that God commanded a holy man to build an ark, wherein he and his family were saved; that the ark was coated within and without with bitumen; that, by Divine direction, the fowl of the air and the beasts of the fields were gathered into the ark of safety; that the rain descended in floods and submerged the earth; that three several times a bird was sent out to report whether the waters had subsided; that the ark rested on a mountain; and that Noah, having been so miraculously delivered, built an altar, and offered thereon a sacrifice to God.

Thus as to all the essential facts touching the Deluge there is remarkable agreement; there are, however, points of difference which are interesting to observe. There is a marked difference as to the size of the ark; as to the construction of the vessel; as to the number of persons saved; as to the duration of the Flood; as to the mountain on which the ark rested; as to the birds sent forth: and as to the end of Noah. According to the Assyrian account, the ark was much larger than the one described by Moses; that the vessel was a regular ship, manned by sailors and navigated by a pilot; that Noah smuggled some of his neighbors on board, who are called "sons of the people;" that the duration of the Deluge was much shorter than stated in the Bible; that a dove, a swallow, and a raven were severally sent forth: that the ark rested on the mountains of *Nizir*, which are supposed to be south of the Lesser Zab, and near Altoon Kupri; and that Noah did not die as men die, but, like Enoch and Elijah, he was translated.

The translation of the Deluge tablet is not perfect. The value and meaning of some of the cuneiform characters are not yet known; the omissions are indicated by stars. As the inscription is in short lines, these lines are reproduced in the translated copy. Mr. Smith is frank enough to say: "The following is rather a free than a literal translation:"

COLUMN I.

Izdubar after this manner also said to Hasisadra afar off:
 "I consider the matter,
why thou repeatest not to me from thee,
and thou repeatest not to me from thee,
thy ceasing my heart to make war
presses? of the, I come up after thee,
* * * how thou hast done, and in the assembly of the gods alive thou art placed."

Hasisadra after this manner also said to Izdubar:
 "Be revealed to thee Izdubar the concealed story,
and the judgment of the gods be related to thee,
 The city Surippak the city where thou standest not * * * * placed.
that city is ancient * * * * the gods within it
* * * * * * * their servant, the great gods
* * * * * * * the god Anu.
* * * * * the god Bel,
* * * * * the god Ninip,
and the god * * * * * * lord of Hades;
their will be revealed in the midst * * * * and
I his will was hearing and he spake to me:
 "Surippakite son of Ubaratutu
* * * * make a ship after this * * * * *
* * * * I destroy? the sinner and life * * * *
* * * cause to go in? the seed of life all of it to the midst of the ship.
 The ship which thou shalt make,
600? cubits shall be the measure of its length, and
60? cubits the amount of its breadth and its height
* * * into the deep launch it."
I perceived and said to Hea my lord:
 "The ship making which thou commandest me, when I shall have made,
young and old will deride me."

Hea opened his mouth and spake and said to me his servant:
* * * * * * * * thou shalt say unto them,
* * * * * * * * he has turned from me and
* * * * * * * * fixed over me
* * * * * * * like caves * * * *
* * * * * above and below
* * * * closed the ship * * * *
* * * * the flood which I will send to you,
into it enter and the door of the ship turn.

Into the midst of it thy grain, thy furniture, and thy goods, thy wealth, thy women servants, thy female slaves, and thy young men, the beasts of the field, the animals of the field all, I will gather and I will send to thee, and they shall be inclosed in thy door."

Adrahasis his mouth opened and spake, and said to Hea his lord:
"Any one the ship will not make * * * *
on the earth fixed * * * * * * *
* * * * I may see also the ship * * * *
* * * * on the ground the ship * * * * *
the ship making which thou commandest me * * *
which in * * * * *

COLUMN II.

strong * * * * *
on the fifth day * * * * * * * it
in its circuit 14 measures * * * its frame.
14 measures it measured * * * over it.
I placed its roof, it * * * * I inclosed it.

I rode in it on the sixth time; I examined its exterior on the seventh time;
its interior I examined on the eighth time.
Planks against the waters within it I placed.
I saw rents and the wanting parts I added.
3 measures of bitumen I poured over the outside.
3 measures of bitumen I poured over the inside.
3 * * * men carrying its baskets, they constructed boxes
I placed in the boxes the offering they sacrificed.
Two measures of boxes I had distributed to the boatmen.
To * * * * * were sacrificed oxen
* * * * * * * * * * dust and
* * * * * * * * * * wine in receptacle of goats
I collected like the waters of a river, also
food like the dust of the earth also
I collected in boxes with my hand I placed.

* * * * * Shamas * * * * material of the ship completed.
* * * * * * * * strong and
the reed oars of the ship I caused to bring above and below.
* * * * * * * * they went in two-thirds of it.

All I possessed the strength of it, all I possessed the strength of it silver
all I possessed the strength of it gold,
all I possessed the strength of it the seed of life, the whole
I caused to go up into the ship; all my male servants and my female servants,
the beast of the field, the animal of the field, the sons of the people all of them, I caused to go up.
A flood Shamas made and
he spake saying in the night: "I will cause it to rain heavily,
enter to the midst of the ship and shut thy door."
A flood he raised and
he spake saying in the night: "I will cause it to rain (or it will rain) from heaven heavily."
"In the day I celebrated his festival
the day of his appointment? fear I had.
I entered into the midst of the ship and shut my door.
To close the ship to Buzur-sadirabi the boatman
the palace I gave with its goods

The raging of a storm in the morning
arose, from the horizon of heaven extended and wide.
Vul in the midst of it thundered, and
Nebo and Saru went in front,
the throne-bearers went over mountains and plains,
the destroyer Nergal overturned;
Ninip went in front and cast down,
the spirits carried destruction;
in their glory they swept the earth;
of Vul the flood reached to heaven.
The bright earth to a waste was turned,

COLUMN III.

the surface of the earth like * * * * * it swept,
it destroyed all life from the face of the earth * * *
the strong deluge over the people, reached to heaven.
Brother saw not his brother, it did not spare the people. In heaven
the gods feared the tempest and
sought refuge; they ascended to the heaven of Anu.
The gods like dogs fixed in droves prostrate.

Spake Ishtar like a child,
uttered the great goddess her speech:
    "All to corruption are turned and
then I in the presence of the gods prophesied evil.
As I prophesied in the presence of the gods evil
to evil were devoted all my people and I prophesied
thus: "I have begotten my people and
like the young of the fishes they fill the sea."
The gods concerning the spirits were weeping with her,
the gods in seats seated in lamentation,
covered were their lips for the coming evil.
Six days and nights
passed, the wind, deluge, and storm overwhelmed.
On the seventh day in its course was calmed the storm, and all the deluge
which had destroyed like an earthquake,
quieted. The sea he caused to dry, and the wind and deluge ended.
I perceived the sea making a tossing;
and the whole of mankind turned to corruption,
like reeds the corpses floated.
I opened the window, and the light broke over my face,
it passed. I sat down and wept,
over my face flowed my tears.
I perceived the shore at the boundary of the sea,
for twelve measures the land rose.
To the country of Nizir went the ship;
the mountain of Nizir stopped the ship, and to pass over it it was not able.
The first day, and the second day, the mountain of Nizir the same.
The third day, and the fourth day, the mountain of Nizir the same.
The fifth, and sixth, the mountain of Nizir the same.
On the seventh day in the course of it

   I sent forth a dove and it left. The dove went and turned and
a resting-place it did not find, and it returned.
I sent forth a swallow and it left. The swallow went and turned, and
a resting-place it did not find; and it returned.
I sent forth a raven and it left.
The raven went, and the corpses on the water it saw, and
it did eat, it swam, and wandered away and did not return.
I sent the animals forth to the four winds, I poured out a libation,
I built an altar on the peak of the mountain,
by seven herbs I cut,
at the bottom of them I placed reeds, pines, and singar.

The gods collected at its burning, the gods collected at its good burning;
the gods like flies over the sacrifice gathered.
From of old also the great god in his course
The great brightness of Anu had created.
When the glory
Of those gods the charm round my neck would not repel;

COLUMN IV.

in those days I prayed for I could never repel them.
May the gods come to my altar,
may Bel not come to my altar,
for he did not consider and had made a deluge,
and my people he had consigned to the deep.
From of old also Bel in his course
saw the ship, and went Bel with anger filled to the gods and spirits:
"Let not any one come out alive, let not a man be saved from the deep."
Ninip his mouth opened, and spake and said to the warrior Bel:
"Who then will be saved?" Hea the words understood,
and Hea knew all things.
Hea his mouth opened and spake, and said to the warrior Bel:
"Thou prince of the gods warrior,
when thou art angry a deluge thou makest;
the doer of sin did his sin, the doer of evil did his evil.
May the exalted not be broken, may the captive not be delivered.
Instead of thee making a deluge, may lions increase and men be reduced;
instead of thee making a deluge, may leopards increase and men be reduced;
instead of thee making a deluge, may a famine happen and the country be destroyed;
instead of thee making a deluge, may pestilence increase and men be destroyed.
I did not peer into the judgment of the gods,
Adrahasis a dream they sent, and the judgment of the gods he heard.
When his judgment was accomplished, Bel went up to the midst of the ship.
He took my hand and raised me up,
he caused to raise and to bring my wife to my side;
he purified the country, he established in a covenant and took the people,
in the presence of Hasisadra and the people.
When Hasisadra, and his wife and the people, to be like the gods were carried away;
then dwelt Hasisadra in a remote place at the mouth of the rivers.
They took me and in a remote place at the mouth of the rivers they seated me.

When to thee whom the gods have chosen also,
for the health which thou seekest and askest,
this do six days and seven nights,
like in a seat also in bonds bind him,
the way like a storm shall be laid upon him."
Hasisadra after this manner also said to his wife,
"I announce that the chief who grasps at health
the way like a storm shall be laid upon him."
His wife after this manner also said to Hasisadra afar off:
"Purify him, and let the man be sent away;
the road that he came may he return in peace,
the great gate open and may he return to his country."
Hasisadra after this manner also said to his wife:
"The cry of a man alarms thee,
this do his *kurummat* (scarlet cloth) place on his head."
And the day when he ascended the side of the ship,
she did, his kurummat (scarlet cloth) she placed on his head.
And the day when he ascended the side of the ship."*

But other and more important results may yet be expected from the labors of Assyrian archæologists. Much has been accomplished, but much more remains to be done. Distinguished success has attended those who have made the cuneiform language a specialty in philology. A grammar and a dictionary have been eliminated, and classes have been formed in London for the study of the language and the interpretation of the cuneiform inscriptions. And sooner or later, the great universities of Europe will organize a department of Assyrian archæology, and the primitive language of Babylon and Assyria will be a recognized branch of philological study.

The success which has thus far attended the efforts of the cuneiform scholars is an inspiration to future endeavor. Their achievements are among the marvels of this marvelous age. They have given to us a new histo-

---

* George Smith's "Assyrian Discoveries," pp. 184–194.

ry. They have made clear what for ages was obscure. They have translated the records of a civilization to be ranked with that of Greece and Rome, and older than either by many centuries. None, more than they themselves, are conscious of the imperfections of their translations of the Assyrian records. There are signs of whose value they are ignorant. There are idioms whose meaning they have not determined. There are chronological and historical differences with well-authenticated facts that they have not been able to reconcile. But all things are possible to him who works. That which these eminent scholars have given us is but the beginning of the end. There are in the British Museum thousands of tablets not translated, whose import may yet astonish the world. There are mounds at Babylon and Nineveh unexplored, whose buried treasures of art and learning invite the discoverer. What seer shall foretell the developments of future exploration? Up to the present moment, Babylon has not been extensively and thoroughly explored. Her vast mounds await the coming of those who will bring to light her too long entombed monuments. It may be that the library of Nebuchadnezzar will be recovered, together with the older annals of the Babylonians. What light such records might throw upon the whole programme of the ancient civilization of mankind! and, perhaps, solve the problem whether the civilization of the East originated on the plains of Assyria or in the valley of the Nile. And who can tell how much more remote such records would carry us into the past? The day may not be far distant when Nimrod's Biography, Noah's History of the Flood, and Adam's Autobiography, shall become standard works among the civilized nations of the earth.

Hitherto, the work of exploration has been advanced

chiefly by France and England; but the time has come when the United States should contribute to a result of such general interest. Ten thousand dollars judiciously expended in the work of excavation might lead to the most gratifying results. It would be a national honor were an accredited agent of our country to discover a new palace with its buried treasures. The Sublime Porte would doubtless accord to the United States the same courtesy extended to England and France, the right of possession of whatever antiquities might be discovered by an authorized representative. It is the opinion of nearly all the distinguished Assyrian explorers that new and valuable discoveries are yet to be made, and that any properly directed effort of exploration would be attended with success. The mounds hitherto explored have been only partially excavated, and the work previously done is preparatory for future effort. But whether new excavations shall be attempted or not, the sum of ten thousand dollars would secure some rare specimens of Assyrian sculpture, such as a pair of the humanheaded lions, a royal statue in high-relief, scenes of war, of the chase, of domestic life, of mechanic art, of devotion, delineated in bass-relief on slabs of alabaster, and a library of histories, poems, and learned works inscribed on terra-cotta tablets, on clay cylinders, on marble slabs. And the facilities for transportation are as great as the antiquities are numerous. Even the heaviest specimens can be floated on rafts down the Tigris to Busrah on the Shaat-el-Arab, where a government vessel might receive them and transport them to the United States, to be added to the splendid collection from Cyprus, of which New York is justly proud.

CHAPTER VII.

Christianity in the East.—Origin of the Nestorians.—Their Great Learning. —Their Vast Missions.—Letter from Mr. Hormuzd Rassam on the Eastern Churches.—Syrian Jacobites.—Syrian Catholics.—Chaldean Nestorians.— Their Chaldean Origin.—Opinions of Ancient and Modern Authors.— Language of the Chaldeans.—History and Creed of the Nestorians.— Their Present and Their Future.

From the Garden of Eden to the snows of Ararat, and from the confines of Persia to the shores of the Mediterranean, Christianity is accepted as a Divine verity. The apostles were the first to preach Christ to the teeming millions of that ancient region, the cradle of humanity. The churches they planted took deep root, and bore abundant fruit. For three hundred years they continued to flourish in the unity of the Spirit; but, in the lapse of time, the union was severed, and the separated parts became sectarian centres of bitter contention. The rival sects strove for the mastery, and displayed a zeal that knew no bounds. Neither the change of governments, nor the power of persecution, nor the lapse of centuries, has been sufficient to extinguish that zeal, or totally destroy those who were inspired therewith. A remnant remains, still tenacious of ecclesiastical life.

The Armenians are by far the most powerful, and the most widely diffused, in the group of purely Oriental churches. Their home is the mountain tract that encircles Ararat, and in wealth, in steadiness, in quietness, they are the "Quakers" of the East. Proud of their founder, they trace their origin to Gregory the Illuminator, whose dead hand is still used for continuing the succession of their patriarchs.

The "Church of Syria" is the oldest of all the Gentile churches, and ancient Antioch is revered as the place of its birth. Its sacred annals are adorned with the immortal names of Ignatius, of Chrysostom, and John of Damascus. Its two divided parts are the Jacobites, who are Monophysites, and the Maronites, who are Monothelitic. The chief city of the former is Diarbekir; the chief sanctuary of the latter is the convent of Kanobin, shaded by the cedars of Lebanon.

The "Chaldean Christians," called by their opponents "Nestorians," live in the secluded fastnesses of Kurdistan, and are the remnant of the ancient church of Central Asia. They trace their descent to St. Thomas the Apostle. They accept as binding, the decisions of the Councils of Nicæa and Constantinople, but reject those of Ephesus, which condemned Nestorius, from whom they are named by those who differ from them.* In the day of their power, Edessa was their sacred city, and the city of Nisibis was their seat of learning and the centre of their grand missionary operations. From their famous schools went forth giants in literature, whose acquirements excite our admiration. Their varied productions were on a magnificent scale, and the authors thereof continued to flourish till crushed by the despotism of the Moslems. Not less than one hundred and fifty authors contributed to advance literature in the East. They were commentators on the whole or parts of the Bible; they were sacred and profane historians: they were lexicographers, grammarians, logicians, metaphysicians, geographers, astronomers, writers on natural

---

* Stanley's "Eastern Church," pp. 91-94.

philosophy; and more than a hundred were poets. Some of them passed beyond the limits of their own language, and carried their investigations into the wide field of Greek literature. They composed Greco-Syriac lexicons, and enriched the Syriac language by the introduction of a great variety of words from the Greek classics. Several of the Nestorian bishops wrote learned treatises in Persian, and one of the number translated the works of Aristotle into that language for the Emperor Chosroes. Some of these monuments of Nestorian learning remain to this day, and can be seen in the libraries at Mosul, Mardeen, and Bagdad. But not a few have been destroyed by the Latin missionaries, who used every possible artifice to exterminate the works of the Nestorian authors. This vandalism is to be deplored, as an irreparable loss to archæology. What light such works might have thrown on the downfall of the ancient Assyrian dynasties, and on the fortunes of the successive kingdoms which rose upon their ruins, and respecting which our information is so scanty! Such information might have solved those difficulties that still baffle the research of the most learned men in Europe, and might have been the key to the remarkable relics of antiquity which are now being exhumed from the mounds of Nineveh and Babylon.*

Impelled by a Divine zeal, the Nestorian missionaries went forth from Edessa and Nisibis to convert the world to Christ. In the sixth century they successfully preached Christianity to the Bactrians, the Huns, the Persians, the Indians, the Persarmenians, the Medes, and the Elamites. The barbaric churches, from the Persian Gulf to the Caspian Sea, were almost infinite; and their

---

* Badger's "Nestorians," vol. ii., pp. 8-15.

faith was conspicuous in the number and sanctity of their monks and martyrs. The pepper-coast of Malabar, and the isles of the ocean, Socotora and Ceylon, were peopled with an increasing multitude of Christians; and the bishops and clergy of those sequestered regions derived their ordination from the Catholic of Babylon. They pursued without fear the footsteps of the roving Tartar, and insinuated themselves into the camps of the valleys of Imaus and the banks of the Selinga. They exposed a metaphysical creed to those illiterate shepherds; to those sanguinary warriors they recommended humanity and repose. In their progress by sea and land, they entered China by the port of Canton and the Northern residence of Sigan; and under the reign of the caliphs, the Nestorian Church was diffused from China to Jerusalem. Twenty-five archbishops composed their hierarchy, and the number of communicants exceeded that of the Greek and Latin communions.*

It was my good fortune while at Mosul to be the guest of Mr. Hormuzd Rassam, who is the most competent living authority as to the creed and condition of the native population of the valley of the Euphrates. Himself a native of Mosul, his parents were Chaldean Christians, and in their faith he was baptized. Educated in Chaldaic and Arabic in the place of his birth, he received his English education at the University of Oxford. His intelligence and character attracted the attention of Mr. Layard, who employed Mr. Rassam to assist him in excavating and exploring the ruins of Nineveh, and who frequently and honorably mentioned him in his "Nineveh and its Remains." At a later period, Mr. Rassam was employed by the British Museum to continue the

---

* Gibbon, vol. iv., pp. 544-546.

work of exploration, and he had the honor to discover the long-buried palace of Asshur-bani-pal, wherein were found important tablets inscribed with the cuneiform characters. From the labors and renown of the explorer, he was called to the responsible position of "First Assistant Political Resident at Aden," under the British Government. While in the discharge of the duties of this office, he was chosen to bear the queen's letter to

HORMUZD RASSAM.

Theodore, King of Abyssinia, a narrative of which "mission" he subsequently published in two volumes. Such was the faithful manner in which he performed the difficult work of that "mission," as to merit the commendation of the queen, and to entitle him to a liberal pension for life. He is now a resident of Twickenham, on the banks of the Thames, where, with his accomplished English wife, he is engaged in literary pursuits.

While at Mosul, and subsequently at Twickenham, I had long and interesting conversations with Mr. Rassam on the present condition of the Christian sects in the valley of the Euphrates, and at my request he prepared the subjoined article on this very important subject:

"TWICKENHAM, January, 1875.

"MY DEAR DR. NEWMAN,—Agreeably to your request, I have the honor to communicate some information as to the Christian communities now existing in and around Mosul, and those scattered through Mesopotamia, Assyria, and Kurdistan. I shall dwell at some length on the terms *Chaldean* and *Assyrian*, because I believe that prior to the great schism which took place in the fifth century the ancestors of the present Christians belonged to the same stock, and held the same belief; and that when Nestorius and Eutychus were excommunicated, all those who adhered to their doctrine were nicknamed after them by their opponents.

"With the exception of a few Armenian families at Bagdad and Diarbekir, and some who are attached to the Greek Church at the latter place, the whole of the Christian community now inhabiting the above-named countries, is divided into four distinct sects: Chaldean Nestorians, Chaldean Catholics, Syrian Jacobites, and Syrian Catholics. The Nestorian community, which is estimated at fifty thousand families, occupies the southern portion of Kurdistan and the vicinity of Lake Oromia, in North-western Persia. The Chaldean Catholics number about thirty thousand families, and reside at Mosul, Bagdad, Diarbekir, and in Southern Kurdistan, bordering on ancient Assyria and Northern Persia. The Syrian Jacobites and the Syrian Catholics are less than thirty thousand strong, and have their chief centres at

Bagdad, Mosul, Mardeen, Diarbekir, and in the Toor Mountains on the extreme south-western limits of Kurdistan.

"The patriarch of the Chaldean Nestorians is styled 'Patriarch of the East,' and resides at Kochannis, in the country of the Kurds. The ecclesiastical head of the Chaldean Catholics is called 'Patriarch of Babylon,' and has his residence at Mosul. The chief of the Syrian Jacobites assumes the title of 'Patriarch of the See of Antioch,' and adds thereto 'Ignatius,' the name of his predecessors. His home is in the monastery near Mardeen, one of the most picturesque spots in all Mesopotamia. And Mardeen is also the official residence of the chief bishop of the Papal Syrians, who also claims the title of 'Patriarch of the See of Antioch.'

"Before I speak at length of the Chaldean Nestorians, I desire to allude briefly to the other Christian sects, already mentioned in connection with them. The Syrian Jacobites are Monophysites, who follow the teachings of Eutychus, who flourished in the fifth century, and who taught that the human and divine natures in our Lord were so blended as to constitute one nature. The Monophysites are divided into four branches—the Jacobites, the Armenians, the Copts, and the Abyssinians. While the last three have retained the name of their nationality, the Jacobites are called after Jacob Baradeus, the zealous defender of their faith in the sixth century, when it was nearly extinct. Of the belief of the Monophysites and of the labors of Baradeus, the historian Mosheim gives the following account: 'Many, while careful to shun the fault of Nestorius, ran into the opposite extreme. The most noted of those was Eutychus, abbot of a certain convent of monks at Constantinople; from whom originated another sect, directly opposite to that of Nestorius, but equally troublesome and mischievous to the interests of Christianity; and which, like that, spread with great rapidity throughout the East, and acquired such strength in its progress, that it gave immense trouble both to the Nestorians and to the Greeks, and became a great and powerful community. In the year 448, Eutychus, now far advanced in years, in order more effectually to put down Nestorius, to whom he was a violent foe, explained the doctrine concerning the person of Christ, in the phraseology of the Egyptians; and maintained that there was only one nature in Christ, namely, that of the Lord, who became incarnate. Hence he was supposed to deny the humanity of Jesus Christ; and was accused by Eusebius of Doryleum, before a council called by Flavianus, perhaps in this very year at Constantinople. And as Eutychus refused to give up his opinions at the bidding of this council, he was cast out of the Church, and deprived of his office; and he, not acquiescing in this decree, appealed to a general council of the whole Church."*

"In book ii., part ii., Mosheim further remarks: 'When the Monophysites were nearly in despair, and very few of their bishops remained, some of them being dead, and others in captivity, an obscure man, Jacobus, surnamed Baradeus, or Zanzalus, to distinguish him from others of the name, restored their fallen state. This indigent monk, a most indefatigable and persevering man, being ordained bishop by a few bishops who were confined in prison, traveled over all the East, on foot, constituted a vast number of bishops and presbyters, revived everywhere the depressed spirits of the Monophysites, and was so efficient by his eloquence and his astonish-

---

* Mosheim, book ii., section xiii.

ing diligence, that when he died, in the year 578, at Edessa, where he had been bishop, he left his sect in a very flourishing state in Syria, in Mesopotamia, in Armenia, in Egypt, Nubia, and Abyssinia, and in other countries. He extinguished nearly all the dissensions among the Monophysites; and as their churches were so widely dispersed in the East, that the Bishop of Antioch could not well govern them all, he associated with him a maphrian, or private of the East, whose residence was at Tagritum, on the borders of Armenia. His efforts were not a little aided in Egypt and the neighboring regions by Theodosius of Alexandria. From this man, as the second father of the sect, all the Monophysites of the East are called Jacobites.'

"It is a fact worthy of note, that the present Jacobites still maintain the old formula, 'Who was crucified for us,' which was introduced in the fifth century by Peter, surnamed 'Fuller, Bishop of Antioch;' and this is used in addition to the celebrated hymn, 'O Holy God, O Holy Almighty, O Holy Eternal.'

"It is just one hundred years ago since the Latin Church succeeded in establishing their Romish principles among the descendants of the ancient Chaldeans. My family, both on the side of my father and my mother, were instrumental in sowing the seed of Popery at Mosul and the adjacent country. Their social position, and their official relations with the Governor of Mosul gave them a great influence with the Chaldeans.

"The Romanists were very careful not to introduce their dogmas in full force upon them. At first they got them to acknowledge the Pope as the head of their Church; substituted the wafer for the leaven bread; abolished the partaking of both kinds by the people; introduced purgatory and auricular confession, with the addition of the Ave Maria to the daily private prayer; and so, little by little, brought in different superstitious practices, such as indulgences, placing pictures and images in their churches, which the Nestorians abhor above all other unchristian innovations. For a long time the Latin Church has been trying to introduce celibacy among the clergy of the Papal Chaldeans, and to do away with some of their rites which are obnoxious to the Papal taste. The present Pope has got so far as to prohibit the Patriarch from consecrating any more bishops without the special approval and sanction of the Vatican. But the Patriarch has ignored the dictates of the Latin Church, and consecrated *three* bishops contrary to its orders.

"The Chaldean community to which I belonged is rightly esteemed the most ancient portion of the population, both as to nationality and Christianity. Our ancestors were the Chaldeans, or Assyrians, mentioned in the Bible; and our forefathers professed the Christian religion as early as the first century. I need scarcely tell you that the origin of the so-called Chaldeans is disputed by those who profess to know a good deal about the history of the Old World, but who can not show from what stock the present Chaldeans really came. They can not help, however, to extend to them the ancient name of 'Assyrians,' because the land which they now inhabit was formerly called by this name. Yet they forget that at one time, especially at the latter end of the Assyrian monarchy, 'Chaldean' and 'Assyrian' were synonymous words, and the nation was sometimes known by one name and sometimes by the other. Take, for instance, the words 'English' and 'British,' which are used frequently one for the other.

"The late Dr. Grant, a member of the American Board

of Missions, who is well known for his philanthropy and Christian love to the Nestorians, published a work entitled 'The Nestorians; or, The Lost Tribes,' wherein he tries to prove that the existing Nestorians are the descendants of 'the dispersed of Israel.' He remarks on the word 'Chaldean,' in the above-mentioned work (page 170), in the following terms: 'Chaldean is a name commonly used to distinguish the Papal, but it is seldom applied to the orthodox, Nestorians; and when so applied, it is used to express their relation to Abraham, who was from "Ur of the Chaldees."' This remark, in my opinion, contradicts itself, because if the Nestorians are related to Abraham, who was a Chaldean, surely they themselves must also be Chaldeans!

"And Messrs. Smith and Dwight, two American missionaries, in a work entitled 'Researches in Armenia,' make the following comment upon the word 'Chaldean:' 'The present Chaldean Christians are of recent origin. It was in A.D. 1681 that the Nestorian metropolitan of Diarbekir, having quarreled with his patriarch, was first consecrated by the Pope, Patriarch of the Chaldeans. The sect was as new as the office, and created for it. Converts to Popery from the Nestorian and Jacobite churches were united in one body, and dignified by the name of the "Chaldean Church." It means no more than "Papal Syrians," as we have in other parts "Papal Armenians," and "Papal Greeks."' Whether this story is a surmise on their part, or they obtained the information from a reliable source, they do not show. If the latter, it is a pity they did not give their authority for such an extraordinary statement, because the Oriental records in Rome will show that, long before the era they quote (when they say the Chaldeans of Diarbekir assumed this name), that there are letters extant from the Nestorian patriarchs and bishops, who style themselves 'Chaldeans;' and, besides, it is absurd to suppose that the Roman pontiff could or would give the new national name of 'Chaldean' to a people who were not living in either Chaldea or Assyria, to say nothing about the converted Nestorians or Jacobites, who have no nationality at all, unless, indeed, Messrs. Smith and Dwight supposed that the present Chaldeans of Diarbekir are descendants of Nestorius or Jacob Baradeus! To show how fallacious are these assertions, I will quote what Assemani says in contradiction thereto. In vol. iv., page 75, he remarks that 'Paul V., *the seventh Pope before Innocent X. (to whom I suppose Messrs. Smith and Dwight refer as having given the name of Chaldean to the Nestorians of Diarbekir*), wrote to Elias, Patriarch of the Chaldeans (who was then a Nestorian) thus, "A great part of the East was infected by this heresy (of Nestorius); especially the Chaldeans, who for this reason have been called Nestorians."' In the same volume, page 1, he also states that 'the Chaldeans, or Assyrians, are called Orientals, from that part of the globe which they inhabit, and Nestorians, from the heresy they profess.'

"The Rev. G. P. Badger, another writer about the Chaldeans and Nestorians, touches also upon the point in dispute, and says, in his 'Nestorians and their Rituals' (vol i., page 180): 'When the Latin missionaries had succeeded in forming a schism among the Nestorians of Diarbekir, they wanted a name to distinguish the proselytes and their Assyrian descent.' It is a pity that Mr. Badger does not give his authority for such a supposition. He allows the Armenians, the Greeks, and *even the Syrians*, to have a name for their nationalities, and yet the poor Nestorians have no nationality whatever, not even as much as the slaves who were imported from

Circassia or Africa; and the important Chaldean community at Diarbekir could only boast of the name 'Sooraye' and 'Nestoraye,' two Chaldean words which mean Christian and Nestorian! With regard to the word 'Sooraye,' if Mr. Badger had examined the word properly, he would have found that it was used by peasants who spoke nothing else but Chaldean; and as the natives of Diarbekir speak merely Arabic and Turkish, the word 'Sooraye' would be foreign to them as much as 'Nestoraye.' All the Roman Catholic Chaldean peasantry speak nothing else but vulgar Chaldean; whereas the respectable Chaldeans, who inhabit the towns, speak the language of the place, Arabic, Turkish, or Persian; and Chaldean is only used like the Latin in the Roman Catholic Church. The peasantry do call themselves 'Sooraye,' and 'Msheehaya;' but they use these words to distinguish themselves from their Mohammedan neighbors, whom they style 'Coordan,' and 'Tayaya.' The meaning of 'Tayaya' is *Mohammedan*, nicknamed after an Arab tribe called Tai, who live at the junction of the Great Zab with the Tigris.

"The words 'Msheehaya' and 'Sooraye' are also applied by the Nestorians to all people who profess Christianity; but the peasantry of the Papal Chaldeans use the term 'Sooraye' for all Christians, and limit the word 'Msheehaya' to Roman Catholics.

"When I was at Faishapoor, living at the chief's house, my host was conversing in Chaldean with some guests about my family, and remarked that my two surviving brothers were 'Msheehaya,' but that I myself was 'Anglaizaia' (English). The poor man was quite dumfounded when he found that I had understood what he said, and when I took him to task for saying that the English are not Christians.

"If 'Sooraye' means 'Syrian,' how can the Nestorians be so named unless they are made to be descendants of Aram, or immigrants from Syria?

"In Chaldean and Arabic, Assyria is called '*Athur*,' as it has always been known by this name in that country; but by the Hebrews it was called 'Asshur.' The *th* has been corrupted into *s*; and in this sense, I conclude, and not in its meaning of Syrian, the word 'Sooraye' has been used by the Chaldean-speaking people to which Mr. Badger alludes. It may be also that as the Fathers of the Church were called 'Syrians,' the Orientals adopted this name to signify their Christian profession.

"Three ancient Arab historians, Yakoot, Aboo Alfoda, and Ibn Saeed, employ the word 'Athur;' the first for Mosul and Mesopotamia, the second for Nimroud, and the third for Nineveh proper. The last-mentioned author (vol. i., page 289, note 11) says, 'The city of Athur, which is in ruins, is mentioned in the Old Testament. There dwelt the Assyrian kings who destroyed Jerusalem.'

"The followers of Nestorius did, and very often do, call themselves Nestorians; but that is merely for the sake of distinguishing themselves from the other sects. Just as a Wesleyan or a Lutheran, if writing upon a religious matter, would say, we are Wesleyans or Lutherans. Surely such words could never be misunderstood to mean nationalities! Moreover, as the Protestants are not ashamed of the name which was given to them by Rome, neither are the Nestorians. But why this doctrinal name should be forced upon them in the sense of a nationality, when they are not connected with Nestorius either in his nationality or patriarchate, is a mystery!

"Now, let us see what ancient historians say with regard to the title of Chaldean, which has been alleged to have been given by a certain pope to the unfortunate obscure people who are theologically called Nestorians.

"Bar Hebræus, who lived in the thirteenth century, in writing about the Aramean language of the Chaldeans, remarks, 'The Orientals, who are the descendants of the Chaldeans, are a wonderful people. In their tongue there is no difference between the Pthaha and Zkapa.' These are two vowels employed by the Chaldeans in their writing, and which the so-called Syrians appear not to understand. Who can these Oriental Chaldeans be, but the people of that name who are the only nation in the world who have these two vowels in their alphabet?

"In another place the same author remarks with regard to the Aramean language under the head of the first Syriac letter 'Alep,' as follows: 'There are three dialects of the Syrian tongue; 1st, The Aramean, or Syriac, properly so called, which is the most elegant of all, and used in Mesopotamia and by the inhabitants of Koha, or Edessa, of Haran, and the Outer Syria. 2d, The dialect of Palestine, spoken by the inhabitants of Damascus, Mount Libanus, and the Inner Syria. 3d, The Chaldee or Nabathean dialect, the most unpolished of the three, current in the mountainous parts of Assyria and in the villages of Kuk and Babylonia?'

"Here, again, no less than five hundred years ago, a Syrian historian mentions the very dialect of the Aramean language which is now used by the Chaldeans. We do not agree, however, with the Syrians that our Chaldean dialect is 'unpolished,' but, on the contrary, we consider it the prettiest of all the Aramean dialects.

"Assemani, another Syrian historian (in vol. iii., page 177), makes reference to the Chaldean Nestorians as follows: 'The Nestorians are not called by this name in the East (for they regard their doctrine as apostolic; and they had never any connection with the person of Nestorius), but are generally called Chaldaic Christians (because their principal or head church is in ancient Chaldea).'

"The Chaldeans, Armenians, and Kurds who inhabited, and do now inhabit, the mountainous country to the north of Nineveh, are mentioned in the 'Anabasis' of Xenophon, which account goes far to show that the very people who existed then exist now.

"In book iv., chap. iii., the following account is written about these tribes: 'At day-break, however, they perceived on the other side of the river a body of cavalry in complete armor, ready to prevent them from crossing, and, on the high banks above the cavalry, another body, of foot, prepared to hinder them from entering Armenia. These were Armenians, Mardians, and Chaldeans, mercenary troops of Orontes and Artuchas. The Chaldeans were said to be a free people, and warlike; for arms they had long shields and spears. The high banks on which these forces were drawn up were three or four hundred feet from the river, and the only road that was visible was one that led upward, apparently a work of art. Here the Greeks endeavored to cross; but as, on making trial, the water rose above their breasts, and the bed of the river was rough with large and slippery stones, and as it was impossible for them to carry their arms in the water, or, if they attempted to do so, the river swept them away (while if any of them took their arms on their heads, they became exposed to the arrows and other missiles of the enemy); they, in consequence, retreated, and encamped at the side of the river.

"'They now perceived the Carduchi assembled in

great numbers, under arms, on the spot where they themselves had been on the previous night. Hence great despondency was felt by the Greeks, as they knew the difficulty of passing the river, and saw the Carduchi ready to attack them if they attempted to cross.'

"Then in 'Cyropædia,' book iii., chap. ii., Xenophon gives the following account of the Chaldeans and Armenians: 'The next day, Cyrus, taking Tigranes with him, and the best of the Median horse, together with as many of his own friends as he thought proper, rode round and surveyed the country, examining where he should build a fortress. Going up to a certain eminence, he asked Tigranes what sort of mountains they were from which the Chaldeans came down to plunder the country. Tigranes pointed them out to him. He then inquired again, "And are these mountains now entirely deserted?" "No, indeed," said he; "but there are always scouts of the Chaldeans there, who give notice to the rest of whatever they observe." "And how do they act," said he, "when they receive this notice?" "They hasten with aid to the eminences, just as each can." Cyrus gave attention to this account, and, looking round, observed a great part of the Armenian territory deserted and uncultivated in consequence of the war. They then returned to the camp; and, after taking supper, went to rest.'

"Again, 'The Chaldeans had each a shield and two javelins. They are said to be the most warlike of all people in that part of the world. They serve as mercenaries, if any one requires their services, being a warlike people, and poor, for their country is mountainous, and but little of it yields any thing profitable. As Cyrus's men approached the heights, Tigranes, who was riding on with Cyrus, said, "Cyrus, are you aware that we ourselves must very soon come to action, as the Armenians will not stand the attack of the enemy?" Cyrus, telling him that he knew it, immediately gave orders to the Persians to hold themselves in readiness, as they would have immediately to press forward as soon as the flying Armenians drew the enemy down so as to be near them. The Armenians accordingly led on; and such of the Chaldeans as were on the spot when the Armenians approached raised a shout, and, according to their custom, ran upon them; and the Armenians, according to their custom, did not stand their charge.

"'When the Chaldeans, pursuing, saw swordsmen fronting them and pressing up the hill, some of them coming up close to the enemy were at once killed, some fled, and some were taken, and the heights were immediately gained. As soon as Cyrus's men were in occupation of the summit, they looked down on the habitations of the Chaldeans, and perceived them fleeing from the nearest houses.'

"Both the Armenians and Kurds (Carduchians) inhabit the same country now, and why not the Chaldeans? The Armenians speak Armenian; the Kurds, Median, or corrupt Persian; and the Chaldeans, Chaldean. Why are the two former tribes acknowledged without any dispute to be the descendants of the ancient Armenians and Carduchians, and why not the Chaldeans? Even in the present time the Nestorians are considered a very warlike people, and the Armenians just the opposite—as they were in the time of Xenophon. Why, then, should the Armenians be called Armenians, but the Chaldeans merely Nestorians?

"All the Armenians profess Christianity, like the Chaldeans; but all the Kurds are Mohammedans, like the Turks and Arabs.

"Having enumerated some testimonies given by different historians with regard to certain people inhabiting Assyria and the mountainous country above it, who were called Chaldeans and Assyrians, and who are now styled Chaldeans, I must say a few words with regard to certain facts which, in my opinion, are convincing proofs that the present Chaldeans are the descendants of the ancient people of that name.

"Firstly, the Chaldeans speak the very same language as is used by that remarkable tribe of Sabeans, or Christians of St. John, as they are vulgarly called, who lived near what was considered to be ancient Chaldea, and who are generally supposed to be descendants of the old Babylonians and Chaldeans.

"Secondly, the present Chaldeans, with a few variations, speak the same dialect used in the Targum, and in some parts of Ezra and Daniel, which is called 'Chaldee.' The Nestorians have no other language but this, and must have inherited it from their forefathers, the Chaldeans; unless, indeed, the fanciful *critiques* can show that the popes of Rome made the converted Nestorians adopt the Chaldee when they bestowed upon them the national name of 'Chaldean.'

"Thirdly, the ten following words, which are pure Chaldean, are understood and pronounced at the present day by the Chaldeans as they were when written in the days of yore. They are as follows: 'Malchites,' 'Yagar,' 'Sahadutha,' 'Rabshakah,' 'Gabrius,' 'Nahr,' 'Malka,' 'Abram,' 'Naharaina,' 'Sarai.'

"'Yagar-sahadutha' was used by Laban when he made a league with Jacob, and means *heap* of witness. (Gen. xxxi., 47).

"'Nahr-malka' is the name of a great canal which is mentioned by many ancient historians as having existed in Babylon, and means *royal*, or *king's river*.'

"'Naharaina' is the name of Mesopotamia in Chaldea, and is found on the Egyptian monuments.

"'Malchites' is the name given by the ancient Oriental Church to the Greek community, which means *kingcraft*, because their doctrine was supported by the emperors of Constantinople.

"'Gabrius' (Chaldean, 'Gabria,' which means *man of God*), mentioned in Herodotus as being an Assyrian follower of Darius.

"'Rabshakah' (Chaldean, 'Rub husheeeka,' which means *the mighty lord*, or *the mighty prince*), the Assyrian general who was sent by Sennacherib, and whom Eliakim and his companions asked to speak to them in the Syrian or Aramean language. *Vide* Isaiah xxxvi., 2.

"'Abram' and 'Sarai' require no explanation, as they are pure Chaldean words which mean, the first, *the exalted father;* and the second, *my lady.*

"I might quote a hundred other words, besides the names of the months, days of the week, and the heavenly host; and find, with a few exceptions, the names used to-day by the Chaldeans are the same as they were mentioned before the Christian era, both by sacred and profane writers.

"What greater proof can there be of the origin of a people than their language? And certainly the Chaldeans are as much entitled to be called by that name as the Jews, Armenians, Greeks, and Arabs, who now speak the language of their forefathers. As the Assyrian or Aramean language became the vernacular dialect of Mesopotamia, Syria, and the Holy Land after the Assyrian conquest, so also, when the Arabians took possession of those countries, they established their language, which has been in use up to the present day. Then, again, all the Chaldeans, whether Nestorians or Papal, still keep strictly the three days' fast of what is called 'Bawoothadnenway,' or *Supplication of Nineveh*, which the Chaldeans assert to have been continued from the time the Ninevites repented at the preaching of Jonah. The Syrians, who, as I said before, must have belonged to the same stock as the Chaldeans, also keep the same fast, but not with the same devotional observances.

"Though, as previously said, Arabic is the vernacular language of Mesopotamia, Syria, and the Holy Land, yet each ancient sect uses its national or mother tongue in its rituals and other ecclesiastical rites; but the Chaldeans in Upper Assyria and Kurdistan, as well as the Kurds, can only speak their own tongue, Chaldean or Kurdish; whereas official work all over the Ottoman dominions is carried on in Turkish.

"The language which is used by the Chaldeans is known in Europe by the name of Syriac; but we ourselves call it Chaldean. We apply the word 'Syriac' to the character used by the so-called Syrians or Jacobites. It is true, there is very little difference between the Chaldean and Syriac, but there is some difference in the pronunciation of certain letters, the vowel-points, and in the formation of the letters, as much as there is between the Old English and the Roman characters.

"Formerly all the so-called Syrians employed the same writing, and pronounced every word the same as the Chaldeans do now; but in the thirteenth century Bar Hebræus, a promoter of the Jacobites, wishing to make a thorough distinction between the writing of the Monophysites and that of the Nestorians, changed the characters and the vowel-points.

"The Chaldean *p* and *a* are changed by the Syrians into *ph* and *o;* for instance, what the former pronounce our Lord's word *eppathaha*, the latter would call *epho-*

thoho. Then such words as 'maranatha,' *our Lord's coming;* 'abba,' *father;* 'talitha,' *damsel;* 'Maria,' *Lord;* 'Allaha,' *God,* the Syrians pronounce 'moronotho,' 'obbo,' 'toletho,' 'Morio,' and 'Olloho.'

"While every one knows that the writing of the present Syriac was invented in the thirteenth century, the Syrian scholars in England disdain to call the old writing of the Chaldeans by any other name than 'Syriac.' Indeed, some scholars have now gone so far as to give to the old Chaldean character, which is said to have existed three hundred years before the Christian era, the extraordinary name of 'Syro-Chaldaic,' which is, in my opinion, a far-fetched misnomer.

"With regard to the doctrine of the so-called Nestorians, their uncharitable enemies have so much exaggerated certain dogmas which were promulgated by Nestorius, that really one would think that the present Nestorians are almost as great unbelievers as the Unitarians; whereas the only difference that exists between them and the Universal Catholic Church, and which has separated them from all other Christian sects for so many centuries, is merely a play upon words. They believe as much as any orthodox Christian in the Trinity in unity, and the unity in Trinity, and that the Word was made flesh, and dwelt among us.

"The fact is, the Eutychian heresy was so obnoxious to the so-called Nestorian Church on account of attributing to our Redeemer only one nature, and confounding the human with the Divine, tending thereby to the blasphemous conclusion that the Godhead suffered, that those who sympathized with Nestorius adopted such Anti-monophysite views as were construed by the Western Church into creating a too wide distinction between the Divine and human attributes. They confess that in our Lord Jesus Christ there are two natures and two persons, *but one Parsopa;* and although by attributing two persons to our Saviour against one person, as professed by the rest of the Christian world, yet they add the *one Parsopa*, which really means *one person*, in the sense it is understood by those who call them heretics.*

"To give you a clearer and fuller account of the history of the Nestorian Church, I do not think I can do better than to quote some apposite accounts from a few ancient and modern authors.

"I must begin with Assemani, who remarks (*vide* Rich, 'Koordistan,' vol. ii., page 120), 'The Chaldeans, or Assyrians, received Christianity in the time of the twelve apostles—Peter, Thomas (Thomas, the incredulous, and the apostle of India), Bartholomew, Matthew, and Judas the son of James, and Thaddeus, also called Lebbeus; also Thaddeus of the seventy, and Mark and Alpheus, are called the apostles of the Syrians and Chaldeans. Addus, or Adi, one of the seventy disciples, was sent into the East by St. Thomas, one of the twelve, and was martyred at Edessa, under the son of the celebrated Abgarus, on his return from preaching in Persia, Assyria, and Babylonia. Mark, a disciple of Addus, proclaimed the Gospel in Babylonia, Assyria, and Persia. He fixed his residence at Ctesiphon and Seleucia, and was called the first Bishop of Seleucia, and became the head of the Oriental Church. He died after a ministry of thirty-three years (from A.D. 48 to 82). St. Thomas, whose surname, according to some, was Jude, not only was the apostle of the Syrians and Chaldeans, but also of the

---

* The Nicene Creed is one of their articles of faith, and I think this is sufficient evidence of their belief in the unity of the two natures. With regard to the procession of the Holy Ghost, however, they agree with the Greek Church.

Parthians, Persians, Medes, and Indians. It has been doubted whether St. Thomas himself ever penetrated into India.'

"Assemani again remarks (vol. iii., p. 177): 'The Chaldeans constitute a large Christian community, which has no connection with others. They have their own forms of worship, their own bishops, and their own ecclesiastical councils. Their church extends through all Asia, and exists partly in the Persian, partly in the Turkish, and party in the Mogul empire. The patriarch resides in a monastery not far from Mosul, and has a great many bishops under him. The enmity of the Persians, and afterward of the Mohammedans and Saracens, against the Romans, contributed much to further the spread of this sect; for they received refugees from the Roman empire, and extended full protection to such Christians as were not tolerated in the Roman provinces, and whom, of course, they could not suspect of any understanding with the Romans. Ibas, Bishop of Edessa, was one of the greatest defenders of the Nestorians among the Orientals; and on that account his epistle to Marin, the Persian bishop of Ardaschir, was rejected by some councils. But the chief persons among them were Barsumas and his assistant, Maanos. After the death of Barsumas, the Archbishop of Seleucia, Babacus, became the head of the party; and from this time onward the patriarchs resided at Seleucia, until, under the caliphs, Bagdad and Mosul were selected for that purpose. This Babacus held a council in the year 499, in which not only the whole Persian Church professed itself to belong to the Nestorian community, but regulations were also made that all bishops and priests must be married, and that second marriages of the clergy were not merely permitted, but declared to be necessary.'

"Mosheim, in his 'Ecclesiastical History,' cent. v., book ii., part ii., says: 'To pass by the minor errors which were attributed to Nestorius, he is said to have divided Christ into two persons, and to have held that the Divine nature joined itself to the full form of man, and only aided him during his life. But Nestorius himself, as long as he lived, professed himself utterly opposed to such sentiments. Nor were such sentiments ever directly stated by him, but only inferred by his adversaries, from his rejection of the epithet, "Mother of God," and from some incautious and ambiguous terms which he used. Hence very many, both among the ancients and the moderns, think that he held the same sentiments that the Ephesian fathers did, though he expressed himself in a different manner; and they cast the whole blame of this most destructive contest upon the restless spirit of Cyril, and his malignant disposition toward Nestorius. Allowing these to judge correctly, still Nestorius must be pronounced guilty of two faults; first that he was disposed, rashly, and with offense to many, to abolish the use of a harmless term which had long been current; and, secondly, that he presumed to express and explain, by unsuitable phrases and comparisons, a mystery which exceeds all human comprehension. If to these faults be added the excessive vanity and impetuosity of the man, it will be difficult to determine which was the principal cause of this great contest, Cyril or Nestorius.'

"Then, again, in cent. v., book ii., part ii., Mosheim says: 'The Nestorian faith is indebted to no one, of all its friends, more than it is to Barsumas, who was ejected from the school of Edessa, with his associates, and created, in the year 435, Bishop of Nisibis. From the year 440 to the year 485, he labored with incredible assiduity and dexterity to procure for Nestorianism a permanent establishment in Persia. Maanos, Bishop of Ardaschir, was his principal coadjutor. His measures were so successful that all Nestorians in Chaldea, Persia, Assyria, and the neighboring countries, deservedly reverence this Barsumas alone, to this day, as their parent and founder. He persuaded the Persian monarch, Pherozes, to expel the Christians who adhered to the opinions of the Greek fathers, and not only to admit Nestorians in their place, but to allow them to make the first cities in Persia, Seleucia and Ctesiphon, their primary seat, which their patriarchs occupied even down to our times. He also erected the famous school at Nisibis, from which issued those who, in this and the following centuries, carried the Nestorian doctrines into Egypt, Syria, Arabia, India, Tartary, and even to China. Before this sect became fully formed and established, there was some difference of opinion in it. Some said that the manner in which the two natures in Christ were combined was wholly unknown; but others denied any other connection than that of will, operation, and dignity. But this disagreement wholly disappeared from the time that the Nestorian community became duly consolidated. For it was decreed by the synods assembled at Seleucia that there were in the Saviour of mankind two persons, or ὑποστάσεις—namely, a divine, that of the Word, and a human, that of Jesus; yet that both persons constituted but one aspect, or, as they (following Nestorius) expressed it, one Barsopa; that is, that this union of the Son of God with the Son of man took place at the moment of conception, and would never end; but that it was not a union of natures or persons, but only of will and affection. Christ, therefore, must be carefully distinguished from God, who dwelt in Christ as in his temple (as Nestorius had said); and that Mary should never be called the mother of God, but only the mother of Christ. They reverence Nestorius as a holy man, and worthy of everlasting remembrance; but they maintain that his doctrine was much more ancient than he, being derived from the earliest ages of the Church; and therefore they wish not to be called Nestorians. And it appears, in fact, that Barsumas and his associates did not inculcate on their followers precisely the doctrines taught by Nestorius, but they in some measure polished his imperfect system, enlarged it, and connected with it other doctrines which Nestorius never embraced.'

"I also quote the following interesting account of the origin of the Chaldean Church from the Rev. W. Badger's work, entitled 'Nestorians and their Rituals' (vol. i., page 136): 'According to ecclesiastical tradition, Mar Addai and Mar Mari were the founders of the Christian Church in Chaldea and Mesopotamia. The latter is regarded by the Nestorians as their first patriarch. From him they derive the validity of their present sacerdotal orders in an unbroken line of spiritual descent; and to him and Mar Addai, his companion in the work of evangelization, they ascribe the authorship of one of their three liturgies, or communion offices. The following is a summary of the labors of Mar Mari, taken from the history of Sleewa Ibn Yohanna, a Nestorian author, who lived in the early part of the fourteenth century. After founding the Eastern see at Ctesiphon, then the seat of the Persian monarchy, and inhabited chiefly by Magians, Mar Mari discipled Doorkan and Cashgar, and traveled on the same mission through the two Iraks, Ell-Ahras, Yemen, and the islands of the Arabian and Indian seas, converting many heathen to Christianity by his preaching, and by the signs and miracles which he wrought, and forming them into churches. On his return to Ctesiphon, he ordained that that city should be raised into a patriarchal see; and before his death, which took place A.D. 82, he intimated that his successor was at Jerusalem, and should be sought for there. Accordingly, after the decease of Mar Mari, the company of the faithful sent to the Holy City to Simon, who succeeded James, the brother of the Lord, as head over the church there, requesting him to send them a patriarch. The person elected was Abrees, who was consecrated at Jerusalem, and sent to Ctesiphon, A.D. 90. Abrees died during the reign of the Emperor Hadrian, having filled the Eastern see for the space of seventeen years.

"'After the lapse of twenty-two years, Abraham, a kinsman of James, the brother of our Lord, was appointed to succeed Abrees, and ruled over the church in the East from A.D. 130 to A.D. 152. During his supremacy, the Christians were sorely persecuted by the Persian king, who was instigated thereto by the Magians. His successor was Yaakoob (James), who also was of the kindred of Mary, the Blessed Virgin. Previous to his death, he gave directions that two of his disciples, Kam-Yeshua, and Aha d'Abhooi, should go to Antioch, in order that one of them might be consecrated patriarch there. They accordingly went, but were seized as spies of the King of Persia, who condemned them, together with Saleeba, the Patriarch of Antioch, to be crucified before the church in that city. Aha d'Abhooi, however, escaped to Jerusalem, and was consecrated there by Mattias, the occupant of that see, in the Church of the Resurrection. He reached Ctesiphon A.D. 205, and presided over the Christians of the East for fifteen years. After another patriarch had been set over Antioch, it was agreed upon by the patriarchs of the four great sees that the Eastern patriarch elect should not again come to Antioch to be consecrated, but that the metropolitans, bishops, elders, and faithful should choose him who was to fill the see, and ordain him thereunto, in the church at Ctesiphon.

"I can not do better than to conclude with the following true and generous remarks made by the great ecclesiastical historian regarding the purity and simplicity of the primitive Nestorian Church: 'The Nestorians, who are also called Chaldeans, reside principally in Mesopotamia and the adjacent countries. These Christians have many doctrines and customs peculiar to themselves; but they are chiefly distinguished from all other sects by maintaining that Nestorius was unjustly condemned in the Council of Ephesus, and by holding with him that there were not only two natures but also two persons in our Saviour. In ancient times this was regarded as a capital error; at this day, it is considered by the most respectable men, even among the Roman Catholics, as an error in words rather than in thought. For these Chaldeans affirm, indeed, that Christ consists of two persons, as well as two natures; but they add, that these two persons and natures are so closely united as to constitute one aspect, or, as they express it, one Barsopa; which is the same with the Greek πρόσωπον, *person*. From which it appears clearly that by *aspect* they mean the same as we do by *person;* and that what we call *natures*, they call *persons*. It is to the honor of this sect, that, of all the Christians resident in the East, they have preserved themselves the most free from the numberless superstitions which have found their way into the Greek and Latin Churches' (Mosheim, cent. xvi., book iv., chap. ii.).

"Although the unfortunate Nestorians have been persecuted, harassed, and even massacred by the thousand, from the time they embraced Christianity, and very often their bitterest enemies were, what I am ashamed to call, Christians, yet their former exploits in preaching the Gospel of salvation to the heathen far and wide, and their courage and fortitude hitherto in keeping themselves from the superstitious practices of different Christian sects around them, have well earned for them the title of 'Protestants of the East.'

"Believe me, my dear Dr. Newman, yours, most sincerely, H. RASSAM.

"The Rev. J. P. NEWMAN, D.D."

CHAPTER VIII.

Departure from Mosul.—Horseback Ride of Six Hundred Miles.—Last View of Nineveh.—First Day's Ride.—A Night with the Devil-worshipers.—Hills of Kurdistan.—The Kurds.—Stuck in the Mud.—Xenophon's Retreat.—Sabbath of Feshapoor.—Crossing the Tigris.—Traveling in Mesopotamia.—Girls of Uznaoor.—Beautiful Scenery.—Nisibeen and the Nestorians.—Roman Ruins at Dara.—The True Ararat.—Heights of Mardeen.—American Mission.—Jacobite Christians.—Missionary Meeting.—Dance of the Devil-worshipers.—Attacked by Robbers.—Great Caravan. —No Water.—Beautiful Orfah.—Abraham's Fishes and Birthplace.—Ur of the Chaldees.—Armenian Christians and their Creed.—A Letter to Christ.—American Church.—Roman Roads and Reservoirs.—Milking Sheep.—Picturesque Town of Birijik.—Crossing the Euphrates.—Traveling in Syria.—American Petroleum.—Three Hundred Camels, and their Habits.—Aleppo and its People.—A Funeral.—Commerce.—American Mission.—A Beautiful Lady.—Charming Scenery.—The Flood.—Roman Roads.—Wild Pass of Beylan.—First View of the Sea.—End of the Journey.

BEFORE us was a horseback ride of six hundred miles. It was a journey from Mosul to the sea. It was a tour through Western Kurdistan, through Central Mesopotamia, through Northern Syria, to Iskenderoon, on the Mediterranean. *En route*, we were to pass through the land of the Yezidis (the Devil-worshipers); through the country of the Nestorians, whose missions had blessed the East; and through Christian villages of the Greek and Latin churches. We were to linger at Uz, where Job suffered and triumphed; at Orfah, where Abraham was born; and at Padan-aram, where Jacob found his beautiful Rachel.

There was a shorter route, west of the Tigris and direct to Damascus; but the certainty of being attacked by robbers on the desert was a sufficient reason why we

A TUKHTERAVAN.

should choose the longer way. We had discarded the clumsy *khajawah*, and taken to the English saddle. For our "elect lady" we had secured a *tukhteravan*, an idea of which is best expressed by the accompanying picture, which is true to life. As we had found it necessary to change dragomans, we were fortunate enough to employ Khidthurs, who was a member of the Protestant Christian community of Mosul, who had been in the employment of the English consul, and who had attended Doctor Leonard Bacon in his tour through Mesopotamia. Khidthurs was a Syrian, standing over six feet high, intelligent and brave, an excellent cook, a polite and obliging servant, and thoroughly honest.

Thursday dawned without a cloud, and at 7 A.M. we were at the river, waiting for the boat. An immense crowd gathered to witness the departure of the Americans. As usual, the Oriental's love of money was manifested, but with intensified greed. Every body expected a present, not for its intrinsic value, but to propitiate Providence to be kind to the travelers. We, however, were willing to bestow a few presents for their intrinsic value, and to trust Providence from other considerations. A "farewell" to Mr. Rassam, who had accompanied us to the river, and we were again on the Tigris, stemming its tremendous current. Safely over, we prepared for our long journey. It required an hour to load the mules, to put our "elect lady" in her *tukhteravan*, and to adjust our English saddles on Arabian horses.

Our path lay along the river, with the mounds of Kuyunjik on our right. It was a temptation not easily resisted to mount the ancient walls of Nineveh and ride thereon, where war-chariots were once driven abreast. We lingered for a moment at the old North-west Gate, and for the last time looked upon those mysterious human-headed bulls, whose vast proportions and admirable workmanship never failed to excite our wonder and admiration.

During the morning, we rode through an undulating country where shepherds were feeding their flocks, and native women were working in the fields. On our right were low mounds, whose summits were covered with grass, and whose sides were stratified with white marble, similar to that found in the ruined palaces of Nineveh. Above the marble mounds rose the deep-gullied hills of Kurdistan, and far away were the snow-capped mountains of Media. At noon the scenery grew picturesque, and added to the pleasure of the tour. The fields on either side were as rich and well cultivated as any in England or America. At 4 P.M. we halted for the night at the small town of Tel-el-Addis, pleasantly located among the low hills. The villagers gathered to see us, for our like had never been seen in their town before. They were tidy and well-dressed, and demeaned themselves in a modest manner. We occupied a *clean* house, for which we paid seven piastres.

At five o'clock the next morning we were again in the saddle. The weather was delightful, and the landscape beautiful. The soil was rich, and productive of grass and grain; but nowhere could be seen a tree or a bush. It is a treeless land. We crossed several mountain-streams, and met one caravan bound for Mosul. We lunched at the Fountain of Feida, near which are the ruins of some unknown town. An hour's rest, and we were again in motion. A ride of three miles brought us to the village of Semail, to reach which we had to cross a rapid stream, and climb a narrow, steep, and rough pass through red hills. Situated on a fertile plain near the mountains, Semail is thirty-six miles from Mosul, and

VALLEY OF SHEIKH ADI.

contains a khan, a military station, and seventy dwellings. But the place has a peculiar interest to the traveler as being one of the many villages of the Yezidis. They constitute a community, and have two principal settlements—one in the hills of Kurdistan, and the other on the plains of Sinjar. They are a politico-religious body, and have chiefs temporal and chiefs spiritual. The head-quarters of the Eastern branch of the tribe are at Baadir, in the Kurdistan mountains. They were once a powerful tribe, brave and thrifty, but have been much reduced in numbers and resources by their Turkish masters. Of their origin there is no certain knowledge, but some regard them as the descendants of the "lost tribes of Israel." In their ordinary habits they are clean, quiet, and industrious. In their physiognomy and general cast of appearance they resemble our American Indians. Their forms are lean and lank; their features are small, sharp, and expressive; their color is not the rich olive of the Turk, nor the glowing sunburned brown of the Arab, but of a deadly or sickly olive of the deepest hue. Their hair is long, black, silky, and glossy, and their beard is thick and full.

Their chief saint is Sheikh Adi, and his tomb is their most sacred shrine. It is in a lonely but lovely valley, and thither the tribe goes once a year to celebrate the annual feast. They believe in one God, but him they never worship. They accept the Old Testament as divinely inspired, and have some knowledge of Jesus. They hold that Christ is a great angel, and that he will come again. It is their custom to baptize their children seven days after birth, and they also practice circumcision, which suggest their Jewish and Christian origin. They reverence fire, into which they never spit; and through the flame they pass their hands, and then kiss them. When they worship, they turn toward the east, and they invariably place the face of their dead toward the rising sun. When they gather around the tomb of Sheikh Adi, at their annual feast, they dance to the music of voice and flute, and abandon themselves to the wildest excitement. The tomb is visited at dead of night. The devotees form in procession, each with a

CHIEF OF THE DEVIL-WORSHIPERS.

blazing torch, and approach the holy shrine and march around it, chanting and dancing till the morning light appears. But their chief peculiarity is their respect for Satan. They never mention his name, and put to death those of their number who dare to do so. They reverence him, not from love, but from fear. They dare not offend him, and seek to propitiate him by never taking

DANCE OF THE DEVIL-WORSHIPERS.

his name in vain. On their annual feast-day, they place a bouquet of scarlet anemones over the entrance to their houses, and hope thereby to please him whose name they never speak. They believe Satan is the chief of all the angels, and that Gabriel, Michael, and Raphael are less than he. Although he now suffers for his disobedience, yet he is still powerful. He is the prince of this world,

HIGH-PRIEST OF THE DEVIL-WORSHIPERS.

and owns all the kingdoms thereof; he is the dispenser of all evil which comes to man, and is, therefore, to be propitiated. They believe that he will be finally restored to his former greatness, and they wish so to demean themselves toward him that he will remember them when he comes into his kingdom. Their symbol of the Evil One is a bronze peacock, around which they march on their festal days, and a duplicate of which their priests carry when they go on missions to raise money.

As we had concluded to keep to the plains and avoid the mountain-passes, where the snow was deep, and as the Turkish soldier from Mosul was not allowed to leave the post-road, we were compelled to take a Devil-worshiper to escort us on our way. He was a young man, of kind and obliging manners, and we felt safe in his company. A short distance beyond Semail, we met a

YEZIDI WOMEN.

party of gayly dressed Kurdish soldiers, who are the sworn enemies of the native Christians, and for whom we had a more respectful fear than we had for Satan. Toward evening, and after having been in the saddle eleven and a half hours, we stopped for the night at the small village of Barsufkee, where we saw fences for the first time during all our tour. The sheikh was absent, but his wife bade us welcome to her new house, built of stone. The *tukhteravan* was placed within the entrance, in which our "elect lady" slept, while we spread our blankets on the cement-covered floor, surrounded by our men.

We were now in Kurdistan, and the villagers were Kurds, brave, fierce, and thievish. They were part of a vast community whose territory extends from near Mosul to the mountain fastnesses of Diarbekir, and from the Desert of the Arabs on the west to their own mountain-range on the east. They are naturally mountaineers, but descend to the plains in quest of pasture. In their

KURDISH WOMEN.

pursuits, they are shepherds and farmers, soldiers and robbers. They are all Moslems, but of the Persian school, and therefore hated by the Turks. They love independence, and are not easily brought into subjection. Like all mountaineers, they are a free, brave, and happy people. They delight in showy costumes, and in the number and brightness of their weapons. Their women are agile as gazelles, but not half so gentle. They pride themselves on their ornaments and the bright colors of their attire. As the men have a passion for war, the women have a passion for love. Their written language is Persian, their oral language is Arabic; their dialects are a corruption of both. They are the bitter enemies of the Chaldean Christians, and in their persecutions they are relentless and blood-thirsty to the last degree. No age, or sex, or condition awakens their sympathy or secures their mercy. In their Mohammedan fanaticism, they have butchered the aged, the infirm, nor spared the helpless infant; they have plundered churches, murdered the priests, robbed and burned the towns, slaughtered the men, and captured the women. They are the enemies of all, the friends of none.

The night passed; the day dawned; the journey was resumed. All promised well for the day. But evil lurked in the air. In exchanging soldiers we were compelled to take one who was sickly, without animation, and indifferent to our comfort. He was a Kurd, and knew that we were Christians. In descending from the hill whereon the town stood, he should have kept to the left, and followed the crest of the hills, and all would have been well; but he led us across a meadow into the thick mud of which our mules and horses sunk to their haunches. In their struggles to rise, the mules capsized the *tukhteravan*, broke the glass windows, and greatly vexed our "elect lady." But she was soon extricated from her embarrassment by good Hadji Merridj, who carried her on his back to where the land was high and dry. But her companions were not so fortunate. Mr. Collins was thrown from his floundering horse, and sprained his knee, which quite disabled him for several days. I had dismounted, and was aiding my horse to get out of the slough, when, in one of his frantic plunges, he nearly crushed my foot. The baggage mules wandered here and there, and floundered in the mud. The

Kurdish soldier contemplated the scene with evident satisfaction. It required two hours before we could resume our journey. The mules had to be unloaded, and each piece of baggage carried by hand to the hill-side. The *tukhteravan* had to be detached and carried by the men to the same place. Nor had our troubles ended. When the men had raised the *tukhteravan* to their shoulders, they disagreed as to which way to go, and then followed a war of words. One party pulled this way and another party pulled the other, and in the struggle all sunk into the mud, upset the *tukhteravan*, and broke a few more panes of glass. Then all swore by their prophet, and gesticulated more vehemently than a stump orator. But the Arabs rarely come to blows, if they only have time to scream and room to gesture. I had to interfere, and take direction of affairs, as neither party was disposed to yield his right of judgment.

Once out of the "Slough of Despond," we followed the ridge of the hills, and passed the first and only tree we had yet seen in the open country. In less than two hours we were opposite the Zakoo Pass, through which Xenophon led his "ten thousand Greeks." We had followed him in his "Retreat," step by step, from the Zabates to the Bumadus, where he defeated Mithridates; from the banks of the Bumadus to Larissa; thence to Mespila, and over the foot-hills to the Kurdistan range, to the Zakoo Pass, through which he fought his way to the higher fords of the Tigris. We here left the historic path to cross the Tigris at the Christian village of Feshapoor.

As we drew nearer to the hills of Kurdistan, we could observe their characteristics more distinctly. Their sides are deeply gullied, and resemble the color of ashes. The higher portions are steep and rugged, and often covered with snow. As we advanced, there was a beautiful opening to the west, through which we saw the Tigris. On our right, and far away, were the high Median mountains, whose snowy peaks were brilliant in the sunlight. Here and there were well-cultivated fields, wherein peasants were plowing with an ox and a donkey yoked together. During the succeeding hours, we forded many rushing mountain-streams, and for miles our path was a series of ascents and descents among steep hills and deep valleys. It was a relief to dismount at Mazareh, a Kurdish town with thatched roofs, and where the children came and sat down on the grass to observe the strangers lunch.

During the afternoon we passed many small farm villages located on the hill-tops, around which, and near the streams that dashed down the ravines, many trees were growing. Later in the day, we rode through a succession of deep valleys and up rugged hills, and caught some pretty landscape views, whose beauty was heightened by sparkling cascades. At 3 P.M. the gray hills of Kurdistan abruptly ended, the north-west end sloping down to the plain. But now appeared a grander range, clad in wintry robes, and beyond was Mount Ararat, a high, long, rounded ridge, white with snow. An hour later we looked down on the green velvet banks of the Tigris, where stands the Christian town of Feshapoor, sixty-six miles from Mosul. We were received by the head-man of the village, and invited to occupy the lower apartments in his two-storied stone house. His residence resembles a fort, and was built for self-defense. A Kurdish chief had threatened him with swift destruction, and he had to pay a ransom of twenty-five hundred dollars. Having completed his stone house, with barred windows and port-holes, he bids defiance to the Kurds, and intends to fight them from his strong castle. The village is well located on the bluffs on the east bank of the Tigris, and on its western side is a rushing mountain-stream, which drives a flour-mill and cherishes a mulberry grove. There is a ferry here over the Tigris, which is a source of revenue to the governor of the town.

Never was the Sabbath of rest more welcome to travelers, sick and weary. Happily it had dawned upon us in a Christian town. The people of Feshapoor are Chaldean Christians, and their better faith was apparent in their thrift, cleanliness, and intelligence. On the banks of the river they have a large stone church, with broad aisles and ornamented chancel. On the walls are pictures of Christ, of Mary, and of the apostles. The high altar is plain, but was brilliantly illuminated. An hour after sunrise the early service began. A hundred men and as many women were present; the former were well dressed, and the latter were richly ornamented. All sat on the floor, the men in front. As the worshipers entered the church, they sprinkled holy water on the brow, and made the sign of the cross. A native priest officiated, whose white beard contrasted with his brown visage. He was robed in white, and on the scapular was embroidered the Greek cross. Six assistants attended him. The services consisted of Scripture readings, of psalms chanted, and responses by the people. The host was elevated amidst the sound of instrumental music. Priest and people smote their breast three times, and all bowed the knee when the name of Christ was pronounced. Clouds of incense rose continually, and surcharged the air with a sweet aroma. At the close of the service, the priest gave his blessing to an attendant, who gave it to a layman near the altar, who in turn gave it to his nearest neighbor, and so it was passed to all the congregation. During the celebration of mass, a European priest was in the confessional, but only two persons were confessed. Originally this was a Nestorian church, but through the zeal of papal missionaries it was transferred to Rome.

Nowhere else in the East had I observed the Sabbath so strictly kept as at Feshapoor. All business was suspended, and no labor was performed. From sunrise till noon, the people attended church. Toward evening they gathered on the house-tops — the men in groups and the women in circles, chatting and laughing in a gleeful manner. Several of the ladies of the place called on Mrs. Newman, and gratified their curiosity by examining her wardrobe. They were excessively adorned with silver ornaments and with mother-of-pearl beads, which the merchants had brought from Bethlehem.

At six o'clock the next morning we were at the river, ready to cross; but the religious boatmen were in church, and could not be induced to leave, notwithstanding their promise of the previous night. After an hour and a half they came; and, to make up for their delay, proposed to crowd into one boat all our mules, horses, and ourselves. They, however, heeded our protest; and, having appropriated one boat to ourselves, we were soon in the strong and rapid current of the Tigris. It was ever a subject of devout thanksgiving to God when we had safely crossed to the other side. The boat returned for the horses and mules, and it was 9 A.M. before all was ready for a start. Had we been Catholics, we might have had an earlier departure; but Rome has made bigots of these simple-minded people, and taught them to hate Protestants.

As we were not on the post-route, and as Turkish soldiers are not allowed to escort travelers on any other road, we were compelled to pay one hundred piastres for two Christian soldiers of Feshapoor to guide us on our way. They were father and son. The former was an old man, who had crossed the plains many times, but was now of little use but as a mentor to his son, who was well mounted, and bore a spear twenty feet long. The old man's mare was as decrepit as himself, and it was a question whether either could endure to the end. We soon entered the hills, and passed many small villages and Arab encampments surrounded with herds and flocks. In an hour we turned westward, and rode through green valleys and over green hills. The hours passed in solitude, during which we met no one on the road, nor saw a human abode. The silence of an uninhabited region reigned unbroken. But beauty held sway in numberless flowers of every hue, and in murmuring brooks of delicious water. Occasionally we saw a deserted village, and after a ride of four hours we lunched near a pretty stream not far from a ruined town. At 5 P.M. we reached Ghoonduck, on a steep mound, containing two houses and twelve persons, who lived amidst a deserted village. The old man and his wife were venerable and pleasant, and their home was extremely humble. Declining to sleep in their hut, we spread our blankets on Jacob's bed, and slept sweetly under the starry sky.

The sun rose on a glorious plain to the south-west, and caused the white crest of Ararat to blush in his earliest light. Our path was over rough hills and through stony valleys. Here and there was a cluster of huts, near rich pasture-fields, wherein were large flocks. At noon we halted at Deroonah, a post-station, but a miserable town. Our Christian soldiers left us here, and in their stead we obtained one soldier, who proved to be an excellent man.

He was a Circassian, and, with thousands of his countrymen, had been conscripted for the Turkish army for a period of four years. He wore a long surtout and a high fur cap. His complexion was bright and his features were regular. He was a splendid horseman and an excellent guide. He informed us that the Sultan had forced a large number of his people to emigrate to this section of Mesopotamia, to be a barrier against the Arabs; but the plan had failed, as many of the emigrants had died.

We were now in Mesopotamia, vast, rich, and beautiful. Extending from the fountains of the Khabour about Mardeen and Nisibeen to Birijik, on the Euphrates, and thence southward, between the Euphrates and Tigris, to Bagdad, it was divided into Upper and Lower Mesopotamia. Since we crossed the Tigris at Feshapoor, our route lay through Upper Mesopotamia, whose fertility is inexhaustible, and whose population is dense and thrifty. From the time we left Deroonah, we had passed on an average a town an hour, and nowhere else had we seen such apparent prosperity. The pastures were rich, the flocks were large and numerous, wheat and barley were abundant, the streams and fountains were frequent, and the water was clear and delicious.

As the shepherds were folding their flocks, and after a ride of eleven hours, we entered the Christian village of Uznaoor. The inhabitants are Jacobite Christians, who have not bowed the knee to Rome, and on the hill in the rear of the town is their little church. We estimated the population at five hundred, and were impressed with the apparent difference between a Christian and a Mohammedan village. In their apparel, their intelligence, their cheerfulness, their thrift, their freedom, their architecture, and comfortable style of living, the Christians are

CHRISTIAN GIRLS OF UZNAOOR.

the superiors of their Moslem neighbors. The head-man of Uznaoor was a splendid specimen of physical manhood, and was hospitable as he was polite. His beautiful daughter, a girl of fourteen, was attractively attired. Her attire consisted of a pair of *shalwar*, and a red robe resembling a surplice, the long sleeves whereof were tied together and thrown behind the shoulders, and secured to the waist by a narrow girdle with two large ornamental silver clasps. Her head-dress was like an archer's helmet, made of a pointed cap, and covered with bright silver coins, laid on like scales, and over it was thrown a veil of thin gauze. The helmet weighed three pounds, and was the maiden's dower. Nearly all the women of the place wore a similar head-ornament, but not half so costly.

At a trifling expense, we were furnished with freshbaked "barley loaves," with sweet and sour milk, with poultry and eggs, with apricots and pomegranates. As we preferred to spread our blankets on the high veranda rather than to sleep even in a Christian Oriental's house, we passed the night unmolested either by voracious animals or the smoke of the Eastern pipe. During the evening the neighbors gathered in the large room to smoke and talk and laugh. Near us two women were churning in a very primitive style. They had erected three poles, and from the centre of the triangle they had suspended a goat's skin filled with milk. One woman took hold of the head, and the other woman took hold of the tail, and churned away to the music of some stirring chant.

The dawn was delightful, and at 6 A.M. we were in the saddle. As we passed through the thrifty town, women were spinning the finest wool, and men were weaving cotton cloth. It was in this same land that

Job wrote those plaintive words: "My days are swifter than a weaver's shuttle." Turning to the north-west, our path lay over a beautiful plain bounded on the north and south by picturesque mountains. The noble plain is dotted with mounds, which may be artificial, having been erected by the Persian Fire-worshipers, and whereon they built their altars; but, whether natural or artificial, these mounds are peculiar to this plain. Either at the base or on the summit of each mound is a village, and during a ride of a few hours we counted not fewer than twenty towns, and all within sight of each other. Three years ago, most of these villages were destroyed by the Mohammedan Arabs, who hate the Christians; but since then the Turkish Government ordered the rebuilding of the houses, which are again occupied by those who had been driven from their homes.

In six hours from Uznaoor, we entered the ancient city of Nisibeen, around which cluster so many historic associations. In strength and grandeur it was the foremost city of the Romans in all their Eastern empire. To capture it, the Persian emperor Shapoor besieged it thrice between A.D. 338 and A.D. 350; but each time he failed in the attempt. Thirteen years later, and after the retreat and death of the Emperor Julian, it was surrendered by the feeble Jovian, and was never retaken by the Romans. Around its walls thousands have fallen in the bloody struggle, and its ruins of to-day are the mournful memorials of defeated armies. Two marble columns, an ancient bridge, a portion of a noble church, are all that remain of its former magnificence. Within the church is a marble sarcophagus, said to have contained the ashes of Saint James, one of the Fathers, who was present at the Council of Nice, and who witnessed the third and memorable siege of the city by the Emperor Shapoor. But

GREEK AND ROMAN REMAINS AT NISIBEEN.

it is now an empty tomb. It was ruthlessly opened and partly destroyed by the conquerors, who had hoped to find therein buried treasure.

There is, however, another and higher historic interest connected with this once renowned city of the East. For centuries it was the ecclesiastical metropolis of the Nestorians, whose missions extended from the Gulf of Persia to the Caspian Sea, and from Jerusalem to the palaces of Ecbatana. Here were their grandest churches: here flourished their schools of learning; and from here went forth their missionaries to the pepper-coast of Malabar, to the spice-groves of Ceylon, and to the walled cities of China. But all now is changed. There is neither church nor college within the precincts of the town. Of the three hundred families of Nisibeen, only twelve are Christian, of which half are Jacobites and half are Armenians, without a church and without a priest. But while they have no memorial in this their former centre of power, yet elsewhere in the East the Nestorians claim to have 7 metropolitans, 7 bishops, 188 priests, 249 churches, and 11,378 families, or a total community of 70,000 souls.

Few cities in Mesopotamia can boast a situation more beautiful than that of Nisibeen. The ancient Mygdonius, now the Jaghjagha of the Arabs, flows clear and rapidly between verdant banks. Across the river is a stone bridge supported by twelve arches. Above the town towers the tall and graceful minaret of the mosque, and toward the west is the residence of the pasha, and near it a large structure used as a military station. The bazaars are considerable, and furnished us with all necessary supplies. We lunched on the grassy banks of the running waters, and, while there, received a call from the military officer in command. He was dressed like a European, except his red fez cap. He was polite and frank, and requested us to write him from Iskenderoon as to the conduct of the soldiers who were our escort. The pretty lawns along the river are the pleasure-grounds of the villagers, and many richly attired ladies were lingering there with their children and domestics, enjoying the music of the running waters.

After a ride of three hours, through a rich farming region, we halted for the night at the miserable Mohammedan village of Kasr-el-Buderveel. It was one of the outposts of the Roman empire in the East, and there still remain two square towers, strongly built of large white stones, and also sections of the wall which inclosed the Roman barracks. It was a relief to leave a place so desolate as that, and in the early dawn we were again on the road. The tedium of the journey was relieved by the coming of the Turkish post. The mail-bags were thrown across the backs of five mules which were in front, and behind them were the mail-agent, three soldiers, and two attendants, mounted on horses, and who urged on the mules to the top of their speed.

During the morning we passed the most remarkable of all the remains of the Roman empire in Mesopotamia. On our right was the famous "Dara in the Mountains," which was built by Anastasius, but improved and strengthened by the Emperor Justinian. Its double walls, its triple ditches, its strong towers, its immense reservoirs, its palace, combined to make it a monument of strength and beauty. It was the pride of the Romans and the dread of the Persians. In the year 529, it was defended by twenty-five thousand Romans under Belisarius, who was attacked by forty thousand Persians. The Romans maintained their position, and the besiegers retired, leaving eight thousand dead upon the field of battle. At a later period the triumphant Chosroës succeeded in reducing this stronghold after it had resisted the flower of his army during a siege of five months. Although now a ruin, yet in its ruins Dara is great. Its remains represent the military architecture of the Romans, and are a monument of their wealth and power. The broken arch, the prostrate column, the fallen wall, the empty tanks, the ruined palace, the two hundred ornamented tombs, proclaim a history as eloquent as it is sad. And where once the Roman Eagles triumphed, and the "standard of Persia" was raised on high, there are now fewer than one hundred and fifty native families, whose huts stand amidst the ruins of ancient Dara.

As we advanced, Jebel Judi was seen on our right—a vast, elongated, rounded mountain, white with snow from base to summit. It is the Mesopotamian Ararat, the rival of the Ararat in Armenia. Both Christians and Moslems believe that it is the mountain whereon the ark rested after the Deluge; and near it is a village called the "Market of the Eight," referring to the number of Noah's family who were preserved from the Flood. This tradition is sustained by the local topography, by the early settlement of Noah's descendants in Lower Mesopotamia, and is not contradicted by any historic facts we now possess. On our left was the large town of Armoodah, and a few miles beyond is the most delicious spring in Asia. Around its crystal waters we rested, and from the bubbling spring we drank, and sung, and laughed, and thanked the Creator for "pure cold water." Again in motion, we passed men on donkeys and women on camels. Away to the north-east was the Mardeen Gap, through which the road passes to Diarbekir. Around us were large and splendid farms, and rich pasture-lands. Just beyond the Mohammedan town of Harreen is one of the most beautiful rivers in the world. Clear, deep, and rapid, it was the image of the "River of Life." An hour farther on, we came to the Christian village of Goeley, which contains a brick-yard, and one hundred and seventy houses. The head-man of the place gave us his new residence, wherein we rested for the night, and most of the next day.

Mounted on a mule and guided by a peasant, I started at an early hour for Mardeen, the Mount Masius of the ancients. It required an hour to reach the base of the mountain, and then, for half an hour, I ascended the most crooked, rough, and intolerable road in Asia. The zigzag path enters a narrow ravine, and thence turns to every point of the compass. Over ledges of sharp rocks, through narrow cuts in some projecting cliff, along the very edge of the precipice, the sure-footed mule struggled till we reached the summit, two thousand four hundred feet above the level of the sea. By the wayside are sweet and brackish fountains, whose waters are conveyed by a series of conduits to the terraces, where the almond-tree was in blossom, and where the vine and the fig-tree were putting forth their tender leaves. On the road, I passed an aged woman, loaded with fire-wood. She was small of stature; her locks were gray; but her Grecian features were worthy the pencil of an Apelles.

CITY OF MARDEEN.

As I reached the summit, the American College bell rang merrily in the clear mountain air, calling the students to their classes; and in honor of my visit, the flag of our country was unfurled to the breeze on Mount Masius. The Rev. Doctor Andrus and Miss Parmley gave me a cordial greeting, and welcomed me to their mission. It was refreshing to be in a Christian home once more, and again look upon the faces of my countrymen. The mission property is well located, and consists of four large buildings, used for residence and school purposes. Under the faithful labors of the missionaries, the mission has proved a success. There is a church of fifty members, and an average congregation of one hundred and thirty persons, in charge of a native pastor. Through the zeal of a Bible reader, one hundred and fifty native women have been induced to study the Scriptures. There are two training schools—one for the education of candidates for the ministry, and the other for the education of their wives. There were ten students in attendance, who seemed to be intelligent and earnest men. The institution is furnished with a philosophical and chemical apparatus and a superior telescope. In the female department there were eleven girls and eight women, who had made commendable proficiency under the care of Miss Parmley. From the theological department several efficient native pastors have gone forth to teach their countrymen the way of life.

Mardeen has a population of twenty thousand, of whom one-half are Moslems, and the other half are Chaldean, Jacobite, Papal Syrian, and Papal Armenian Christians, and a few Jews. The principal streets are so many terraces cut in the side of the mountain, and rise one above the other; and the small streets which run at right angles to the former are a series of steps in the native rock. The buildings are of stone, and, being the color of the gray rocks, it is difficult to distinguish them at any considerable distance from the place. Around the town is a wall two miles in circuit. On the highest peak is the ruin of an old Roman castle, now a military station. The view from the citadel is vast and commanding.

The Moslems are in power, and have eight mosques.

They are fanatical in the extreme, and have the well-earned reputation of being the greatest quarrelers in Mesopotamia. Their Christian neighbors are more pacific, but not less bigoted. Mardeen is a religious centre. It is the head-quarters of the Syrian Papal patriarch; the residence of the Papal Armenian bishop; the home of the Chaldean bishop, and the stronghold of the Jacobite Christians. To the south of the town, and amidst scenery wild and grand, is the Yellow Monastery of the Jacobites. The structure is plain and roomy, but gloomy as a prison. The adjoining church is small and filthy, and in a side apartment are the tombs of the patriarchs and bishops. In the library is a Syriac copy of the Gospels, as old as the year A.D. 1150. The supreme spirit of the monastery is the patriarch, who is not allowed to eat flesh, drink wine, use tobacco, nor have a wife. The priests are allowed the last-named luxury, and their families reside with them in the dark monastic halls.

That night we slept at Tel-Ermine, twelve miles from Mardeen. It is a small Jacobite village near the ruins of a large Mohammedan town, whose ruined mosque and two square minarets are seen from afar. It is located at the base of one of the many mounds which dot this great plain. Near it is a stream of crystal water, wherein we enjoyed a delightful bath. Although these villages are so near each other, yet the people of each speak a different language, which made it probable that we were near the place where the "Lord did confound the language of all the earth." We were entertained by a family, superior in comforts, cleanliness, and politeness. In the evening we were joined by Doctor Andrus and Miss Parmley from Mardeen, and by Rev. Mr. and Mrs. Bell, and Miss Sears, just from America, who were to devote themselves to the work of missions. It was a joyous meeting, and the evening was passed in pleasant conversation, in hymns of praise, and in earnest prayers. After their long and fatiguing overland journey, the new missionaries were cheerful and hopeful. The ladies especially had endured much to reach their field of labor, and were not unmindful of the toil and self-denial before them. The Master had demanded much of them, but he had highly honored them in calling them to his work, and their future reward will be great.

In the gray of the morning we were in the saddle, and for hours rode through rich meadow-lands without a flock or a herd. Near Meshkoke the ground is covered with volcanic rocks, or perhaps cinders from another planet. At 5 P.M. we reached Hellalu, and pitched our tent on the grassy banks of a flowing stream. Near us were the tents of Kurdish shepherds, from whom we purchased milk, eggs, and poultry. They were gayly dressed, and wore their hair long and flowing.

The rain-clouds, which had threatened us all the night, were driven before a north-west wind, and the Sabbath dawned in beauty upon earth and sky. The sweet rest of the holy day was thrice welcome to the weary travelers, whose ears were banqueted by the music of running waters, whose senses were perfumed with the odor of the lovely flowers, whose vision was entranced by the glorious landscape of snow-capped mountains, of far-extending valleys, and of a sky as soft and pure as that of Eden. The pleasures of the hour were interrupted by the coming of a band of wandering musicians, who belonged to the sect of Devil-worshipers. Each had a donkey, and they traveled from place to place in quest of a few piastres. They approached our tent, and played, and danced, and begged. Their music was as simple in composition as it was rude in execution, and we gladly gave them a few coins as the price of their departure.

As the sun was declining, we crossed the Hellalu River, and rode over the hills to Deda, five miles beyond. In passing, a peasant woman, loaded with firewood, looked inquiringly upon our "elect lady," and tartly asked, "Why does she ride in a *tukhteravan*, and I go on foot with this load on my back?" It was in substance the old question which has agitated humanity from the beginning, and which has never been satisfactorily answered. On the hills were many encampments of shepherds, and also of muleteers whose beasts were bearing grain to the Mediterranean. On our left was the small tent village of Deda, and near it an octagonal tomb of some Moslem saint, much revered by the faithful. The Deda river is broad and deep, and flows through a glen of limestone rock, bold and rugged. The steep sides of the glen were as a vast wall, fringed with a few young pines. The shades of the evening rendered the deep chasm more gloomy, and we paused to enjoy the solemnity of the hour. Our Circassian soldier attempted to ford the river, but found the water above his horse's neck. Lower down are the five remaining piers of an old Roman bridge, and there we successfully crossed. Ascending the hill beyond, we encamped for the night. It was a bold venture, and so it proved. At one o'clock in the morning, the cry of "Robber! Robber!" resounded through our camp. In that dread hour of the night, when weary men sleep most soundly, some Kurdish robbers had forded the stream, and had crept stealthily up the slope where our animals were tethered. Jebarah first discovered the approaching thief, and gave the alarm. Shots were exchanged in quick succession; and in the excitement our servant rushed into our tent, and shouted, "Shall I shoot one?" "No, you must not kill any one." "But if I shoot one, all will run." What the honest fellow meant was, to discharge one barrel of the revolver. When his meaning was clearly comprehended, permission was given, and he blazed away in a most soldierly manner. The robbers had failed to surprise us, and, having been detected, they were content to give us a parting shot, which was returned with interest.

We waited patiently for the morning, and, "while it was yet dark," we started across a vast and rich meadow. On our left was a solitary tree, to be known hereafter as "The Robber's Shrub." There were many streams to ford, the broadest and deepest of which was the beautiful Bussameer. At night we halted beside the deeper, broader waters of the Oslonchi, or the "Lion Water." Here is an immense limestone glen, the sides of which are alternately concave and convex. The deep chasm curves in all directions, now almost in parallel lines, again in a majestic sweep. In the sides of the glen are immense caves, wherein one hundred persons could lodge, and wherein travelers often sleep. This deep stream is fed by the rains and the melted snow on the Taurus range.

On the west bank of the glen we encamped, and listened to the music of the rapids. As I stood on the verge of this great chasm, one hundred horses, mules, and donkeys came down the opposite side, with bells on their nose, bells on their neck, bells on their breast, bells behind, and bells before, which tinkled on the evening air. The animals were loaded with wheat for the Mediterranean, where it was in great demand. It is a slow method of transportation, as they travel but four hours a day, or twelve miles. The custom is to travel two hours and rest four hours, so that the whole distance is equally divided between the morning and the afternoon.

At 5 A.M. the tents were struck, the animals loaded, and the caravan was in motion. Then came the sound of bells, from the smallest sleigh-bell to the largest cow-bell. Poe should have heard those bells and added another stanza. Inspired by the music of the bells, we joined the caravan. In an hour we came to a Roman reservoir, fifteen feet wide and sixty feet long, and well preserved. During four mortal hours thereafter, we traveled through a succession of interlaced limestone hills, rocky and barren. In some places the deep glen was not twenty feet wide, while on either side, like cyclopean walls, the rocks rose above us one thousand feet perpendicularly. At times we seemed completely shut in, and our only outlook was up to the clear blue sky. There was a rugged grandeur in the scene, and the silence was impressive. It was ours also to know by experience what is meant by a "dry and thirsty land where no water is." Faint and weary, we would have rested in the "shadow of a great rock;" but there was no water for man or beast. We stopped from sheer exhaustion. There was but one small jug of water, while seven persons and seven animals were sorely athirst. A passing traveler informed us of water half a mile beyond. All hastened to the spot, where we found a pond of muddy rain-water, but of which all were glad to drink. Five miles farther on were the ruins of a Mohammedan khan, and near it was another Roman reservoir half full of impure rain-water. Around it the shepherds gathered with their scanty flocks. As we advanced through the glen, we observed the remains of a Roman road paved with round stones, and flanked with well-dressed blocks of limestone. Other reservoirs were passed, some in ruins, some in good condition. In the days of the empire, this was one of the military roads of the Romans, who made ample provision to supply their armies and caravans with water.

At length we emerged from the "valley of the shadow of death," to traverse "wide extended plains," where the fields were green with grass and grain, and whereon murmured a hundred rivulets. It was here we witnessed the sport of the natives. To relieve the tedium of the journey, the muleteers of a large caravan threw their sticks high in the air, each attempting to hit the first one thrown; and when done, it was the signal of a wild shout. After having been in the saddle thirteen hours, we halted at Tel-el-Merdge, near a pretty stream, where we pitched our tent, and were soon fast asleep.

The rainless weather continued. The dawn was cloudless. A ride of half an hour brought us to Jellab, a charming spot. On either bank of the river are the cottages of the Syrian Christians, around which the apricot was in blossom, and near which were long avenues of young poplars. As far as the eye could reach, the land was in a state of cultivation. An hour from Jellab, and beautiful Orfah was in view. The approach thereto was singularly picturesque. The intervening space of twelve miles was rich in the variety of its landscape. The young grain of spring, the flowers of the field, the winding stream through grassy banks, the distant mountains, the city on the hills, with dome and minaret and castellated towers looming up from out groves of the apricot, the fig, and the pomegranate, with, here and there, the dark and graceful cypress, contrasting with the red tower and white minaret, delighted the eye and animated the soul. A broad mountain-stream flows along the base of the hills, and is spanned by a well-constructed

CITY OF ORFAH.

stone bridge. We preferred to ford the stream, and follow the wall to the north-east gate, where we encamped. The people gathered in crowds to see the strangers, nor were the veiled women the least curious to see us. We were courteously received and entertained by the Rev. Mr. Hagap Aboohagatian, of the American mission. He was educated in Germany, and is reputed a good scholar. The mission premises are admirably located on the hillside, and the church is spacious and accessible. There is a membership of one hundred and fifty, and a congregation of seven hundred. A large school is supported by the church and community. We occupied the apartments wherein the American missionaries reside, when in town; and here we rested for a day and a night, and thanked God for a Christian bed.

For beauty of situation and for historical associations, Orfah is one of the most interesting cities of Mesopotamia. It rivals Damascus in garden scenes and in architectural ornamentation. From the plain the town rises in terraces up the gentle slope of the mountains on the west, surrounded with gardens which cover an area of ten miles beyond the walls on the east and south-east. Through the city flows the pretty Kara Kozoon, which is spanned by three bridges, and which runs through the gardens to the open country beyond. The city walls are high and penetrated by three imposing gates. The streets are narrow but clean, and paved on either side, with a causeway for pedestrians. The buildings are constructed of limestone, and not a few are substantial and ornamental. The bazaars are tastefully arranged, and are well supplied with native and foreign goods. The manufactures of India, Persia, Cashmere, and Europe are displayed for sale. The domestic articles are cotton and woolen cloths, which are purchased by the poor. In the numerous coffee-houses the traveler is served with iced milk, sherbets of honey, cinnamon-water, and a variety of rich perfumes. In the markets may be had the delicious white mulberry, the apricot, the quince, the fig, the grape, the pomegranate, and the pistachio-nut, together with oranges, lemons, and melons.

The population of Orfah is about equally divided into Moslems and Christians. Of the fifty thousand people who reside within the walls, some are Chaldeans, some are Armenians, some are Arabians, and not a few are Syrians. They display toward each other the fanaticism peculiar to the sects in the East, and are intolerant one toward the other. There is a display of wealth and refinement in the street apparel of both men and women not seen in towns to the south and south-east. The average thrift of the people is greater than at Mosul or Bagdad, and the standard of education is proportionably higher. The ladies excel in beauty and in the richness of their ornaments, and delight to display both in the lovely gardens and on the shaded terraces.

As a historic place, Orfah presents many points of interest. Traditions, antiquities, and names indicate its great age. It is, no doubt, the "Ur of the Chaldees," and a very ancient tradition makes it identical with the "Land of Uz." Near the Haran Gate is "Job's Well," from which the patriarch drank, and which is a sacred shrine with the people. The tradition seems to be confirmed by the fact that Job dwelt among a people called Sabeans and Chaldeans,* who plundered him of his flocks and herds, and the descendants of whom reside here now in the persons of the Yezidis, some of whose doctrines and rites are connected with Sabeanism and Magianism. But if their religious tenets are not proof of their descent, their thievish propensities are, as they are ready to plunder Job, or any one else they may chance to meet.

There is, however, much stronger evidence for the tradition that Orfah is the birthplace of Abraham. It is recorded in Genesis that "Terah took Abram his son, and Lot the son of Haran his son's son, and Sarai his daughter-in-law, his son Abram's wife; and they went forth with them from Ur of the Chaldees, to go into the land of Canaan; and they came unto Haran, and dwelt there. And the days of Terah were two hundred and five years: and Terah died in Haran."† The site of Haran is less than twenty miles to the south-east, and

---

* Job i., 15–17.   † Genesis xi., 31–32.

within its now ruined walls is the traditional grave of Terah, the father of Abraham. On the two hills are the remains of the Roman castle where the Parthians defeated the Romans, and where occurred the death of Marcus Licinius Crassus. Somewhere between these two cities was the Padan-aram where the beautiful Rebekah lived before she was wedded to Isaac, and where Jacob served Laban, and received Leah and Rachel as his wives.

To the people of Orfah the name of Abraham is a household word. They point to his birthplace with evident pride, and have reared monuments to his memory. To the south-east of the town, and at the base of the mountain, is the cave wherein he was born, and over it is a mosque so holy that only Moslems are allowed to enter therein. And not far from the cave, and within the most lovely portion of the city, is a pool of crystal water, filled with Abraham's fishes. It is called "Birket-el-Ibrahim el Khaleel"—"Abraham the Beloved, or Friend of God." It is one of the most enchanting spots on earth. The clear water is conducted from a perennial spring into a marble basin, three hundred feet long, twenty feet wide, and six feet deep. At the eastern end, where the waters are allowed to escape, there is a rustic bridge; at the opposite end is a pretty marble kiosk, from beneath which the waters flow; on the south side are green lawns, and gardens of flowers, and groves of the white mulberry, the tall and sombre cypress, the drooping willow, the bright oleander, the lofty sycamore, and the shady fig and pomegranate. From out the grove rises a mosque, and above the mosque towers a graceful minaret. On the opposite side is a well-paved causeway for promenades, whose very edge is washed by the waters of the lake. Above this noble path is the grand façade of the Mosque of Abraham, whose name it bears. This marble mosque is crowned with three domes of equal size, surmounted with gilded crescents, and a lofty minaret, springing up from amidst a cluster of tall and solemn cypress-trees. Within the sacred inclosure, silver lamps, filled with the choicest olive-oil, burn night and day in honor of the Father of the Faithful. The sylvan lake is filled with fine carp, to the number of not

ABRAHAM'S MOSQUE AND POOL.

less than twenty thousand. They are sacredly called "Abraham's fish," the descendants of those cherished by the patriarch. As the water in which they swim is beautifully transparent, they are seen to good advantage; and, as they are not allowed to be caught or in any way molested, they multiply exceedingly. It is deemed an act of piety to feed them; it is considered a crime to eat them. To prevent any person from catching these fish, the Moslems have invented the superstition that he who purloins from the sacred waters will be smitten with idiotcy. But the Christians of Orfah have such a reverence for Abraham that they are never so happy as when they can feast on a dish of his fish, cooked with wine-sauce, and eaten as a royal dainty.

From this enchanted spot, where turbaned Turks and veiled women repose in the music of its waters, and beneath the shade of its trees, we passed to examine the old Roman castle seated on the summit of the adjacent mountain, and whose walls are two thousand feet in extent. In the outer wall, as if to mark the entrance to a palace, are two Corinthian columns crowned with beautiful capitals, and on each the stork had built its nest. Around the walls is a moat, fifty feet deep, cut in the solid rock. Within the walls reside a few poor families, where once Roman emperors dwelt. The view from the castle is commanding and grand. Far away on the plains were the groves of the fig, the apricot, and the pomegranate; at our feet were the gardens around the Pool and Mosque of Abraham; and above them rose the swelling dome, the slender minaret, the square red tower of some early Christian church, and the tall, dark cypress that gave shade to the beautiful picture.

Few cities in Mesopotamia are richer in Greek, Roman, and Christian antiquities than Orfah. It is the Edessa of the Greeks, and the Antoniopolis of the Romans. It was here that Macrinus assassinated Antoninus Bassianus Caracalla, son of the Emperor Severus. It was enlarged and beautified by the Emperor Justinian, who may be regarded as the great church-builder in the East. It was so highly esteemed as a military centre that, around its walls, Greeks and Romans, Persians and Par-

thians, Saracens and Crusaders, fought for its possession.
But its chief historic significance is in connection with
early Christianity. Here was the residence of King Abgarus, who wrote a letter to Christ, and requested therein that the artist who bore the letter might be permitted
to paint a portrait of Our Lord. According to the pious
tradition, the Saviour declined to sit for his picture, but
condescended to make a miraculous impression of his
countenance upon a napkin, which he sent to the King
of Edessa. For centuries this image was esteemed the
palladium of the city, and was finally worshiped by a
deluded people.

Although Orfah early became a Christian city, yet it
is notorious for its religious errors and factions. During
the time of Julian the Apostate it became a stronghold
of the Arians, whose disorders led to the confiscation of
their church property; and one hundred years later the
heresy of the Nestorians was accepted as Divine truth,
notwithstanding it had been driven from Ephesus and
Chalcedon. At present the Christian community is divided into Syrian Jacobites and Armenians. The former
are few in number and weak in influence; but the latter
are strong in numbers, in wealth, and social position.
Their community is estimated at fourteen thousand, and
annually increasing. On our return from the castle, we
visited their large and imposing church. It stands in a
spacious court, and connected therewith is the episcopal
residence and the parish school. The church is one hundred and fifty feet long and seventy-five feet wide. The
interior is divided into three aisles by a double row of
Saracenic columns, which support graceful arches. One
of the aisles is partitioned off by a trellis-work, to screen
the female portion of the congregation. From the ceiling depend large lamps, and the floor is covered with

Persian carpets. The high altar is exceedingly imposing. Fifty feet high and thirty feet broad, it is a Gothic arch, richly gilded. In the centre is a representation of the Holy Family, and on either side are images of the apostles, while above them all is Christ sitting in judgment. On the right of the altar is an image of Mary and her Son, encased in silver, and said to have been painted by Thaddeus, one of the Seventy. A lamp ever burns before that image, and a contribution-plate is ever there to receive the gifts of the people. Although vespers were ended, yet many worshipers were present. It is customary for the working people, before they return home, to stop at the church and offer their prayers. Some stood like statues, others touched their foreheads to the ground and breathed forth their devotions. Around the church are the graves of the sainted dead, and over some of the tombs are tasteful monuments.

The Armenians have communities in nearly all the principal towns, from Bagdad to the Black Sea, and from Kurdistan to the Mediterranean. They trace their origin back to apostolic times. In the fourth century of our era they accepted as truth the Nicene and Athanasian creeds, and continued in this belief for two hundred years. But in the sixth century they were induced to change their religious views by Jacob Baradæus, who taught that the human nature of Christ had been absorbed by his Divine nature; and that the procession of the Holy Ghost was from the Father alone. In these false doctrines they still abide, and are to-day a formal and powerless church. They invoke the saints and worship images; they practice a triune immersion in the administration of baptism; and they believe in transubstantiation in the holy eucharist. They have patriarchs, bishops, and priests; they have monasteries and convents and parochial schools. At present their community is divided into Monophysites and Roman Catholics; but the Papists have had less success in perverting Armenians than in converting Nestorians. The American missionaries are now exerting a wholesome influence over the Armenian youths by extending to them the privileges of education.

The storm of the previous night had been succeeded by a charming morning, and at 8 A.M. we were again in motion. On the outskirts of the town were extensive Mohammedan cemeteries, and beyond them were large graperies and fig orchards. Our path lay up an ascent two thousand feet high, from the summit of which we obtained a glorious view of the plains below and of the snow-capped mountains that rose above us on the north. Fragments of an old Roman road appeared here and there as we advanced, and now and then we saw the remains of ancient reservoirs. After leaving the summit of the ridge, and for eighteen miles beyond, we traveled through a rough and hilly region. About 5 P.M. we halted for the night at Charmelik, and encamped at the base of a mound, near which is a Roman reservoir, one hundred feet long, six feet wide, and fifty feet deep. The huts of the villagers are of mud, with roofs of sun-dried bricks, which resemble bee-hives. In the dusk of the evening I strolled through the town, and examined these ingeniously constructed dwellings. The entrance is a descent into an under-ground apartment, above which is the conical roof. Upon the earthen floor was spread the coarse rug whereon the occupants sleep, and on the walls were suspended the sword and gun for protection against the midnight thief. There was a hum of busy life in the little village. Youthful shepherds were returning with their flocks; the men were feeding their camels and donkeys; and the women were carrying wood and water for the night. One poor girl, who had lost the use of her lower limbs, moved over the ground by aid of her hands, and seemed to be pitied and caressed by her companions.

The night was severely cold. The thermometer indicated a change from seventy-eight to forty degrees in less than twelve hours. We were near the Taurus range, which was covered with snow; and as the wind blew from the direction of the snowy mountains, it was intensely cold. But the sun came forth clear and bright, and his earliest rays were welcomed by the icy peaks, which blushed in the rosy light. Nearly all the morning we followed the line of the telegraph, which imparted to the soul a sense of home. Having lunched near a small stream, we resumed our tour, and rode over chalk-hills so white as to be exceedingly painful to the eyes. Here in this dry region the Romans had constructed immense reservoirs for the accommodation of their armies and for the comfort of caravans; and so admirably were they made, they have suffered but little from the lapse of the ages, and the constant neglect by the subsequent occupants of the country. At 1 P.M. we passed the watershed, and an hour thereafter we saw the Euphrates. The large town of Birijik was now full in view, and the prospect thereof was the most picturesque we had seen in Mesopotamia. The toil of the journey was relieved by the pleasant approach to the city through extensive graperies, and fig and apricot orchards. On either side of the road, the clear water flowed rapidly in its descent to the Euphrates. In the rocks are large caves where travelers repose during the night, and in the quarries natives were at work dressing the soft stone for building purposes. Passing through the crowded bazaar, we reached the ferry with difficulty. Large quantities of grain in sacks were there to be ferried over the river, and an immense throng of people were waiting to cross. We applied to the authorities for permission to cross, but, after a tedious delay of an hour, we were informed that we must wait till morning. This was a disappointment, as we preferred tenting on the green banks beyond to remaining in a Turkish town. We dispatched our

TOWN OF BIRIJIK.

servant to the pasha, but that placid dignitary consoled us by affirming that there would be less water in the river in the morning, and that it would then be much safer crossing. This polite reply was to cover his purpose to detain us till the morrow. Reluctantly we returned through the narrow, crowded streets, and stopped for the night in a large khan, where all manner of animals had their abode.

In the light of the setting sun, and in the light of

the full moon, we viewed with delight the terraced streets, the embattled towers, the dome and minaret of many a mosque, and the white dwellings, rising in tiers to the summit of the bluffs, which combine to make Birijik the most picturesque town on the banks of the Euphrates. It is, no doubt, the Birtha of antiquity, and near it has been a ferry across the Upper Euphrates, between Syria and Mesopotamia, from the days of the patriarchs to the present time. The town is built upon three white chalk bluffs, which are from five hundred to one thousand feet high. The streets are so many terraces cut in the rocks, and extend from the water's edge to the summit of the hills. The buildings are of the same materials as the hills, and it is difficult to distinguish them apart at any considerable distance from the place. The sight was pleasing as we looked up from the margin of the river and saw the people on the flat roofs of their dwellings enjoying the beautiful sunset. Of the twenty thousand inhabitants, some are Turks, some are Arabs, some are Christians, and a few are Jews. The Moslems have five mosques, the Armenians have one church, and the Jews have a synagogue. The people speak Turkish and Arabic, and most of them are merchants and craftsmen. In the fantastically excavated caves, both within and without the city walls, the Arab shepherds live and fold their flocks. On the summit of the most northern bluff, whose base is washed by the river, is an old castle, now shattered, but still imposing. Rising two hundred feet above the Euphrates, the old Roman tower is oblong in form, with a double row of apartments on the eastern side, crowned with a parapet, and beneath them are two tiers of galleries cut in the solid rock, with loop-holes for archery. The entrance is through a narrow gate-way, and within is a covered passage-way which leads to the river. Some of the larger chambers remain in good condition, and in one of the arched apartments is a bass-relief. A few Corinthian columns and a broken frieze indicate the former elegance of the place.

At six o'clock the next morning we were at the ferry. At our feet rushed and foamed the ancient Euphrates. Having its source in the mountains of Armenia, its volume is increased in the spring by numberless tributaries, and swollen by the melting snows on Mount Taurus. Larger than the Orontes and the Jordan, about equal in breadth to the Thames at Blackfriars Bridge, it is not wider than the Hudson opposite West Point. It is of the color of the Nile, and the dull yellowish earth which discolors its waters is borne southward, to form alluvial plains around the ruins of Babylon. Where the banks are steep, they are here composed of a chalky soil; and where they are flat, they are covered with trees and verdure. Both to the north and south of the town there are woods and green fields and extensive groves. Looking northward, it was a pleasing sight to watch the classic river as it flowed toward us, meandering as it does among the distant hills. It is one of the few rivers mentioned in the Bible which still retain the Scriptural name. It was familiar to the patriarchs, for it is said, "In that same day the Lord made a covenant with Abram, saying, Unto thy seed have I given this land, from the river of Egypt unto the great river, the river Euphrates."[*]

Where we stood, the eastern bank was steep, and the opposite one was flat, covered with dark sand and pebbles of white quartz. As the recent rains had melted the snows on the Taurus Mountains, the river was swollen

---

[*] Genesis xv., 18.

beyond the memory of man. The current was strong, not less than twenty feet deep, and rushed by with a rapidity equal to six miles an hour. The boats in which we were to cross were rude and unwieldy. Each one was forty feet long, ten feet broad, fifteen feet high at the bow, and only two feet high at the stern. These boats have neither keel, stem-piece, nor stern-post; the bottoms are formed by planks nailed beneath the cross-timbers of the flooring; and the stern gradually rises from the bottom till above the level of the water. On the high bow is a long oar, formed of a trunk of a young tree, with its thickest end inboard, and so fastened as to nearly balance. By this Oriental arrangement the rudder is in the bow of the boat. At the stern and on either side were immense oars, each pulled by three men. When ready to cross, the boat is pushed upon the beach, stern on, and then loaded.

During the night many caravans had arrived, and the excitement at the ferry was intense. Thousands of sacks of grain had been brought there for transportation, and the impatient merchant was furious at the delay. Horses, mules, camels, donkeys, cattle, sheep, men, women, and children, were there to be ferried across, and the neighing of the horse, the groaning of the camel, the braying of the ass, the bleating of the sheep, mingled with the cry of the child, the scream of the women, and the harsh guttural of the men. We were detained in this noise and crowd for more than an hour; not from necessity, but from sheer love of money. In addition to the ordinary ferriage, we were required to pay fifty piastres for the privilege to cross at once, or otherwise we must wait the pleasure of the ferry-masters. We paid it, and thought " What thieves these Turkish officials are!"

The amount was given, and we were soon out in the

powerful current, which swept us down the river, despite the efforts of the boatmen. It was an anxious moment. The men lost control of the boat; our horses became restive; the Arabs grew pale; and the boatmen shouted and screamed, as if blowing were better than rowing. We had been carried half a mile below the proper landing, but thanked God that the crossing was over.

We were now in Syria, which extends from the Euphrates to the Mediterranean, and from Armenia to Palestine and Arabia. We were to cross its rugged mountains and follow its narrow, tortuous valleys. We were to scale the heights of its Libanus and Antilibanus, and look upon the icy crown of Hermon. We were to visit Aleppo, its chief commercial inland city, and embark at Iskenderoon, one of its largest sea-port towns. Our tour through Mesopotamia had been completed; we had looked upon the Euphrates for the last time; and we were now to traverse Northern Syria, through which had so often marched the proud armies of the Assyrians, of the Greeks and Romans, of the Persians and Parthians, and over which Solomon had swayed his mighty sceptre.

All were ready for a start at 9 A.M.; but, at the moment of starting, our Turkish soldier proved himself a rogue. He pretended that the pasha had commanded him to take us by the longer route to Aleppo; this, however, was but a pretense to get a present to go the shorter road. We dismissed him at once, and an hour beyond we saw him lying by the wayside awaiting our coming, and still hoping that we would employ him. Having acquainted the pasha with the facts, he sent us an excellent guide, and also his apology for what had occurred. Our path was among the dark hills, and in three hours we crossed a new bridge that spans a pretty stream, near which is a beautiful cascade.

On the way we met three hundred camels, loaded with English dry-goods and with American petroleum, bound for the inland towns as far south as Mosul. We halted to see them pass. It was a grand sight. There was majesty in the slow, measured movement of the three hundred, as each waved its head on high as if conscious of the review. Each was a noble specimen of its kind; each had a bell suspended around its long and curving neck; each had its name, and knew the voice of its driver. They recalled the patriarchal past, for "Job had six thousand camels,"* and they formed in part the great wealth of Abraham. As beasts of burden they are indispensable in a country like this, and are here esteemed of great value. They are domestic animals, and are never found wild. In their structure, they are adapted to the climate, to the soil, and to the condition of society in the East. Their feet are adapted to the sands of the desert, and to the plains of Syria and Mesopotamia. Consisting of two long toes, a hard, elastic cushion, and a tough, bony sole, the camel's foot bespeaks the wisdom that formed it for a purpose. Where they are compelled to make long journeys, and often through dry and barren regions, their power of endurance is wonderful. They can travel for twenty days, a distance of six hundred miles, without food; and although they require ordinarily as much water as other animals, yet they are furnished with a series of cells into which the water runs, and wherein it is preserved for future use. Sometimes the camel is killed to supply the famishing owner or driver with water. When first taken from the cells it is of a greenish color, but soon becomes fresh again. A camel can drink as much as

---

* Job xlii., 12.

twenty gallons at one time. They are so endowed that they can scent water a great way off, and many a thirsty traveler has been encouraged to hope by the motion of his camel. As beasts of burden their strength is great. They can carry from five to six hundred pounds, and travel on for many days. Although they are revengeful and never playful, yet they become attached to their driver, and seem charmed with his song, of which this is a specimen:

> "Dear unto me as the sight of mine eyes
> Art thou, O my camel.
> Precious to me as the health of my life
> Art thou, O my camel.
> Sweet to my ears is the sound
> Of thy tinkling bells, O my camel;
> And sweet to thy listening ears
> Is the sound of my evening song."

While the ordinary camel is slow of pace, yet the deloul is exceedingly swift. In appearance, the deloul is lank, gaunt, and ungainly, but it can go ten miles an hour, and can endure a continuous journey of five hundred miles. The color is light brown and white, and the limbs seem formed for rapid motion. Delouls are employed by Turkish and European officials in the East, to carry a special messenger when business requires dispatch. To this the prophets allude: "Thou art a swift dromedary traversing her ways;"* and, "The multitude of camels shall cover thee, the dromedaries of Midian and Ephah; all they from Sheba shall come: they shall bring gold and incense; and they shall show forth the praises of the Lord."†

There is a very marked difference between the camels of Mesopotamia and those of Bactria. The Bactrian cam-

---

* Jeremiah ii., 23.   † Isaiah lx., 6.

el is adapted to a colder climate by the thickness of its hair, and to a mountain region, by a long, projecting toe, which enables it to climb the rocky passes. Those of Bactria are draught-camels, employed to draw huge carts and lighter vehicles. To these Isaiah refers: "And he saw a chariot of camels."* Some suppose that the distinction between the camel and the dromedary is in the

THE DROMEDARY.

supposition that the former has one hump, and the latter has two humps. But such is not the case. The double-humped camel is found only in Bactria, and in countries north and east of Persia; and is shorter, thicker, more muscular, covered with a dark and shaggy hair, and is heavier and stronger than the single-humped camel found

* Isaiah xxi., 7.

in Mesopotamia, Arabia, Syria, Egypt, and Africa. The latter are taller, more slender, of a paler color, lighter in form and in flesh, and are covered with a short, sleek hair. From the single-humped camel comes the dromedary, which is trained for speed, and holds the same relation to other camels that the race-horse holds to other horses.

Having passed the great caravan, we rode on, and lunched at Saracosh. During the afternoon our path

ARAB CAMELS.

lay through a beautiful section of country, where the soil was red, rich, and well cultivated. Crossing the charming Sarjure, we halted for the night at the small village of Karaguz. From the peasants we replenished our exhausted larder, and after a good supper on what the dairy, the hennery, and the flock could furnish, we rested for the night.

The morning was bright, but a strong north-west wind blew hard all day, which detracted from the pleasure of traveling. At noon we rested for two hours at Chobombegjee, where is a small mosque shaded by three young trees. The pretty maidens of the place were milking the sheep, which their youthful brothers had driven in from the fields. Both men and women were engaged in brickmaking, and the bricks produced resembled in size and color those I had seen at ancient Babylon and Nineveh. After our too brief rest, we were again in the saddle, and, during the afternoon, rode through a rich country, and more thickly settled than any other portion of Syria we had yet seen. As the sun declined, we pitched our tents for the night at the village of Barazur.

Cheered by the prospect of reaching Aleppo by noon, we started the next morning at four o'clock. At 6 A.M. we forded a stream whose waters flow to the sea, which clearly indicated that we had commenced our descent to the Mediterranean. The road was stony, and rougher than on any previous day. While resting for an hour near a half-ruined town, a caravan of Persian pilgrims passed us, who were returning from Mecca to their distant homes. In an hour beyond, the Castle of Aleppo was seen to the south-east, and the sight thereof filled our hearts with gladness.

The approach to the city was through extensive suburban gardens, wherein the vine, the fig, the pomegranate, the apricot, the lemon, and the orange blended their foliage and their blossoms, producing a pleasing scene. Above the groves rose the domes and minarets, the walls and towers, of the most elegant city in inland Syria. On our left was the old Roman castle, crowning the highest of the surrounding hills, and which has been the scene of many bloody struggles for the conquest of the place. From its geographical position, Aleppo represents the older civilization of the East and the better civilization of the West. A fortified town, its walls are forty feet high, penetrated by seven gates, and defended by towers ten feet higher than the parapet. The buildings within are of stone, and many of them are superior in construction and ornamentation. The city contains two hundred fountains, sixty baths, one hundred coffee-houses, one hundred mosques, and many schools and churches.

HALT OF A CARAVAN.

Of the one hundred thousand inhabitants, three-fourths are Moslems, and the remainder are Syrian, Greek, Chaldean, Armenian, Catholic, and Protestant Christians, together with native and foreign Jews. The Catholics have divided the Greeks, the Armenians, and Syrians, and greatly outnumber those who have remained steadfast in the faith of their fathers. In commercial importance and wealth Aleppo is second to Damascus. Being but three days from the sea-port town of Iskenderoon, the trade of Europe passes through its gates to all inland towns as far south as Mosul; and through it flows the return commerce of Mesopotamia, Kurdistan, and North-eastern Syria, for shipment at Iskenderoon for Egypt, the Levant, Europe, and America. In refinement of manners, in style of living, in social intercourse, the citizens of Aleppo are the most polished people in the East. Those who are rich reside in spacious dwellings, which are furnished in a manner representing the elegance of the West and the luxury of the East; and around such dwellings are gardens wherein flowers bloom, fountains sparkle in the sunlight, and orchards yield the most luscious fruits.

During our stay of three days in Aleppo, we were entertained at the American mission. The property is well located, and is admirably adapted to the purposes for which it was purchased. Within is a paved court with fountain, vines, and flowers. On one side of the quadrangle is the church, capable of seating four hundred persons; adjoining it is the school-room, wherein were thirty boys and girls under the care of a native Christian lady; on the other sides of the square are the residences of the missionaries, for the accommodation of two families. The membership of the mission is fifty, and the congregation averages one hundred. Some of the most enterprising young men of Aleppo are members of this community, whose influence is a power for good. The pastor in charge is a native, and is highly esteemed for his piety and learning.

While a guest at the mission, I was invited to attend the funeral of one of the most wealthy and influential members of the congregation. A walk of twenty minutes brought me to the residence of the departed, where a large concourse of people had assembled. The coffin was placed on the floor, and around it sat the relatives and friends of the dead, singing hymns appropriate to the sad occasion. The deceased was wrapped in a winding-sheet, and about his head was a napkin. In the absence of the pastor, one of the elders of the church offered prayer, and then invited the mourners to take a farewell look of the beloved dead. The voice of weeping and lamentation touched all hearts present with deep sympathy for the afflicted family. At the head of the procession were four swordsmen, who were followed by four hired pall-bearers, dressed in red. The coffin was borne by four coolies, who were alternately relieved by four others. The officers of the church marched in front of the coffin, and sung hymns full of Christian hope, which seemed a cheerful way to bury the pious dead. The procession increased in numbers as it advanced to the tomb, and all joined in the funeral song. Women in white thronged the streets, and preceded the solemn cortége to the grave. The cemetery is near the English consulate, and covers an area of many miles. When the coffin was lowered into the grave, a human skull and arm-bones were placed on the casket as the ghastly emblems of death. Then the great congregation sung a hymn, the officiating elder offered an affecting prayer, and the dead was left in peace.

In company with Mr. Frederic Poche, the American consular agent, and Doctor Hagopian, the consular dragoman, we strolled through the large bazaars, which were filled with English, French, Swiss, American, and native goods. Among the latter were elegant silk and gold-embroidered robes, such as are worn by the Syrian ladies, and which would be highly prized by the ladies of our own country. During our stroll we passed several places where American petroleum was sold, and which is in great demand throughout the East. In the evening we were the guests of Mr. Poche at dinner. He and his brother are the most extensive and successful European merchants in Aleppo. His style of living indicates his wealth and the refinement of his taste. Madam Poche is a lady of great personal beauty, in whose complexion blend the lily and the rose, and whose large, black, lustrous eyes shone like resplendent diamonds.

At 2 P.M. the next day, we resumed our journey to the sea. According to a beautiful Oriental custom, Messrs. Poche and Hagopian accompanied us to the gardens to the north-west of the city, from which point is obtained the most imposing view of elegant Aleppo. After a ride of four hours through a hilly region and over a rough road, we halted for the night at Auwaggeal, a village that had seen better days.

The rainless weather continued. The sun rose in a cloudless sky. The balmy breath of spring was laden with the odor of wild flowers. The birds carroled the melody of their song from their sylvan coverts. The sparkling waters of the cascade leaped with delight, and the murmuring brook flowed musically by. The fresh grain imparted beauty to the hills, and the rich meadows were teeming with herds and flocks. Amidst such pleasures of nature we rode on, hour after hour. We had passed Tarkot on the left, and at noon we lunched in a charming valley near a well of delicious water. Late in the afternoon we entered a glorious valley, bounded by lofty mountains and smaller hills, dotted with towns and encampments, rich in grain and grasses. In the meadows, hundreds of camels were browsing, and near them were their burdens of foreign goods *en route* for Aleppo. On our left were hot sulphur-springs, where bath-houses had been erected for invalids. Here we met the only European traveler in all our journey of forty days. He was bound southward, and had a military escort. In the stillness of the evening hour, we stopped for the night at the little village of Inonabarsh, in the north-west end of the valley. We had been in the saddle eleven hours, and rest was sweet. The peasants received us kindly, and supplied us with fruits and eggs, with milk and poultry. The cottages are constructed of reeds, and are cool in summer, but cold in winter. They were furnished with more comforts than any we had yet seen. The family of our host was large and interesting. The mother and daughters were gayly attired, and their head-dress was high and ornamental. Our comfort was increased by clean beds and mosquito-bars, rare luxuries in the East.

As the rosy light of the dawn appeared, we were descending the foot-hills, and soon entered the north-west branch of the magnificent valley we had crossed yesterday. On our right, and far away, appeared gray mountains capped with white clouds; on our left, and before us, were meadows, rich and vast. Across the head of the valley extended a stone causeway built by the Romans, and repaired by the Turks; but the recent rains and the melting of the snows had rendered it useless. The whole meadow was submerged to the depth of three feet. Our soldiers led the way, and we rode for miles through the water to reach the high ground on the east. During the morning we regained the broad and well-made road, constructed of blocks of limestone; and, as part of the same, we crossed four bridges, the largest of which is twelve hundred feet long, twenty feet wide, and is supported by twelve arches. We subsequently traced this road as far as Beylan. But it is now a ruin.

Under the present sultan, there is neither public spirit in the people nor official honesty enough in the country to keep such a road in good condition.

Once out of the wet meadow-lands, we were again on the highway to the sea. As we approached the coast, caravans were larger and more frequent. We passed not fewer than one thousand camels; some were at rest, others were in motion. In one caravan were three Syrian ladies, who rode with graceful ease, and whose beautiful faces could be seen through their light gauze veils.

At noon we entered the grand pass of Iskenderoon, and halted at Khan Diarbekir, where a Teuton and his Syrian wife provided us with luncheon. Here the mountain-streams met, and our ears were banqueted with the music of running waters. We now began the ascent of the magnificent but difficult pass. In two hours we reached a broad plateau covered with the fig, the olive, and the oleander. Another ascent was before us, but neither so rough nor dangerous. Here and there could be traced the old Roman road, that answered well enough for the valley, but not for this steep pass. Up the winding way we toiled, the wind sighing softly through the mountain pines. In three and a half hours we had gained the summit, and had therefrom a noble view of the near ravines, the distant mountains, the valley we had left behind. Here the telegraph crosses the ridge; here a new khan has been erected for travelers; here a broad macadamized road was in process of construction. As the sun went down, we halted for the night at Beylan. Like a Swiss village, Beylan is in the mountains, where the valleys are deep and the peaks are high. The nine hundred houses are of stone, with flat, thatched roofs, and are built on the side of the mountains from base to summit. The streets are narrow and tortuous. The six thousand inhabitants are Moslems, Jews, and Armenian Christians. Down the mountains rush cascades whose united waters form in the deep gorge a stream of much power, but which the villagers fail to utilize from lack of mechanical skill. Our stopping-place was a coffee-house overhanging the deep valley, and therein we spent the last night of our memorable journey.

Amidst the charms of another bright morning we commenced the descent of the Beylan Pass. A train of camels loaded with Syrian wool blockaded the narrow path, and compelled us to halt. Patience conquers all things, camels and Arabs included. Permitted at length to pass, we were soon beyond the limits of the town. An hour's ride, and we saw the sea, a sight long anticipated, and now realized with gratitude to Him "who is over all, and God blessed forever." All nature sympathized with the joyfulness of the moment. The wild scenery; the deep gorges; the high mountains; the tumultuous rush of the waters; the fresh foliage of the pine, the cedar, the oak, and oleander; the scream of the eagle, and the song of birds, delighted the senses, and enhanced the joy of the soul. Having accomplished the descent in two hours, in less than an hour thereafter we were at Iskenderoon, in whose placid bay lay the steamer that was to bear us on our homeward voyage.

THE END.

www.ingramcontent.com/pod-product-compliance
Lightning Source LLC
Chambersburg PA
CBHW031153020526
44117CB00042B/963